MYŎNGDO'S
KOREAN

by A. V. Vandesande
Revised by Yunsook Hong

U-SHIN SA PUBLISHING CO.
Seoul Korea
1990

All inquiries should be addressed to :
U-Shin Sa Publishing Co.,
2-1 Yangjae-dong Sŏch'o-gu, Seoul 137-130, Republic of Korea

ACKNOWLEDGMENTS

Myŏngdo's Korean '68 is based on the teaching system adopted by Myŏngdo Institute and owes much to the experience of the teachers of the Institute. I thank all the teachers for their valuable assistance.

I feel greatly indebted to Mr. Francis Park, without whose continued devotion and great skill the book could not have been completed. I also wish to thank Miss Marian Chŏn, for the diacritic marking and for assisting in the preparation of the phonetic charts and Mr. Harold F. Cook and Fr. Donald Haven for helping with the English. Mr. Harold F. Cook not only helped with the English but also took upon himself the arduous task of reading and correcting the proofs. With Fr. Luke A. Pirone, Mr. F. Park and Miss Chŏn he saw the book through the final stages of preparation.

I owe much to the encouragement and assistance of Very Rev. A. van Leeuwen, superior of the Franciscans in Korea. May this text be a reward for his great efforts.

Realizing the *Myŏngdo's Korean '68* is only a first and imperfect effort, I take all responsibility for its shortcomings and look forward to any suggestion and criticism which may help improve a future edition.

Seoul, October 1, 1967

Anthony V. Vandesande

FOREWORD TO THE REVISED EDITION

The first edition of this book was published in 1968. Its revision has long been overdue. Teachers of Korean who have used the first edition in the past have strongly felt the need for it in accordance with great social change as well as language change in Korea as witnessed, in particular, in the 1988 Revised Spelling and Pronunciation of Korean (in South Korea).

The Myŏngdo Institute in Seoul was originally where the textbook was made and used. It no longer does any teaching, but its textbook has since gained popularity in Korean schools as well as in foreign universities. For over two decades, however, no revision has been done. The present revised edition was initiated to accomodate such need and to update obsolete information found in the earlier version.

For two years (1984-1986), the revisor taught the Korean language courses at the University of Pennsylvania (Philadelphia). It was during those years that she made notes of points for correction while using the Myŏngdo books. Miss S. H. Hwang, assistant teacher initially and successor after the revisor left Penn to resume her teaching at Hanyang University in Seoul, subsequently provided her with several suggestions and comments.

Some characteristics of the revised edition are as follows: the main dialogs in each lesson were maximally retained except in Lessons 1 and 2, which have been substantially revised. All in all, each volume was reduced to approximately two thirds of the first edition to be adequate to be taught in a semester. Substantially cut down were example sentences in sections other than main dialogs. Also, drills were made compact by schematizing them.

This Volume 1 retains the first 15 lessons of the 1968 edition. Volume 2 includes 16 lessons which were abridged from 23 lessons (Lessons 16 through 38 in the old edition):

Lessons 18 and 19 of the old edition were put together into one (as Lesson 18) ; Lessons 20, 24, 32, 33, 34 and 35 were deleted. But most of the relevant grammatical points therein were incorporated into later lessons for the sake of continuity. While little change was made in Vol. 1, active reorganization of lessons was undertaken in Vol. 2. Vol. 1 and Vol. 2 roughly correspond to Part I and Part II of the old edition.

Korean spelling follows the 1988 Revised Spelling and Pronunciation System of Korean : most notably for example, -읍니다 was revised to -습니다 as in 있습니다, 먹습니다, and 없습니다.

Among many textbooks of Korean, *Myŏngdo's Korean '68*, inspite of its numerous weaknesses, is known to have been most loved by teachers as well as students of Korean abroad. Its merits seem to lie in its rich humor and casual conversational style that are real in daily life in Korea. Not only do the dialogs come alive but also the sample sentences in the Remarks to the Text, Structural Patterns and Drills in each lesson are inexhaustive and comprehensive.

The 1968 edition was written to be used for students learning Korean four hours daily and five days a week (approximately 20 hours per week). Considering the fact that this textbook may be used for Korean classes in universities abroad that cannot afford so many hours, the reduction in volume was inevitable. Such classes are usually held two hours daily, three days a week (plus language lab listening) —hence nine hours at the most.

As for the social information newly incorporated in this volume, some typical examples are living expenses, prices of goods, newly developed communications systems, urban topography including high buildings and widened streets and roads, and changed attitudes of the younger generation. Ideas and values have changed. Younger women of Korea today, for instance, can join men in the beer-drinking evening dinner.

Efforts were made to maintain the original value of this textbook by way of minimal revision. It is hoped that users of this revised edition find it useful and convenient at home and abroad as well.

Finally, many thanks are due to three people at least : Father S. I. Yoo of the Myŏngdo Language Institute and Mr. Y. H. Roh, president of the U-Shin-Sa Publishing company, who have made the long-overdue decision to undertake the revision of *Myŏngdo's Korean 1968* (Parts 1 and 2) and who have not spared their heartfelt moral and financial support since our first meeting in the summer of 1987 ; Miss Ellen Eisenlohr, who has learned Korean with Volume 1 (first printing) of the revised edition, was kind enough to provide the revisor with many valuable questions about grammatical points and inconsistencies.

Although efforts have been made, still, errors may be found. All of them are the responsibility of the revisor.

May 7, 1991   Yunsook Hong

CONTENTS

Key to the Abbreviations and Symbols Used in this Textbook

S.P.	Structural patterns
R.T.	Remarks to the text
A.V.S.	Action verb stem
D.V.S.	Descriptive verb stem
V.S.	Stem of any verb
i.e., e.g., viz.	For example
vs	Voiceless
vd	Voiced
=	Equals
≠	Contrasts
→	Becomes or changes into

Heavy print at the beginning of a word indicates a slight rise of pitch.

◦	Voicing
›	Glottalization, tensing
∨	Pause
↗	Rise of pitch
↘	Fall of pitch
⌒	Dip of pitch
⌒/	Dip-and-rise of pitch
⌐	Unreleased (This symbol comes after syllable-final voiceless consonants.)

Note : The Romanization used in this textbook is a modified from of the McCune—Reischauer System, more specifically, "The Romanization of Korean" in *The Revised Korean Spelling and Pronunciation System of 1988,* as promulgated by the Mirry of Education, Seoul, Korea.

Classroom Instructions

1. 잘 들어 보세요. ⌒   Please listen well.

2. 말씀해 보세요. ⌒   Please try to say (it).

3. 다시 말씀해 보세요. ⌒   Please try to say (it) again.

4. 한국말로 말씀해 보세요. ⌒   Please try to speak in Korean.

5. 영어를 쓰지 말아 주세요. ⌒   Please don't use English.

6. 책을 펴 주세요. ⌒   Please open (your) book.

7. 책을 봐 주세요. ⌒   Please look at (your) book.

8. 책을 보지 말아 주세요. ⌒   Please don't look at (your) book.

9. 책을 덮어 주세요. ⌒   Please close (your) book.

10. 다 같이 말씀해 보세요. ⌒   Please say (it) in chorus.

11. 한 사람씩 말씀해 보세요. ⌒   Please say (it), one person at a time.

12. 더 빨리 말씀해 보세요. ⌒   Please speak more quickly.

13. 더 똑똑히 말씀해 보세요. ⌒   Please speak more clearly.

14. 더 큰 소리로 말씀해 보세요. ⌒   Please speak in a louder voice.

15. 김선생님에게 물어 보세요. ⌒   Please ask Mr. Kim.

16. 따라 읽으세요. ⌒   Please repeat after me.

17. 한 사람씩 따라 읽으세요. ⌒   Please repeat after me, one person at a time.

18. 대답해 주세요. ⌒   Please answer.

제일과 한글 (Lesson 1 Han-gŭl)

Language is basically a stream of structured sounds, and writing not more than a secondary graphic representation of language. When learning a new language, learning problems should not be multiplied unnecessarily. Each should be tackled separately. If these statements are true, logically it should follow that writing be introduced only after the beginning problems of the spoken language have been overcome. Yet we prefer the student to become familiar with the writing system from the very beginning. The reasons are : 1) the Korean writing system is relatively simple ; 2) romanization is hardly used by anyone and therefore not practical, for the transition from romanization to the use of the Korean alphabet in a later stage of learning has proved to be difficult ; 3) the new language learner is assumed to be an adult who has therefore passed the linguistically critical age of 12 or so. When a learner passes the age, he or she starts to analyze the new language while learning, instead of memorizing it by rote. For these reasons, introduction of the writing system as well as grammar from the very beginning will prove to be more efficient for the learner.

The native name for the Korean writing system is *han-gŭl*. The graphic symbols of *han-gŭl*, unlike, e.g., the Japanese *kana,* represent phonemes rather than syllables. Therefore, *han-gŭl* is an alphabetic writing system. Phonemes are groups of sounds which by virtue of their phonetic similarity belong together, yet at the same time show at least one feature of sound contrast. For example, in Korean, p (as in 방[pang] 'room'), b (as in 가방[kabang] 'bag') and p-unreleased (as in 납[nap⁻] 'lead') all belong to the group of bilabial stops and so are phonetically similar. However, b contrasts with p-unreleased in being voiced ; p-unreleased contrasts with p and b in being unreleased ; and p contrasts with b and p-unreleased in being neither voiced nor unreleased. Each of the above three subsounds is represented by the graphic symbol ㅂ. The subsound in each case is determined by the nature of the immediate phonetic environment of ㅂ.

Han-gŭl consists of forty letters. Twenty-one of these represent simple vowels and diphthongs, nineteen represent consonants. Twenty-four are basic, while the others are compounds of the basic lettrers.

1. Korean Vowels and Consonants

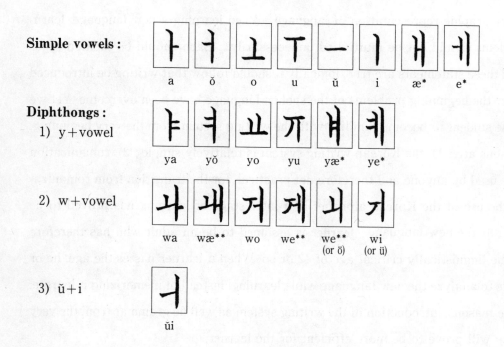

Simple vowels :

ㅏ ㅓ ㅗ ㅜ ㅡ ㅣ ㅐ ㅔ
a ŏ o u ŭ i æ* e*

Diphthongs :
1) y+vowel

ㅑ ㅕ ㅛ ㅠ ㅒ ㅖ
ya yŏ yo yu yæ* ye*

2) w+vowel

ㅘ ㅙ ㅝ ㅞ ㅚ ㅟ
wa wæ** wo we** we** wi
              (or ö) (or ü)

3) ŭ+i

ㅢ
ŭi

---

*The distinction between ㅐ and ㅔ is being lost among the younger generation in Standard Korean. Those older than 40 of age still maintain the distinction but those younger than 40 do not, particularly in casual speech.

**As a result of loss of distinction between ㅐ and ㅔ, the three vowels ㅙ, ㅞ and ㅚ are not normally distinguished in Standard Korean speech today. Also, the vowels ㅚ and ㅟ are rarely pronounced as simple vowels(i. e., as [ö] and [ü]) in Standard Korean. Therefore, these are put together with diphthongs. They are more often pronounced as diphthongs, i. e., as [we] and [wi] respectively

Consonants:

1) Plain (Lax)

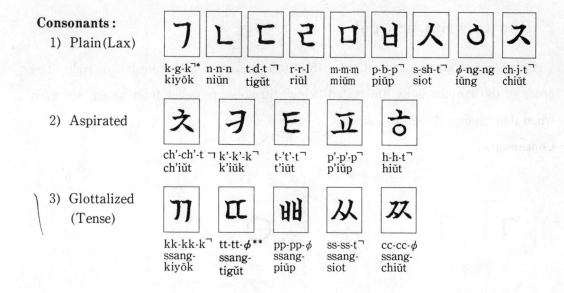

ㄱ	ㄴ	ㄷ	ㄹ	ㅁ	ㅂ	ㅅ	ㅇ	ㅈ
k-g-k⌐*	n-n-n	t-d-t⌐	r-r-l	m-m-m	p-b-p⌐	s-sh-t⌐	φ-ng-ng	ch-j-t⌐
kiyŏk	niŭn	tigŭt	riŭl	miŭm	piŭp	siot	iŭng	chiŭt

2) Aspirated

ㅊ	ㅋ	ㅌ	ㅍ	ㅎ
ch'-ch'-t⌐	k'-k'-k⌐	t-'t'-t⌐	p'-p'-p⌐	h-h-t⌐
ch'iŭt	k'iŭk	t'iŭt	p'iŭp	hiŭt

3) Glottalized (Tense)

ㄲ	ㄸ	ㅃ	ㅆ	ㅉ
kk-kk-k⌐	tt-tt-φ**	pp-pp-φ	ss-ss-t⌐	cc-cc-φ
ssang-kiyŏk	ssang-tigŭt	ssang-piŭp	ssang-siot	ssang-chiŭt

---

*The syllable structure of Korean is typically CVC (Consonant-Vowel-Consonant).
k-g-k⌐ means that in initial position of the Korean syllable, ㄱ is pronounced as [k]
as in 거리 ; in intervocalic position (or between vowels) it is voiced as [g] as in 아가 ;
in final position it is unreleased as [k] as in 막.

**φ (This symbol) means that the consonant in question does not occur wherever the
symbol φ appears.

2. How to write han-gŭl

All symbols of *han-gŭl* are written   from top to bottom and from left to right. The order of the strokes is as illustrated below. Strokes are never interrupted, not even when they change direction halfway.

Consonants:

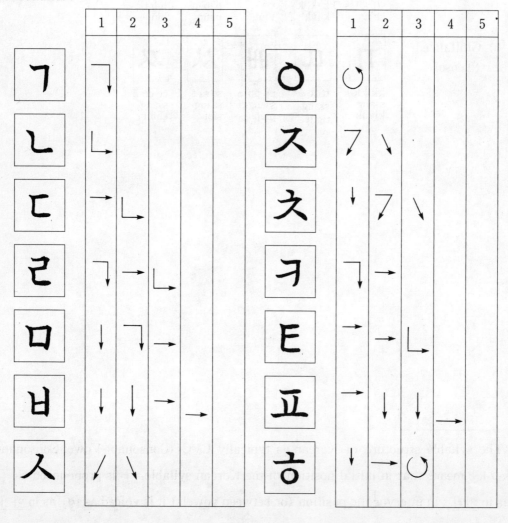

Vowels :

	1	2	3	4	5
ㅏ	↓	→			
ㅐ	↓	→	↓		
ㅑ	↓	→	→		
ㅒ	↓	→	→	↓	
ㅓ	→	↓			
ㅔ	→	↓	↓		
ㅕ	→	→	↓		
ㅖ	→	→	↓	↓	
ㅗ	↓	→			
ㅘ	↓	→	↓	→	
ㅙ	↓	→	↓	→	↓

	1	2	3	4	5
ㅚ	↓	→	↓		
ㅛ	↓	↓	→		
ㅜ	→	↓			
ㅝ	→	↓	→	↓	
ㅞ	→	↓	→	↓	↓
ㅟ	→	↓	↓		
ㅠ	→	↓	↓		
ㅡ	→				
ㅢ	→	↓			
ㅣ	↓				

3. Formation of some vowels and diphthongs

ㅐ = ㅏ + ㅣ [æ]   ㅚ = ㅗ + ㅣ [we] or [ö]

ㅒ = ㅑ + ㅣ [yæ]   ㅘ = ㅗ + ㅏ [wa]

ㅔ = ㅓ + ㅣ [e]   ㅙ = ㅗ + ㅐ [wæ]

ㅖ = ㅕ + ㅣ [ye]   ㆎ = ㅜ + ㅓ [wŏ]

ㅢ = ㅡ + ㅣ [ŭi]   ㅞ = ㅜ + ㅔ [we]

ㅟ = ㅜ + ㅣ [wi] or [ü]

4. How to compose syllables

The vowel in all vowel-consonant combinations is usually written somewhat larger than the accompanying consonant or consonants. The consonants never dominate the combination. For example 가 and 브, not 가 and 브.

1. Consonant-Vowel :

   a) Vowel symbols which have their main or longer stroke standing upright have the consonant at their left side. They are the nine vowels which occur in the following consonant –vowel combinations :

      가, 냐, 더, 려, 미, 배, 걔, 제, 폐.

   b) Vowel symbols which have their main or longer stroke lying in horizontal position have the consonant on top. They are the five which occur in the following syllables :

      고, 묘, 수, 쥬, 브.

   c) The following seven combinations of vowel symbols have the accompanying consonant symbol written on top of the left vowel in place of ㅇ [*iŭ*ng] in the combination :

      외, 위, 의, 와, 왜, 워, 웨. → 뇌, 귀, 희, 봐, 쇄, 둬, 췌.

16

2. Consonant-Vowel-Consonant and Consonant-Vowel-Consonant-Consonant: The closing consonant or consonants in a syllable are written below the main vowel:

밥, 국, 적, 길, 문, 설, 값, 맑, 덟, 몫, 젊.

3. Vowel-Consonant: in vowel-consonant combinations, the vowel always appears in combination with the consonant symbol *iŭng* ㅇ, having it either at its left side or on top according to the rules for consonant-vowel combinations (See 1 above):

압, 엇, 운, 은, 잇, 얼, 옻.

If these rules are more technically described, a maximal Korean syllable structure is CVCC, where C represents "consonant" and V "vowel". While C is optional, V is obligatory. The Korean syllable structure can therefore be re-written as (C) V (C) (C). All the possible combinations of the syllable occurrences are exemplified as the following:

V : 아, 오, 애   CV : 가, 보, 세

CVC : 낙, 불, 강   VC : 얼, 움, 은

VCC : 않, 없, 읊   CVCC : 값, 몫, 덟

Iŭng ㅇ, preceding vowels, is phonetically of no value (example : 아[a]). Only the one following vowels within a syllable has phonetic value (ex : 강[kaŋ]).

5. Exercises

1. One or two letter syllables (C) V

가*	나	다	라	마	바	사	아	자	차	카	타	파	하
개	내	대	래	매	배	새	애	재	채	캐	태	패	해
갸	냐	×	랴	×	×	×	야	×	×	×	×	×	햐
걔	×	×	×	×	×	×	얘	×	×	×	×	×	×
거	너	더	러	머	버	서	어	저	처	커	터	퍼	허
게	네	데	레	메	베	세	에	제	체	케	테	페	헤
겨	녀	×	려	며	벼	셔	여	져	쳐	켜	×	펴	혀

계	네	×	례	×	×	×	예	×	×	×	×	페	혜
고	노	도	로	모	보	소	**오**	조	초	코	토	포	호
과	놔	×	×	×	봐	×	와	좌	×	콰	×	×	화
괘	×	돼	×	×	×	쇄	왜	×	×	쾌	×	×	홰
괴	뇌	되	뢰	뫼	뵈	쇠	외	죄	최	×	퇴	×	회
교	뇨	×	료	묘	×	쇼	**요**	죠	×	×	×	표	효
구	누	두	루	무	부	수	**우**	주	추	쿠	투	푸	후
궈	눠	둬	뤄	뭐	붜	숴	워	줘	춰	쿼	퉈	×	훠
궤	×	×	×	×	×	×	웨	×	췌	×	×	×	훼
귀	뉘	뒤	×	×	×	쉬	위	쥐	취	퀴	튀	×	휘
규	뉴	듀	류	뮤	뷰	슈	**유**	쥬	츄	큐	튜	퓨	휴
그	느	드	르	므	브	스	**으**	즈	츠	크	트	프	흐
긔	늬	×	×	×	×	×	의	×	×	×	×	×	희
기	니	디	리	미	비	시	**이**	지	치	키	티	피	히

*The order of the sound sequences in the first horizontal line is the order used in current Korean dictionaries. The line 가 나 다 라 마 바 사 아 자 차 카 타 파 하 should therefore be learned thoroughly by heart. Also, it is good to know that all native Koreans know by heart the sequence of 아 야 어 여 오 요 우 유 으 이 along with the 가 나 다 라 sequence. The two sequences are in bold-faced letters in the above chart. These are 24 basic letters in Korean, while the others are compounds of the basic letters.

As of January 15, 1988, however, a new sequence of the Korean alphabet for the dictionary entry was promulgated. It consists of 19 consonants and 21 vowels : ㄱ ㄲ ㄴ ㄷ ㄸ ㄹ ㅁ ㅂ ㅃ ㅅ ㅆ ㅇ ㅈ ㅉ ㅊ ㅋ ㅌ ㅍ ㅎ, ㅏ ㅐ ㅑ ㅒ ㅓ ㅔ ㅕ ㅖ ㅗ ㅘ ㅙ ㅚ ㅛ ㅜ ㅝ ㅞ ㅟ ㅠ ㅡ ㅢ ㅣ.

2. Three letter syllables CVC

각 난 넥 덮 렝 멀 밭 살 실 삽 갓 짙
칩 탑 갖 낟 녘 덴 린 멜 뱀 샐 십 앨
작 집 침 택 갱 납 님 딤 릴 몇 뱁 생
싫 잔 찰 칵 턴 갈 낮 닢 딩 릿 명 벌
삼 겉 잘 찾 칼 텃 건 낱 단 락 링 백
석 선 잿 창 캥 텍 멘 쟁 척 캘 텡 겸
낳 닻 란 만 밉 별 선 곁 냇 닿 람 망
밋 볏 셈 점 천 컴 팀 팁 긴 냉 댕 랍
많 밑 빗 셈 젓 첨 컵 넉 댈 런 맷 반
별 셋 식 젠 쳇 켄 깊 넘 덕 먼 반 빛
짖 친 킬

3. Four letter syllables CVCC

Four letter syllables are those which end in two consonants. In Korean, you never pronounce two consonants simultaneously but only one of them is pronounced in the final position. The question therefore is which consonant is pronounced and which one is not. An exhaustive list of 13 double consonants in modern Standard Korean can be classified into three groups:

Group 1 : The nine clusters and examples that belong to this group are as follows. The first two are geminates ㄲ and ㅆ and are pronounced as if they are single consonants ㄱ and ㅅ respectively. For the others in this group, the rule is to pronounce the first member of the cluster. For example, 넋 is pronounced as 넉, 값 as 갑, 많 as 만, etc.

ㄲ : 넋 닦 밖 섞 솎   ㅆ : 있 았 었 왔

ㅄ : 값 없   ㄳ : 삯 몫 넋

ㄽ : 돐 곬   ㄵ : 앉 얹

ㄾ : 핥 훑   ㄶ : 않 많 끊

ㅀ : 싫 앓 옳 끓

Group 2 : There are three clusters in this group. Free variation is practiced for this group in modern Standard Korean. That is, either consonant is pronounced. For example, 읽 can be read as 일 or 익.

ᆲ : 짧 넓 얇   ᆵ : 읊

ᆰ : 읽 굵 늙 맑 밝 닭

Group 3 : This group has only one cluster in it. The second member of the cluster is pronounced.

ᆱ : 젊 곪 삶 옮 굶

In short, a simple rule is to know that in all except the last cluster you pronounce the first member of the double consonant cluster.

4. Words

위, 폐, 표, 집, 문, 칼, 신, 책, 봄.

그저, 누구, 어느, 회사, 모두, 어디, 우리, 아이, 구두, 가다, 시계, 모자, 여자, 아마, 이제, 기차, 수녀, 여기, 모레, 어서, 오다, 의자, 너무, 수사, 아래, 부인, 요일, 가을, 부산, 글피, 겨울, 책상, 학교, 주일, 미국, 내일, 연필, 공일, 영국, 제일, 저것, 공부, 그림, 그때, 양복, 지금, 물건, 사람, 좋다, 다음, 신부, 운동, 양말, 영어, 정구, 같이, 교실, 농구, 말씀, 야구, 처음, 칠판, 이등, 학생, 많이, 여름, 아직, 쉽다.

아니오, 지우개, 그리고, 부치다, 안녕히, 이즈음, 한국말, 독일어, 그러면, 어떻게, 날마다, 교과서, 프랑스, 그저께, 일본말, 백화점, 손수건, 대합실, 선생님.

해바라기, 할아버지, 기다리다, 미안하다.

5. Short Phrases :

가십시오.   한국말을 가르칩니다.

잘 있습니다.   또 오십시오.

그저 그렇습니다.   수요일입니다.

고맙습니다.   목요일입니다.

어디 가십니까?   월요일입니다.

책입니다.   화요일입니다.

이것은 연필입니다.   공부합니다.

같이 갑시다.
좋습니다.
이것이 문입니다.
참 쉽습니다.
어렵습니까?
그림을 봅니다.
안녕하십니까?
책을 읽습니다.
정구를 칩니다.
농구를 합니다.
요즈음 어떻습니까?
저것은 얼마입니까?
이것을 삽시다.
비싸지 않습니다.
책을 사려고 합니다.
내일 갈 것 같습니다.
무엇을 사시겠습니까?
알고말고요.
모릅니다.
김 선생이시죠.
처음 뵙겠습니다.
부쳐 주십시오.
한 시간이 남았습니다.

일을 합니다.
무엇하십니까?
어서 오십시오.
너무 비쌉니다.
그럼 그럽시다.
드리겠습니다.
무엇을 드릴까요?
그만두겠습니다.
갔었습니다.
자지 않겠습니다.
좋았습니다.
나쁘지 않았습니다.
무엇을 사셨습니까?
실례했습니다.
괜찮습니다.
집으로 갑시다.
다 되었습니다.
도와줍니다.
집에 가고 싶습니다.
참 빠릅니다.
짐을 찾읍시다.
그래도 좋습니다.
또 만납시다.

6. Longer Sentences :

요즈음 어떻게 지내십니까?
안녕히 주무셨습니까?
같이 가도 좋습니까?
이것이 우리 학교입니다.
여기서 영어도 가르칩니까?

부인께서도 안녕하십니까?
천만에 말씀입니다.
예, 좋습니다. 같이 갑시다.
선생님은 어느 분입니까?
학생이 모두 몇 사람입니까?

오늘 폐 많이 끼쳤습니다.

선생님은 날마다 무엇하십니까?

선생님은 무엇을 가르칩니까?

선생님은 책을 많이 읽습니까?

저는 봄에는 야구를 합니다.

종이에 싸 드리겠습니다.

우리는 백화점에 갔다가 옵니다.

물건 값이 퍽 비쌉니까?

다음 달에 갈 것 같습니다.

한 주일의 첫째날은 무슨 요일입니까?

우리 아이 옷과 양말 그리고 책상을 사려고 합니다.

어제는 무슨 요일입니까?

나는 회사에서 일을 합니다.

제가 지금 이 그림을 봅니다.

이 학생은 운동을 많이 합니다.

칠천 삼백 오십원입니다.

김 선생님 댁에 갔었습니다.

김 선생님, 무엇을 사셨습니까?

이 다음에 사려고 합니다.

선생님 안녕하십니까? 지금 어디 갔다 오십니까? 예, 지금 백화점에 갔다 옵니다. 한 선생님께서도 잘 있습니까? 예, 잘 있습니다. 지금 백화점에 같이 갔다 오다가 그 분은 극장에 갔습니다. 아! 그렇습니까? 선생님 언제 부산에 가시겠습니까? 아마 모레 갈 것 같습니다. 무엇으로 가시겠습니까? 기차로 가려고 합니다. 누구와 같이 가십니까? 혼자 갔다 오겠습니다. 부산에 가는 기차는 몇 시에 있습니까? 오후 세시에 서울역에서 떠납니다. 그러면 부산에 가셨다가 언제 오시겠습니까? 다음 목요일에 오겠습니다. 그러면 다음 금요일에 학교에서 또 뵙겠습니다. 예, 안녕히 가십시오. 예, 안녕히 가십시오.

제이과 한국어의 음성구조
(Lesson 2 The Korean Sound System)

1. Vowels

ㅣ	i	high-front-unrounded
ㅔ	e	mid-front-unrounded
ㅐ	æ	low-front-unrounded
ㅡ	ŭ	high-back-unrounded
ㅓ	ŏ	mid-back-unrounded
ㅏ	a	low-back-unrounded
ㅜ	u	high-back-rounded
ㅗ	o	mid-back-rounded

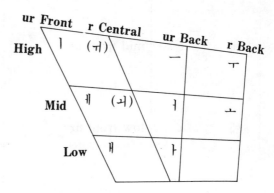

Korean Vowel Chart

Note : **ur** stands for "unrounded" and **r** stands for "rounded".

ㅟ ü high-front-rounded : this vowel does not exist for many speakers. They pronounce [wi] instead. Hence the parentheses in the chart.

ㅚ ö mid-front-rounded : this vowel does not exist for many speakers. They pronounce [we] instead. Hence the parentheses in the chart.

a) Sequences of vowels

Vowels in sequence are usually pronounced distinctly and separately. For example, 아우 "younger brother", 오이 "cucumber", 우애 "friendship". The sequences 이오 io and 이아 ia, however, frequently become 요 yo and 야 ya.

b) "Purity" of vowels

Vowels are pronounced "pure" without having them slip into diphthongs. Individuals with an English speaking background should give this particular attention. For example, 우 is pronounced **u**, not **uw**, **wu** or **wuw** ; 오 is pronounced **o**, not **ow**, **wo** or **wow**.

c) Description of Korean Vowels

Symbol		Description	Examples*		
이	i	high front **ur**	이웃	시민	사치
			이름	미신	소나기
			이성	비밀	보슬비
에	e	mid front **ur**	에미	세상	지게
			에우다	베다	기세
			에이다	체육	사제
애	æ	low front **ur**	애기	새집	축배
			애인	채소	물개
			애호	시내	새해
으	ŭ	high back **ur**	으뜸	그림	사르르
			으쓱하다	스승	흐리다
			으레	으레	
어	ŏ	mid back **ur**	어머니	버릇	서거
			어깨	서리	유서
			어느 것	저녁	상처
아	a	low back **ur**	아버지	타국	전차
			아들	파도	과자
			아이	사탕	허파
우	u	high back **r**	우승	우울	추수
			우량	구경	부부
			우리	수선	폭풍우
오	o	mid back **r**	오리	조사	사고
			오염	보리	시조

*For translation of the examples, see the list following the description of the Korean consonants.

24

Symbol		Description	Examples*		
			오인	모자	폭포
예	ye	Semi-vowel y+에	예의	계란	세계
		mid front **ur**	예정	폐물	은혜
얘	yæ	Semi-vowel y+애	얘기	개	얘
		low front **ur**			
의	ŭi	으+이	의사	의지	하의
		High back **ur**	의견	의의	사의
여	yŏ	Semi-vowel y+어	여름	겨울	등뼈
		mid back **ur**	여자	처녀	쌀겨
			여가		
야	ya	Semi-vowel y+아	야근	갸륵하다	얘야!
		low back **ur**	야심	야초	가느냐?
			얼마나 좋으랴!		
유	yu	Semi-vowel y+우	유서	휴양	절규
		high back **r**	유람	공휴일	난류
			유치원	규수	우유
요	yo	Semi-vowel y+오	요령	묘지	상표
		mid back **r**	요인	교수	관료
			요망	효험	비뇨
웨	we	Semi-vowel w+에	훼손	발췌	궤도
		mid front **ur**	금궤	췌담	
왜	wæ	Semi-vowel w+애	왜간장	쇄도	연쇄
		low front **ur**	왜가리	쾌히	쾌쾌
			왜곡	돼지	불쾌
워	wŏ	Semi-vowel w+어	싸워	가둬	가줘
		mid back **ur**	워낙	잡쉬 보세요	춤춰

Symbol	Description	Examples*		
와 wa	Semi-vowel w+아 low back **ur**	뭐야 와해 와병 와언	나눠 놔두어 좌우 기와	성과 가봐
위 wi(ü)	Semi-vowel w+이 high front **r**	위 위험 위치	쉬다 취미 휘파람	갈퀴 마귀 박쥐
외 we(ö)	Semi-vowel w+에 mid front **r**	참외 외국인 외교	죄인 쇠고기 되다	파괴 열쇠 사죄

2. Consonants

a) Korean Consonant Chart

What happens ? \ Where does it happen ?		Bilabial		Alveolar		Alveo-palatal		Velar		Glottal
Stops										
Plain	vs*	p	ㅂ	t	ㄷ			k	ㄱ	>
	vd	b	ㅂ**	d	ㄷ**			g	ㄱ**	
Glottalized	vs	pp	ㅃ	tt	ㄸ			kk	ㄲ	
Aspirated	vs	p'	ㅍ	t'	ㅌ			k'	ㅋ	
Affricates										
Plain	vs					ch	ㅈ			
	vd					j	ㅈ			
Glottalized	vs					cc	ㅉ			
Aspirated	vs					ch'	ㅊ			
Fricatives										
Plain	vs			s	ㅅ					h ㅎ
Glottalized	vs			ss	ㅆ					
Resonants										
Nasal	vd	m	ㅁ	n	ㄴ			ng	ㅇ	
Lateral	vd			l	ㄹ					
Flap***	vd			r	ㄹ					

* **vs** stands for voiceless, **vd** stands for voiced.

**[b, d, g] are produced between vowels or between a sonorant and a vowel.

***The flap [r] is produced initially or medially while [l] is heard finally in the syllable, as in 라디오 [radio], 사람 [saram], 과일 [kwail], etc.

b) Description of Korean Consonants

Symbol	Position	Description	Examples
ㅂ piŭp	**Initial**	Voiceless bilabial stop (slight local aspiration)	바 버 벼 뵈 브 배 베 보 부 비
	Medial ㅂ between vowels	Voiced bilabial stop (ㅂ→b*)	이발 이불 아버지 자본 기분
	Medial ㅂ following voiceless consonants	Glottalized bilabial stop (ㅂ→ㅃ)	각본 앞발 늦바람 곱배기 팥밥 꽃병 돋보기 촛불 동녘바람
	Medial ㅂ(ㅍ)preceding, ㅁ, ㄴ, ㄹ	Bilabial nasal resonant (ㅂ→ㅁ)	잎만 겁나다 협력 업무 합니다 법률 십만 집념 십리
	Medial ㅂ following ㅁ, ㄴ, ㄹ, ㅇ	There is no clear rule. 1) In certain cases : voiced bilabial stop (ㅂ→b) 2) In other cases : glottalized bilabial stop(ㅂ→ㅃ)	금방 번번이 팔방 동복 함부로 헌병 일본 공부 겸비 신부 갈비 낭비 마음보 문법 달밤 방바닥 봄비 산보 풀비 등불 여름밤 산불 불법 용법
	Final	Voiceless bilabial stop unreleased (ㅂ→ unreleased ㅂ).	밥 굽 법 읍 톱 집

*Roman symbols are used where Korean symbols are lacking.

Symbol	Position	Description	Examples				
ㄷ tigŭt	**Initial**	Voiceless alveolar stop (slight local aspiration)	다	디	도	두	드
			대	데	되	뒤	디
	Medial ㄷ between vowels	Voiced alveolar stop (ㄷ→d)	바다 두더지	구두 아들	지도 더디다		
	Medial ㄷ following voiceless consonant except ㅎ	Glottalized alveolar stop (ㄷ→ㄸ)	밉다 듣다 깍두기 윗도리	낚싯대 앞뒤 낱돈	동녘달 빗돈 꽃동산		
	Medial ㄷ following ㅎ changes places with ㅎ	ㅎㄷ→ㄷㅎ→ㅌ (h t→t h→t')	낳다 좋다	놓다 넣다	닿다 누렇다		
	Medial ㄷ(ㅅ, ㅆ, ㅈ, ㅊ, ㅌ) preceding ㅁ, ㄴ, ㄹ	(ㅅ, ㅆ, ㅈ, ㅊ, ㅌ) in final position unreleased ㄷ) Alveolar nasal resonant (ㄷ→ㄴ)	빗 낱말 윗마을 첫물	있 낱낱이 윷놀이 있는	빚 잇노라 만며느리 빗나가다	빛	밭

	Medial
	ㄷ following ㅁ, ㄴ, ㄹ, ㅇ
		There is no clear rule.
		  1) In certain cases :
		Voiced alveolar stop (ㄷ→d)
		  2) In other cases :
			험담
			성당
			말더듬이
			관대
			굶다
				판단
				감동
				생도
				돌도끼
				논둑
					졸다
					운동
					삼등
					몽둥이
					발달		

Symbol	Position	Description	Examples
	Medial ㄷ preceding 이	Glottalized alveolar stop (ㄷ→ㄸ) 디→di or 디→지	손등　갈대　장독대 신다　검디검다 물독 맏이　곧이듣다 굳이
	Final	Voiceless alveolar stop, unreleased (ㄷ→ unreleased ㄷ)	낟　낮　낫　낱　낮 왔다
ㄱ kiyŏk	**Initial**	Voiceless velar stop (slight local aspiration)	가　갸　거　겨　고　교 귀　그　기　개　개　게 계　괴　구　규　긔
	Medial ㄱ between vowels	Voiced velar stop (ㄱ→g)	자가　고구마　우그리다 사거리　수고　고기
	Medial ㄱ following voiceless consonants except ㅎ	Glottalized velar stop (ㄱ→ㄲ)	겹겹이　깎기　부엌기구 듣기　깊게　늦게 학교　밭갈이　숯가마 옷감　만났고
	Medial following ㅎ changes places with ㅎ	ㅎㄱ→ㅋ (hk→kh→k)	파랗게　많기에　좋고
	Medial ㄱ(ㅋ, ㄲ) preceding ㅁ, ㄷ, ㄹ	Velar nasal resonant (ㄱ→ㅇ)	한국말　독나비　박람회 식모　숙녀　격려 국물　부엌만　깎는

Symbol	Position	Description	Examples

	Medial
	ㄱ following
	ㅁ, ㄴ, ㄹ, ㅇ
		There is no clear rule :
		  1) In certain cases :
		voiced velar stop
		(ㄱ→g)
		
		  2) In other cases :
		glottalized velar stop
		(ㄱ→ㄲ)
			음계 한국 밀고 장갑
			감기 긴급 출가 창고
			금고 건강 절교 용기
			
			염가 인기 물가 성격
			소금기 본과 물고기 정가
			감고 안고 술김에 상과

	Final	Voiceless velar stop unreleased (ㄱ→unreleased ㄱ)	낙 북 턱 극 독 식
ㅃ ssang- piŭp	**Initial** **Medial** **Final**	Voiceless bilabial stop, glottalized idem Does not occur.	빠르다 뿌리 뽕나무 뼈 뺨 빨래 아빠 고삐 뽈뽈이 예뻐 뽀뽀 기쁨
ㄸ ssang- tigŭt	**Initial** **Medial** **Final**	Voiceless alveolar stop, glottalized idem Does not occur.	땅 뚱보 때 떡 뜻 띠 이따금 어떻게 똑똑히 허리띠 오뚝이 으뜸
ㄲ ssang- kiyŏk	**Initial** **Medial** **Final**	Voiceless velar stop, glottalized idem Voiceless velar	까마귀 꾸지람 거꾸로 끄다 꼬리 끼니 아까 가꾸다 세모꼴 지껄이다 토끼 이끌다 밖 안팎

Symbol	Position	Description	Examples		
		stop, unreleased (ㄲ→unreleased ㄱ)			
ㅈ chiŭt	**Initial**	Voiceless alveo-palatal affricate (slight local aspiration)	잠 즉시	준비 조사	저울 지도
	Medial between vowels	Voiced alveo-palatal affricate (ㅈ→j).	모자 요즈음	아주 지조	수저 처지
	Medial ㅈ following voiceless consonants except ㅎ	Alveo-palatal affricate, glottalized (ㅈ→ㅉ)	어렵지 받자 학적	깎지 깊지 얕잡다	낮잠 꽃전차 이웃집
	Medial ㅈ following ㅎ changes places with ㅎ	ㅎ+ㅈ→ㅈ+ㅎ→ ㅊ (h+ch→ch+h →ch')	좋지	낳지	
	Medial ㅈ following ㅁ, ㄴ, ㄹ, ㅇ	There is no clear rule. 1) In certain cases : voiced alveo-palatal affricate(ㅈ→j) 2) In other cases : three segments voiceless alveo-palatal affricate, glottalized	감자 상자 몰지각 운전수 문자 몸짓 손짓 질주	신자 참조 공지 물주다 망조 손재주 상장	살자 전진 염전 상점 철저히 건망증 골자

Symbol	Position	Description	Examples
	Final	(ㅈ→ㅉ) Voiceless alveolar stop, unreleased (ㅈ→unreleased ㄷ)	낮 빛 젖
ㅉ ssang- chiŭt	**Initial** **Medial** **Final**	Voiceless alveo- palatal affricate, glottalized idem Does not occur.	짜다 쭈그리다 찌다 쩔쩔매다 쪼개다 짝짝이 여쭈다 언제쯤 쩔쩔매다 이쪽 어찌
ㅊ ch'iŭt	**Initial** **Medial** **Final**	Voiceless alveo- palatal affricate, aspirated idem Voiceless alveolar stop, unreleased (ㅊ→unreleased ㄷ)	차 추리 처지 측면 초 침대 자동차 고추 천천히 차츰 십초 처치 낯 꽃 빛 돛 숯
ㅅ siot	**Initial** **Medial** ㅅ preceded by any consonant In either ini-	Voiceless alveolar fricative (slight local aspiration) Voiceless alveolar fricative, glottalized (ㅅ→ㅆ) idem, but palatalized	사랑 수사 스승 서울 소 시사 악사 뱃사람 같습니다 듣습니다 늦습니다 깊숙이 설사 꽃송이 닿소리 시 쉽다

Lesson 2 The Korean Sound System 33

Symbol	Position	Description	Examples		
	tial or medial position when preceding the vowels 이 or 위	(ㅅ→sh, as in sheep)			
	Final	Voiceless alveolar stop, unreleased (ㅅ→unreleased ㄷ)	낫 빗	이웃 지긋지긋	돗 빗
ㅆ ssang- siot	**Initial** **Medial** **Final**	Voiceless alveolar fricative, glottalized idem Voiceless alveolar stop, unreleased (ㅆ→unreleased ㄷ)	쌀 쓰다 쌀쌀하다 말씨 있(다)	쑥 쏘다 말씀 말쑥하다 갔(다)	썰매 씨름 말썽
ㅎ hiŭt	**Initial** **Medial** **Final**	Glottal fricative (glottal aspiration) idem Voiceless alveolar stop, unreleased (ㅎ→unreleased ㄷ)	하늘 흐리다 초하 호흡 낳(다)	후사 호기심 오후 기호	허리 힘 공허 오히려
ㅁ miŭm	**Initial** **Medial**	Bilabial voiced nasal resonant idem	말 미국 이마 가려무나	무 모양 나무	머리

Symbol	Position	Description	Examples		
	Final	idem	할머니 담 모범	사모 곰 어려움	의미 금 김
ㄴ niŭn	**Initial**	Alveolar voiced nasal resonant	나 느리다	누구 노인	너 님
	Medial ㄴ preceded or followed by ㄹ	Lateral voiced alveolar resonant (ㄹㄴ and ㄴㄹ→ㄹㄹ)	찰나 신라	난로 불능	불놀이 산림
	Final	Alveolar voiced nasal resonant	만	온천	전진
ㄹ riŭl	**Initial**	Alveolar voiced flap: Does not occur except in the name of the symbol ㄹ and in a few foreign loan words.	리을	러시아	라디오
	Medial ㄹ between vowels	Alveolar voiced flap	사람 기러기	마루 가로수	모르다 버리다
	Medial ㄹ following any consonant except ㄴ ㄹ ㅎ	Alveolar voiced nasal resonant (ㄹ→ㄴ)	압록강 압력	십리 남루한	심리
	Final	Alveolar voiced resonant (ㄹ → l)	발 절	수술 솔	슬슬 실

Symbol	Position	Description	Examples		
ㅇ iuŋ	Initial Medial Final	Does not occur. Velar voiced nasal idem	궁전 사랑	증가 공중	빙과 실증
ㅍ p'iŭp	Initial Medial Final	Bilabial stop, strong- ly aspirated idem Voiceless bilabial stop, unreleased (ㅍ→unreleased ㅂ)	팔 퍼렇다 한파 아프다 앞 늪	풀 포도 부풀다 대포 무릎 숲	프랑스 피리 시퍼렇다 모피 헝겊 짚
ㅌ t'iŭt	Initial Medial Final	Alveolar stop, strongly aspirated idem Voiceless alveolar stop, unreleased (ㅌ→unreleased ㄷ)	탈 털 낙타 집터 낱 숱 겉 끝 솥 뒤곁	투지 트집 사투리 도토리	토지 티 틈틈이 버티다
ㅋ k'iŭk	Initial Medial Final	Velar stop, strongly aspirated idem Voiceless velar stop, unreleased (ㅋ→unreleased ㄱ)	칼 컴컴하다 조카 컴컴하다 부엌	쿨쿨 코 삼키다 웅크리다 동녘	크다 키 넝쿨 큰코 윗녘

3. List of examples to the description of the vowels and consonants and their meanings

【이】 이웃   neighborhood

이름   name

이성   reason, rationality

시민   citizen

미신   superstition

비밀   secret

사치   luxury

소나기   shower

보슬비   drizzling rain

【에】 에미   (dialect or humble form of) mother

에우다   encloses, surrounds

에이다   scoops (out), puts out

세상   world

베다   cuts, gives a cut

체육   physical education

지게   A-frame

기세   spirit, ardor

사제   master and pupil, priest

【애】 애기   baby

애인   lover, sweetheart

애호   protection

새집   new house

채소   vegetables

시내   downtown

축배   toast

물개   sea lion

새해   new year

【으】 으뜸   the first

으쓱하다   is thrilling

으레   no doubt

그림   picture

스승   teacher

호리다   is cloudy

사르르   gently

【어】 어머니   mother

어깨   shoulder

어느 것   which one

버릇   habit

서리   frost

저녁   evening

서거   death

유서   will (*n.*)

상처   hurt

【아】 아버지   father

아들   son

아이   child

타국   foreign country

파도   billow, wave

사탕   candy

전차   streetcar

과자   confectionery, cake

허파	lung
【우】 우승	victory
우량	superiority
우리	we, cage
우울	melancholy
구경	visit, sightseeing
수선	repair
추수	harvest
부부	man and wife
폭풍우	rainstorm, storm
【오】 오리	duck
오염	pollution
오인	misconception
조사	investigation
보리	barley
모자	hat
사고	accident
시조	founder
폭포	waterfall
【예】 예의	manners
예정	previous arrangement
계란	eggs
폐물	useless article (thing)
은혜	grace
세계	world
【애】 얘기	story
얘	this child
걔	that child
【의】 의사	doctor

의견	opinion
의지	will, trust, artificial
	limb
하의	trousers, skirt
사의	resignation
의의	meaning
【여】 여름	summer
여자	woman
여가	spare time, leisure
겨울	winter
등뼈	backbone
쌀겨	rice-bran
처녀	virgin, maiden
【야】 야근	night duty
야심	ambition
야초	wild grass
갸륵하다	is praiseworthy
애야	my boy !
가느냐	Do you go ?
얼마나 좋으랴	How nice it is !
【유】 유서	written will
유람	sightseeing
유치원	kindergarten
휴양	rest, repose
공휴일	holiday
규수	maiden
절규	scream
난류	warm current
우유	milk

【요】	요령	gist (of a matter)		가둬	Jail (him) !
	요인	factor, element		춤춰	Dance !
	요망	demand		가줘	Go !
	묘지	graveyard	【와】	와해	fall, downfall
	교수	professor		놔두어	Leave it there !
	효험	efficacy, effect		와병	sick in bed
	상표	trademark		좌우	left and right
	관료	bureaucracy		와언	groundless rumor
	비뇨	urination		성과	result, outcome
【웨】	훼손	damage, injury		가봐	Go !
	궤도	orbit, circle		기와	tile
	췌담	superfluous	【위】	위	upside
	발췌	excellence, superior-ity		위험	danger
				위치	position
	금궤	money-chest		쉬다	rests
【왜】	왜간장	Japanese soy sauce		취미	hobby
	왜식	Japanese style		휘파람	whistle
	왜곡	distortion		갈퀴	rake
	쇄도	rush, flood		마귀	devil
	쾌히	pleasantly		박쥐	bat
	돼지	pig	【외】	참외	melon
	연쇄	chain, link		외국인	foreigner
	홰홰	brandishing repeat-edly		외교	diplomacy
				죄인	criminal
	불쾌	unpleasant		쇠고기	beef
【워】	워낙	originally		되다	to become
	잡숴 보세요	Please eat !		파괴	destruction
	싸워	Fight !		열쇠	key
	뭐야	What !		사죄	apology

【ㅂ】	이발	haircutting		번번이	each time
	아버지	father		헌병	military policeman
	자본	capital, fund		신부	bride, Father(Rev.)
	이불	quilt		팔방	every direction
	십이	twelve		일본	Japan
	기분	feelings		갈비	rib
	각본	libretto		동복	winter clothes
	곱배기	double-the-ordinary (cup of liquor)		공부	studies
	돋보기	glasses for far vision		낭비	waste
	앞발	paw		마음보	temper
	팥밥	rice boiled with red beans		봄비	spring rain
	동녘바람	east wind		여름밤	summer night
	늦바람	evening breeze		문법	grammar
	꽃병	flower vase		산보	stroll
	촛불	candlelight		산불	forest fire
	잎만	leaves only		달밤	moonlit night
	업무	business		풀비	paste-brush
	십만	100,000		불법	unlawfulness
	겁나다	fears		방바닥	floor of a room
	합니다	does		등불	lamp light
	집념	attachment		용법	way to use
	협력	cooperation		밥	cooked rice
	법률	law		법	law
	십리	10 *li*		톱	saw
	금방	just now		굽	hoof
	함부로	carelessly		읍	town
	겸비하다	combines		집	house
			【ㄷ】	바다	sea
				두더지	mole

지도	map	감동	emotion
구두	shoe	삼등	third class
아들	son	판단	judgment
더디다	is slow	운동	movement
빗	comb	관대	broad-mindedness
빚	debt	졸다	dozes
빛	light	말더듬이	stammerer
밭	field	돌도끼	stone ax
밉다	is hateful	성당	church, cathedral
듣다	hears	생도	schoolboy (girl)
깍두기	kind of kimch'i	몽둥이	stick
낚싯대	fishing rod	굶다	starves
앞뒤	before and behind	좀도둑	sneak (thief)
낱돈	small money	검디검다	is jet-black
동녘달	east moon	논둑	dikes around a rice-field
빚돈	debt		
꽃동산	flower garden	손등	back of a hand
웃도리	the upper part of the body	신다	wears
		발달	development
있다	exists	갈대	reed
낱말	vocabulary	물독	water jar
맏며느리	first daughter-in-law	선생댁	house of the teacher
첫물	period pending the first wash	장독대	jar stand
		맏이	the eldest
낱낱이	one by one	곧이듣다	takes (one's word) seriously
웃마을	village up the road		
윷놀이	*yut* game	굳이	solidly
빗나가다	misses the mark	낳다	gives birth to
험담	slander	닿다	arrives, reaches

넣다	puts (a thing) into	식모	kitchen maid
놓다	puts, sets	국물	soup
좋다	is good	독나비	poisonous butterfly
누렇다	is deep yellow	숙녀	lady
낟	a grain	부엌만	only the kitchen
낫	grain sickle	깎는	cutting
낮	daytime	박람회	exhibition
낯	face	격려	encouragement
낱	a piece	음계	musical scale
왔다	came	감기	a cold
		금고	money safe
【ㄱ】 자가	one's own house	한국	Korea
사거리	crossing	긴급	emergency
수고	trouble	건강	health
고구마	sweet potato	밀고	secret information
우그리다	crushes	출가	marriage
고기	meat	절교	breach of friendship
겹겹이	ply on ply	장갑	gloves
듣기	hearing	창고	storehouse
학교	school	용기	courage, tool
깎기	beats down the price	염가	low price
깊게	deeply	소금기	saltiness
밭갈이	cultivating	감고	winds and
부엌기구	kitchen tools	인기	popularity
늦게	late	본과	the regular course
숯가마	charcoal kiln	안고	embraces and
옷감	cloth	물가	prices
만났고	met and	물고기	fish
한국말	Korean (language)	살결	the texture of skin

술김에	while intoxicated		떡	rice cake
성격	character		또	again
정가	fixed price		뚱보	fat person
상과	commercial course		뜻	meaning
파랗게	blue		띠	belt
많기에	because there are many		때	time
좋고	is good and		이따금	occasionally
낙	pleasure		똑똑히	clearly
턱	jaw		오뚜기	tumbler
독	poison		어떻게	how
북	drum		허리띠	belt
극	drama		으뜸	the first
식	ceremony			

【ㅃ】 빠르다	is fast		【ㄲ】 까마귀	crow
뼈	bone		거꾸로	upside down
뽕나무	mulberry		꼬리	tail
뿌리	root		꾸지람	scolding
뺨	cheek		끄다	turns off
빨래	laundry		끼니	meal
아빠	daddy		아까	some time ago
예뻐	pretty		지껄이다	chats
기쁨	joyfulness		세모꼴	triangle
고삐	rein		가꾸다	cultivates
뽀뽀	kiss		토끼	rabbit
뿔뿔이	scatteredly		이끌다	guides
			밖에	to the outside
【ㄸ】 땅	land, soil		안팎이	the interior and exterior

【ㅈ】 잠　　sleep

저울　　scale

조사　　investigation

준비　　preparation

즉시　　immediately

지도　　guidance

모자　　hat

수저　　spoon and chopsticks

지조　　constancy

아주　　very

요즈음　　these days

처지　　situation

어렵지　　It's difficult, isn't it ?

받자　　Let's receive it.

학적　　school register

깎지　　Peel !

깊지　　It is deep.

얕잡다　　treats with contempt

낮잠　　nap

꽃전차　　floral streetcar

이웃집　　next door

좋지　　is good

낳지　　is born

감자　　potato

참조　　reference

염전　　saltfield

신자　　believer

전진　　forward movement

운전수　　driver

살자　　Let's live.

몰지각　　indiscretion

물주다　　pours water

상자　　case

공지　　open area

상점　　store

몸짓　　gesture

문자　　letter

손재주　　skillfulness

손짓　　signal with the hand

망조　　signs of declining fortune

건망증　　amnesia

상장　　certificate of merit

철저히　　thoroughly

질주　　scamper, speeding

골자　　main point

낮　　daytime

빚　　debt

젖　　breast, milk

【ㅉ】 짜다　　is salty

쩔쩔매다　　is confused

쪼개다　　splits

쭈그리다　　crouches

찌다　　steams

짝짝이　　in pairs

이쪽　　this way

여쭈다　　tells

언제쯤	about when	
어찌	how	

【ㅊ】

차	car
처지	situation
초	candle
추리	reasoning
측면	side
침대	bed
자동차	automobile
천천히	slowly
십초	ten seconds
고추	red pepper
차츰	gradually
처치	disposition
낯	face
돛	sail
꽃	flower
숯	charcoal
빛	light

【ㅅ】

사랑	love
서울	Seoul
소	cow
수사	investigation
스승	teacher
악사	bandsman
듣습니다	hears
곱셈	multiplication

설사	even though, loose bowels
뱃사람	seaman
늦습니다	is late
꽃송이	a flower
부엌세간	kitchen utensils
얕습니다	is shallow
깊숙이	deeply
닿소리	consonant
낫이	sickle
벗이	friend
못이	nail
이웃이	neighborhood
빗이	comb

【ㅆ】

쌀	rice
썰매	sled
쏘다	shoots
쑥	mugwort
쓰다	uses
씨름	wrestling
쌀쌀하다	is chilly
말썽	trouble
말쑥하다	is neat, is smart
말씀	saying
말씨	the use of words
있어요	It is ; I have.
갔어요	(He) went.

【ㅎ】 하늘	sky	【ㄴ】 나	I
허리	the waist	너	you
호기심	curiosity	노인	old man
후사	warm thanks	누구	who
흐리다	is cloudy	느리다	is slow
힘	strength	님	an honorifix suffix
초하	early summer	찰나	moment
공허	vacancy	불놀이	playing with fire
기호	mark, taste	불능	impossibility
오후	afternoon	난로	stove
호흡	breath	신라	shilla(dynasty)
오히려	on the contrary	산림	forest
		만	10,000
【ㅁ】 말	horse	온천	hot spring
머리	head	전진	advance
모양	shape		
무	radish	【ㄹ】 리을	the letter "r"
미국	America	러시아	Russia
이마	forehead	라디오	radio
할머니	grandmother	사람	man
사모	longing	기러기	wild goose
나무	tree	가로수	trees along a street
의미	meaning	마루	floor
담	wall	모르다	does not know
모범	model	버리다	throws away
곰	bear	압록강	Amnok River
어려움	difficulty	십리	10 *li*
금	gold	심리	psychology
김	laver	압력	pressure

남루한	poor	모피	fur
발	foot	앞에	in the front
절	temple	헝겊	small piece of cloth
솔	brush	숲에	in the bush
수술	operation	무릎에	on the knee
슬슬	softly	늪에	in the swamp
실	thread	짚으로	with a straw

【ㅇ】 궁전	royal palace	【ㅌ】 탈	mark
증기	steam	털	fur
빙과	ice-candy	토지	land
사랑	love	투자	investment
시렁	shelf	트집	split
악몽	nightmare	티	dust
공중	the public	낙타	camel
실증	actual proof	집터	building land, lot
상징	symbol	도토리	acorn
		사투리	dialect
【ㅍ】 팔	arm	틈틈이	at odd moments
퍼렇다	is deep blue	버티다	support
포도	grapes	낱낱에	for each piece
풀	grass, paste	뒤곁에	behind
프랑스	France		
피리	flute	【ㅋ】 칼	knife
한파	cold wave	컴컴하다	is dark
시퍼렇다	is deep blue	코	nose
대포	cannon	쿨쿨	snoring
부풀다	expands	크다	is big
아프다	hurt	키	height

조카	niece, nephew		큰 코	big nose
넝쿨	vine		부엌에	in the kitchen
웅크리다	crouches		동녘에	in the east
삼키다	swallows		윗녘에	upper side

4. Intonation, Final Contours, Pitch and Pause

In the intonation patterns of the Korean language, pitch (difference in voice levels) is much more important than stress (voice volume). Students with any of the European languages as their linguistic background must be very careful not to carry over their stress type intonation system into Korean !

There are, generally speaking, four levels in the Korean intonation system: 1. extremely high; 2. high; 3. mid; 4. low. These four voice levels are combined within the sentence in three different ways resulting in rises, falls and dips. In our text, they are marked by lines, especially at the end of phrases and sentences (final contours). Heavy print at the beginning of a word indicates a slight rise of pitch. Rises are marked by a rising line ↗, falls by a falling line ↘ and dips by some sort of bent line ⌒, or ↝

Stress exists in Korean but one could perhaps say that it is more noticeable on certain consonants, e.g., those that are aspirated or glottalized (and perforce also on the vowels following those consonants), than on the vowels or on the whole syllable, as in some other languages.

5. Syllabification

An important feature in the Korean sentence is its syllabification. If in a sequence of words the first word ends in a consonant while the next word begins with a vowel, very frequently in normal speech the final consonant of the first word combines with the initial vowel of the second word to form a syllable of their own. For example, 잘 있습니다→자리씀니다(chal issŭmnida→cha-ri-ssŭm-ni-da) ; 재미있습니다→재미씀니다 (chaemi issŭmnida→chae-mi-ssŭm-ni-da).

제삼과 인사 (Lesson 3 Greetings)

TEXT I

〔VOCABULARY〕

제삼	the third	좋아요(좋지-)	is(are, am) good
과	lesson	요즈음	these days, nowadays
인사	greeting	재미	interest, enjoyment
선생	Mr., Mrs., Miss, teacher, doctor	어떠세요	how is ? how are ?
안녕	peace, good health, well-being	그저	just
날씨	the weather	그렇지요	am(is, are) so so
참	very		

1. 김일환 : **안녕하세요?** ↗ How are you ?
2. 이영숙 : 예, ⌒ **안녕하세요?** ↗ Fine (thank you), and you ?
3. 김일환 : 날씨가 **참 좋지요?** ↗ Very fine weather, isn't it ?
4. 이영숙 : 예, ⌒ 참 **좋아요.** ⌒ Yes, it's very nice !
5. 김일환 : 요즈음 **재미가 어떠세요?** ⌒ How are you getting along these days ?
6. 이영숙 : 그저 그렇지요, ↗뭐. ↘ (Just) so so. (I can't complain.)

TEXT II

〔VOCABULARY〕

참	exclamation indicating sudden remembrance	안부	regards, best wishes
-님	personal suffix (honorific)	전해요(전하지-)	conveys, transmits, passes
-께서	nominative(honorific)	주세요(주지-)	give
-도	also	드리지요(드리지-)	honorific form of '주세요'
잘	well, all right		
있어요	is, am, are	그럼	well, then
그분	he, she, that person (honorific)	또	again
-한테	to	뵈어요(뵙지-)	meets (honorific)

7. 김일환 : 참, 한 선생님께서도 안녕하   By the way, how is Mr. Han ?

          세요?

8. 이영숙 : 예, 잘 있어요.   He's fine.

9. 김일환 : 그분한테 안부 전해 주세요.   Please give him my best regards.

10. 이영숙 : 예, 전해 드리지요.   I certainly will.

11. 김일환 : 그럼, 또 뵙겠어요.   Well, I'll see you again.

12. 이영숙 : 예, 안녕히 가세요.   Good-bye !

TEXT III

[VOCABULARY]

어디 where	아주 extremely
가요(가지-) goes	바빠요(바쁘지-) is busy
오래간 (for) a long time	한국 Korea
만이에요 elapsed since	말 word, language
요새 lately, nowadays	한국말 Korean (language)
지내요(지내지-) lives, spends, gets along	공부해요(공부하지-) studies

13. 전성철 : 노 선생님, 어디 가세요?   How do you do, Miss Roh ? (Lit :

                                Where are you going, Miss Roh ?)

14. 노진희 : 아, 전 선생님, 오래간만이   Oh, Mr. CHŏn ! It's a long time since we

          에요.   met.

15. 전성철 : 요새 어떻게 지내세요?   How have you been lately ?

16. 노진희 : 아주 바빠요.   I've been very busy.

17. 전성철 : 왜요?   Why ?

18. 노진희 : 한국말 공부하느라고요.   Because I am studying Korean.

REMARKS TO THE TEXT

Text I

The Arabic numbers below refer to the sentence numbers in the main text.

1. ○안녕하세요? ↗ : This expression is an honorific greeting used in addressing people whose social level is actually or supposedly superior to that of the speaker, e. g., grandparents, parents, teachers, employers, strangers, etc. It is not used when speaking to children, servants, etc., where forms such as : 잘 있었니? ↗ 잘 있니? ↗ are used. Since the subject is not expressed, it can be either "you", "he", "she", or "they", according to the circumstances. The expression may be used at any time of the day : morning, noon and evening.

2. ○예 and its variant 네 are used when one wants to be positive if called, spoken to, greeted, etc. More people favor the latter in casual speech. 예 is used more often among men in formal situations and older people.

3. ○-가 is a particle indicating the subject of the sentence.

   ○참 is the abbreviated form of 참으로 : really, truly, very.

   ○좋- is the stem of the verb 좋아요 : am(is, are) good.

   ○The ending -지요 together with the intonation pattern↗ indicates a casual question corresponding to the English tag question : statement plus "isn't it", "aren't they", etc.

6. ○그렇- is the stem of the verb 그래요. The ending -지요 in combination with the intonation pattern↘ indicates a statement.

Text II

7. ○참! or 아, 참! is an exclamation pronounced in a slightly abrupt way and followed by a pause. It is used when you suddenly recall something completely

forgotten.

○선생 is a title of respect and consequently never used for oneself. Its approximate English equivalent is "Mister", "Mrs.", "Miss", and it may be used either alone or attached to the family name. In its place nowadays the titles 미스터 for "Mister" and 미스 for "Miss" are frequently used. 선생 is also a noun meaning "teacher" and "doctor".

○-님 is a noun suffix expressing reverence. It is never used for oneself.

○-께서 is the honorific form of the subject particle -가 (See R.T., No.3).

9. ○-한테 is a noun particle expressing direction toward both people and animals.

○전해 주세요 is a polite request. As a verbal it consists of two parts 전해 and 주세요. 전해, being the main verb, expresses the main action "passes", while the dependent verb 주세요 expresses the idea that the action of the main verb is requested in favor of the speaker ("Please").

10. ○전해 드리지요 means the same as 전해 주지요 except that the former is more polite. Here the dependent verb 드리지요 is a polite form of 주지요 and expresses the idea that the action is being done in favor of the one spoken to (for you). Do not overly concern yourself with these forms now. Learn them by heart just as they come. Later you will hear more of them.

12. ○예, 안녕히 가세요. This expression means literally : "Please, go in peace". When two people meet on the street, both use this expression to say good-bye. When A visits B at home, in the office, etc. B bids good-bye to A when A leaves with the expression : 안녕히 가세요, "Please, go in peace". A, however, says to B, who stays behind : 안녕히 계세요, "please, stay in peace".

Text III

13. ○이 선생님 : the intonation pattern ↗ plus a short pause after -님 sets off the form as a vocative.

○어디 가세요? : The literal meaning of this question is : "Where are you going ?" The cultural meaning, however, is different. The person addressing you merely wants to be kind and to greet you. This expression is one of the elementary meaning units in the culture of Korea. Feeling offended when addressed this way only shows you have failed to understand. Consequently, you may or may not answer the question, offer some pleasant remark, etc. Nothing further is expected or required.

k-sound, a sound transposition(metathesis) takes place : The k-sound is pronounced

14. ○아! is an interjection of delight, surprise or astonishment.

15. ○어떻게 means : how?, in what way ? In all cases where h-sound precedes k-sound, a sound transposition(metatheses) takes place : The k-sound is pronounced first and is followed by a strong aspiration(h) : 어떠케 ŏttŏkhe.

18. ○The ending -느라고 directly attached to the verb stem expresses reason or causality.

Note :

Voicing the consonant between vowels in a sentence is not fixed ; it often depends on whether there is a pause before the consonant in question or not. If there is a pause prior to it, then the consonant is not voiced as it behaves as an initial consonant. On the other hand, even if the consonant is initial of a word, if it comes in the middle of a breath group(i. e., a sentence or sentences spoken in one breath), then it is voiced. By now, you have already discovered this rule by yourself. Here are some examples:

예, 전해 드리지요 : 예, 전해 드리지요.

or, 아주 바빠요 : 아주 바빠요.

상용어 : Everyday Expressions

1. **고맙습니다.** ⌐
"Thank you." (pure Korean)

   감사합니다. ⌐
"Thank you." (derived from Chinese)

2. **실례합니다.** ⌐
Literally : "I am committing a rudeness." The expression is used for excusing oneself from someone's presence for either a short time or an extended period. (present tense)

   a) "Excuse me for a moment."

   b) "Excuse me, I'll have to go."

   실례했습니다. ⌐
Literally : "I have committed a rudeness." The expression is an apology for something supposedly wrong which has already been done. (past tense)

3. **천만에요.** ⌐
"You are welcome." or "It's all right." A formal response to apologies, expressions of thanks and compliments.

4. **미안합니다.** ⌐
"I'm sorry." Used to apologize or to express gratitude when one takes leave or has been the subject of a little service or favor. In such cases 고맙습니다 or 감사합니다 is sometimes added to the above expression.

5. **수고하십니다.** ⌐
Literally : "You are taking great pains !" Used when you see somebody who is working hard. (present tense)

6. **수고했습니다.** ⌐
Used to say "thank you" for the work somebody has already done. (past tense)

7. **수고하세요.** ⌐
Used when you part from somebody who is actually working.

8. 안녕히 주무세요. ⌐↘

"Good night." Greeting used before going to bed

9. 안녕히 주무셨어요? ↗

"Good morning." Or, literally, "Did you rest well?" Greeting used in the morning.

10. 놀러 오십시오. ↘

"Why don't you come and see us(me)?"

11. 또 오십시오. ↘

"Come again." Used when someone leaves your place after a visit.

12. 그저 밤낮 그렇지요, ↗뭐. ↘

"No change!" (as a possible answer to "How are you?")

DRILLS

─── [ADDITIONAL VOCABULARY] ───────────────────────────

신부   (Catholic) father   부인   your (or his) wife

Text I

A. Substitution Drill : The student is to substitute each of the words given in the box on the right, one by one, for the underlined word in the model sentence given on the left.

1. <u>김 선생님</u> 안녕하세요? ↗
   How are you, Mr. Kim ?

전 선생님,	노 선생님,
이 선생님,	선생님

2. <u>김 선생님</u>이 참 좋지요? ↗
   Mr. Kim is very nice, isn't he?

임 선생님,	마 선생님,
장 선생님,	선생님

3. <u>이</u> 선생님이 참 좋아요. ⌒
   Mr. Lee is very nice..

김 선생님,	전 선생님,
최 선생님,	박 선생님

4. <u>요즈음</u> 재미가 어떠세요? ⌒
   How are you getting along these days ?

안 선생님,	김 선생님,
이 선생님,	선생님

B. Response Drill (based on the Basic Dialogues and Everyday Expressions)

1. 안녕하세요?   예, ⌒ 안녕하세요. ↗
2. 날씨가 참 좋지요?   예, ⌒ 참 좋아요. ⌒
3. 요즈음 재미가 어떠세요?   그저 그렇지요, ↗ 뭐. ↘
4. 고맙습니다.   천만에요. ⌒
5. 감사합니다.   천만에요. ⌒
6. 실례합니다.   천만에요. ⌒

7. 실례했습니다.　　　　　　　　천만에요. ⌒

8. 미안합니다.　　　　　　　　천만에요. ⌒

C. Expansion Drill

어떠세요? ⌒

재미가˘ 어떠세요? ⌒

요즈음˘ 재미가˘ 어떠세요? ⌒

김 선생님 ˘요즈음˘ 재미가˘ 어떠세요? ⌒

How are you getting along these days, Mr. Kim ?

Text II

D. Substitution Drill

1. 김 선생님께서도˘ 안녕하세요? ↗

   And how is Mr. Kim ?

전 선생님,	장 선생님,
정 선생님,	부인

2. 김 선생님께서도˘ 안녕하세요. ⌒

   Mr. Kim is fine, too.

한 선생님,	전 선생님,
장 선생님,	정 선생님

3. 그분한테˘ 안부 전해 주세요. ⌒

   Please give him my best regards.

전 선생님,	장 선생님,
정 선생님,	부인

4. 그럼˘ 또 뵙겠어요. ⌐

   Well, I'll be seeing you again.

신부님,	한 선생님,
김 선생님,	장 선생님

5 한 선생님˘ 안녕히 가세요. ⌐

   Good-bye, Mr. Han.

김 선생님,	전 선생님,
장 선생님,	정 선생님

E. Response Drill

1. 한 선생님께서도 안녕하세요?　　　예, ⌒ 잘 있어요. ⌒

2. 그분한테 안부 전해 주세요.　　　예, ⌒ 전해 드리지요. ⌒

3. 그럼 또 뵙겠어요.   예, ⌒ 안녕히 가세요⌐

4. 수고하십니다.   **안녕하세요?** ↗

5. 수고했습니다.   **천만에요.** ⌐

6. 안녕히 주무세요.   예, ⌒ **안녕히 주무세요.** ⌐

F. Expansion Drill

전해 주세요. ⌒

안부 전해 주세요. ⌒

그분한테 ˇ **안녕** 전해 주세요. ⌒

박 선생님, ˇ 그분한테 ˇ **안부** 전해 주세요. ⌒

Mr. Park, please give him my best regards.

Text III

G. Substitution Drill

1. **미스터 김,** ˇ **어디** 가세요? ⌒

   How do you do, Mr. Kim ?

미스터 최	미스 장
미스 전	미스 박

2. 아, ⌒ **박** 선생님, **오래간만이에요.** ⌒

   Oh! Mr. Pak! I haven't seen you in

   ages.

신부님	**이** 선생님
김 선생님	**장** 선생님

3. **김** 선생님, ˇ **요새** **어**떻게 지내세요? ⌒

   How have you been lately, Mr. Kim ?

박 선생님	**장** 선생님
미스 마	**미스 정**

H. Response Drill

1. 이 선생님 어디 가세요?   아, ⌒ **오래간만이에요.** ⌒

2. 요새 어떻게 지내세요?   **아주** 바빠요. ⌒

3. 왜요?   **한국말** 공부하느라고요. ⌒

4. 놀러 오십시오.   예, ⌒ **고맙습니다.** ⌐

5. 또 오십시오.   예, ⌒ **감사합니다.** ⌐

6. 안녕히 계세요.   예,⌒ 안녕히 가세요.⤳

I. Expansion Drill

지내세요?⌒

어떻게 지내세요?⌒

요새ˇ 어떻게 지내세요?⌒

미스터 김,ˇ 요새ˇ 어떻게 지내세요?⌒

How have you been lately, Mr. Kim ?

제사과 학교 (Lesson 4 At School)

TEXT I

[VOCABULARY]

제사 the fourth	책 book
학교 school	무슨 what(kind of)
이것 this thing	-을 (object particle)
-이 (subject particle)	-(에)서 (happens) at, in
무엇 what	명도원 Myŏngdo Institute
-이에요 am, is, are	

1. 권순제 : **이것이 무엇이에요?** ⌒   What is this ?

2. 장신자 : **책이에요.** ⌒   It's a book.

3. 권순제 : **무슨 책이에요?** ⌒   What (kind of a) book is it ?

4. 장신자 : **한국말 책이에요.** ⌒   It's a Korean language book.

5. 권순제 : **그럼, 한국말을 공부하세요?** ↗   You mean you are studying Korean ?

6. 장신자 : **그럼요.** ⌒   Sure !

7. 권순제 : **어디(에)서 공부하세요?** ⌒   Where do you study ?

8. 장신자 : **명도원에서 공부해요.** ⌒   I'm studying at the Myŏngdo Institute.

TEXT II

[VOCABULARY]

어때요 how is(are)	정동 Chŏng-dong
그런데 but, well	-에 at, in
-는 (topic particle)	그래요 I see, is that so

9. 권순제 : **그 학교가 어때요?** ⌒   How is that school ?

10. 장신자 : **글쎄요.** ⌐   That's hard to say...

11. 권순제 : 그런데 그 학교는 어디 있어요?   (I see but) where is that school located?

12. 장신자 : 정동에 있어요.   It's located in Chŏng-dong.

13. 권순제 : 그래요? 한국말이 재미있어요?   I see. Do you find Korean interesting?

14. 장신자 : 예, 참 재미있어요.   Yes, very much so.

TEXT III

[VOCABULARY]

학생 student	모두 altogether, in all
많아요(많지-) are many(is much)	열다섯 fifteen
아니오 no	가르쳐요(가르치지-) teaches
그리(+neg. verb) not very, not too	내(가) I
몇 분 how many people	엉터리 noncompetent person or a
-은 (topic particle)	person taking it easy

15. 권순제 : 그 학교에 학생이 많아요?   Are there many students in that school?

16. 장신자 : 아니오, 그리 많지 않아요.   No, not very many.

17. 권순제 : 선생님은 몇 분이에요?   How many teachers are there?

18. 장신자 : 모두 열다섯 분이에요.   There are fifteen altogether.

19. 권순제 : 모두 잘 가르쳐요?   (Do they all teach well?) Are they all good teachers?

20. 장신자 : 그럼요. 그런데 내가 엉터리에요.   Yes, of course, but I take it easy.

REMARKS TO THE TEXT

Text I

1. ○ 이것 refers to things close to the speaker : "near me". 그것 refers to things removed from the speaker but close to the person spoken to : "near you". It is also used to indicate a certain thing already under discussion. The English equivalent is "it" or "that". 저것 refers to things removed from both the speaker and the person spoken to : "over there". See the examples below :

이것은 무엇이에요 ? ⌒	What is this ?
그것은 무엇이에요 ? ⌒	What is that ?
저것은 무엇이에요 ? ⌒	What is that over there ?

○ 이- is a demonstrative modifying the following noun. Others of the same category are 그- and 저-. See S.P. No. XI of this lesson.

이것	this (thing)	이사람	he, she (Lit., this person)
그것	that (thing)	그사람	he, she (Lit., that person)
저것	that (thing) over there	저사람	he, she (Lit., that person over there)

○ 무엇. Depending on intonation and pitch, 무엇 functions either as an indefinite pronoun or as an interrogative pronoun. With normal initial pitch(3) and the final contour of the intonation of the sentence going up(↗), 무엇 functions as an indefinite pronoun. With the higher initial pitch(4) and the final contour going down(⌒), it functions as an interrogative pronoun. Other forms behaving in the same way are 누구 "who", 어디 "where", 언제 "when" and some others. See the examples below :

1) a. 무엇을 공부해요 ? ⌒	What do you study?
b. 무엇을 공부해요 ? ↗	Are you studying (something)?

2) a. 누구를 만나요? ⌒　　　　　Whom will you meet ?

　　b. 누구를 만나요? ↗　　　　　Will you meet somebody ?

3) a. 어디 있어요? ⌒　　　　　　Where is it ?

　　b. 어디 있어요? ↗　　　　　　Is it somewhere ?

4) a. 언제 가요? ⌒　　　　　　　When do you go ?

　　b. 언제 가요? ↗　　　　　　　Will you go sometime ?

3. ○무슨- is a noun modifier meaning "what kind of". It is a bound form. See this lesson under S.P. No. XI. See the examples below :

　　무슨 책이 있어요? ⌒　　　　　What book do you have ?

　　무슨 일을 하세요? ⌒　　　　　What work do you do ?

　　무슨 말을 가르치세요? ⌒　　　What language do you teach ?

Text II

9. ○그 학교(가) 어때요? In this sentence the subject particle -가 is omitted. See S.P. No. III.

10. ○글쎄요 "well" is an exclamatory expression of uncertainty.

11. ○그런데 is a contraction of 그러한데. Practically, the contracted 그런데 is much more used. Depending on the context and situation, it has the following meanings : "but", "however", "and", "and yet", "such being the case", etc.

14. ○참 is a contraction of 참으로. It is pronounced in a high pitch (3, 4) and followed by a short abrupt pause. It is used when you hear or see something for which you were not prepared or when you suddenly recall something.

　　○재미있어요 is a descriptive verb, meaning "is interesting", "is delightful". Its literal meaning is "Interest (pleasure, enjoyment) exists". The opposite verb is 재미없어요. Modifier form (or adjective) : 재미있는. Adverb : 재미있게. See the following examples :

　　재미가 어떠세요? ⌒　　　　　How are you feeling ?

　　이 책이 재미있어요? ↗　　　　Is this book interesting ?

이것은 ˅재미있는 ˅책이에요. ⌒   This is an interesting book.

그분은 ˅재미있게 ˅공부해요. ⌒   He finds studying interesting.

한국말은 ˅재미없어요. ⌒   Korean is not interesting.

Text III

15. ○많아요,   "is many", "is much" is used for number as well as for quantity. The opposite word is 적어요. Modifier form: 많은, Adverb: 많이.

학생이 ˅많아요. ⌒   There are many students.

물이 ˅많아요. ⌒   There is much water.

많은 학생이 ˅공부해요. ⌒   Many students study.

이 학생이 ˅공부를 ˅많이 해요. ⌒   This student studies hard (a great deal).

17. ○몇 is a noun modifier meaning "how many" (number).

학생이 ˅몇 사람이에요? ⌒   How many students are there?

선생님이 ˅몇 분이에요? ⌒   How many teachers are there?

이 교실에 ˅책상이 ˅몇 개 있어요? ⌒   How many desks are in this classroom?

20. ○엉터리 is (1) an unreliable or clumsy person;

(2) something made to appear otherwise than it actually is.

그것은 ˅엉터리 회사예요. ⌒   That is a bogus company.

그분은 ˅엉터리 작가예요. ⌒   He is a hack writer.

그분은 ˅엉터리 의사예요. ⌒   He is a quack doctor.

저분은 ˅엉터리예요. ⌒   He is clumsy.

STRUCTURAL PATTERNS

Text I

I. The structure of the Korean sentence

General rule : The more important a word or phrase, the nearer it is placed to the end of the sentence ; the less important, the nearer to the beginning.

Data :

1. The most important item of the Korean sentence is the <u>verb</u>. Its place, therefore, is at the <u>end</u> of the sentence. Korean is a SOV language while English is a SVO language, where S is subject, O is object, and V is verb.

2. Object, place, time or subject are placed before the verb in the order laid down in the above general rule. The order of items in the Korean sentence, therefore, is quite flexible. If all the items in a sentence are of about equal importance, their usual order is : time, subject, place, indirect object, direct object, verb.

  Ex. 오늘 나는 학교에서 친구에게 책을 주었다.

   Today I school-at friend-to book-OP gave. (OP : object particle)

3. Any part of the sentence, with the exception(usually) of the verb, may be omitted from the sentence whenever its meaning is already conveyed to the hearer by the context and / or the situation.

II. The verb -예요(-이에요) : is, equals. This verb is often called copula.

  Examples :

  이것이 교과서예요. ⌒   This is a textbook.

  그것이 책이에요. ⌒   That is a book.

  저것이 연필이에요. ⌒   That over there is a pencil.

  Notes :

  1. This verb expresses identification. It is used whenever you tell <u>what</u> a thing

is, or, to express it somewhat differently, it is used in all sentences that can be reduced to the following pattern: this is the same as that.

2. Being a bound form, it can never occur alone but must always combine in pronunciation with a preceding form. Never pause in front of it.

3. It occurs in two forms:

    a) -예요 after a word ending in a vowel(Ex. 1);

    b) -이에요 after a word ending in a consonant(Ex. 2, 3).

III. The subject particle -가/-이.

Examples:

1. 날씨가 참 좋아요. ⌢	The weather is very fine.
2. 이 교과서가 좋아요. ⌢	This textbook is good.
3. 이것이 책이에요. ⌢	This is a book.
4. 한국말이 재미있어요. ⌢	Korean is interesting.

Notes:

1. The particle -가/-이 marks off the word to which it is added as the subject of the sentence. Later you will see, however, that in a great many cases subjects take the particle -는/-은 instead of -가/-이. When do subjects take the particle -가/-이? Generally stated, they do so whenever you do not want to bring out any particular contrast between the subject and any other expressed or implied matter, event, person, etc.

    In those sentences where the subject takes the particle -가/-이, you might say that the most important piece of information conveyed by the sentence is contained in the subject. For the example:

이것이 무엇이에요? ⌢   What is this?

2. The subject particle occurs in two different forms:

    a) -가 after a word ending in a vowel(Ex. 1, 2);

    b) -이 after a word ending in a consonant (Ex. 3, 4).

3. Being a bound form, the subject particle is directly preceded by the noun. Never pause in front of it.

4. If content and/or situation do not require clear marking of the subject, the subject particle is often omitted. But before you develop the habit of omitting this particle, it is better to first learn thoroughly how to use it correctly.

IV. The object particle -를/-을

Examples:

1. 이 학교를 좋아해요. ⌒   I like this school.
2. 한국말을 공부해요. ⌒   I'm studying Korean.

Notes:

1. The direct object of the verb in the Korean sentence is marked by the particle -를/-을.

2. The particle has two forms:

   a) -를 after words ending in a vowel (Ex. 1);

   b) -을 after words ending in a consonant (Ex. 2).

3. Never pause in front of it.

4. If context and/or situation do not require clear marking of the object, the object particle is often omitted.

V. The honorific infix -시-/-으시-

Korean custom requires an expression of reverence in speech whenever certain categories of people are spoken to or spoken about (parents, grandparents, elder brothers and sisters, high officials, guests, etc.). This is done by using humble forms in referring to oneself, certain items of vocabulary, or certain grammatical devices. All of these are called honorifics. In Lesson Three we studied two of them, the suffixes -님 and -께서. Later we shall meet others. Here we shall limit ourselves to the honorific infix -시-/-으시-. (cf. Lesson 11 S.P. III for the non-honorific polite formal style -ㅂ니까/-습니까 below.)

Examples:

1. 어떻게 지내십니까? ↘ (honorific)   어떻게 지냅니까? ↘   (non-honorific)
   How have you been?

2. 옷을 입으십니까? ↗ (honorific)   옷을 입습니까? ↗   (non-honorific)
   Are you getting dressed?

3. 어떻게 ˅지내세요? ⌒   (honorific)   어떻게 ˅지내요? ⌒   (non-honorific)

How have you been ?

4. 옷을 ˅입으세요? ↗   (honorific)   옷을 ˅입어요? ↗   (non-honorific)

Are you getting dressed ?

Notes :

1. Most verbs which do not have a specific counterpart are easily made honorific by inserting the infix _-시-/-으시-_ between the verb stem and the endings.

2. The honorific appears in two different forms:

   a) _-시-_ after verb stems ending in a vowel(Ex. 1 and 3);

   b) _-으시-_ after verb stems ending in a consonant(Ex. 2 and 4).

Verb Stem	infix	ending	completed form
지내-	-시-	-ㅂ니까	지내십니까
입-	-으시-	-ㅂ니까	입으십니까

3. As you have noticed in examples 3 and 4, whenever the honorific infix _-시-_ is followed by the verb ending _-어요,_ the vowel 이 of the infix amalgamates with the vowel 어 of the ending. The resulting vowel is 여. _-시+어_ becomes 셔; _-셔요_ then becomes _-세요_ in modern Korean.

4. The honorific infix _-시-_, like all other honorifics, is frequently used in addressing other persons. When used in this way it has the meaning of a polite "you".

5. The infix _-시-_ can be used with most of the speech styles.

VI. The particle _-에서_ : (happens) at, in

Examples :

어디에서 ˅공부하세요? ⌒   Where do you study?

학교에서 ˅공부해요. ⌒   I study at school.

교실에서 ˅한국말을 배워요. ⌒   I learn Korean in the classroom.

Notes :

1. _-에서_ denotes location, but <u>only dynamic location</u> : It is used only with an action

verb, i. e., if someone <u>does</u> something at a certain place.

2. The <u>-에</u> of <u>-에서</u> is frequently dropped for no other reason than ease.

Text II

VII. The particle of contrast <u>-는/-은</u>

Examples :

이 교과서는 좋아요. ⌒	This textbook is good.
이 연필은 좋아요. ⌒	This pencil is good.
한국말은 재미있어요. ⌒	Korean is interesting.

Notes :

1. While the particle -가/-이 can only be attached to the subject of the sentence, the particle -는/-은 can be added to almost any part of the sentence, even to the verb (but only in its negative form).

2. The particle -는/-은 is added to the subject (object, etc.) of the sentence whenever you want to bring out a contrast between the subject (object, etc.) and some other expressed or implied matter, event, person, etc.   In sentence where -는/-은 is added to the subject (object, etc.) you might say that the most important piece of information conveyed by the sentence is contained not in the subject (object, etc.) but somewhere else in the sentence.

3. In building Korean sentences, the subject you are going to say something about (the topic) is sometimes put in front of everything else, almost as if it had structurally no relation with the rest of the sentence. In those cases usually the particle -는/-은 is added to the topic. It implies a vague contrast with things you could be speaking about but actually are not.

   Example : 한국은 날씨가 좋아요. ⌒ In Korea   (I'm not speaking of, e.g., India) the weather is fine.

4. There are a great many sentences showing more than one contrast.

   Example : 한국은 날씨는 좋아요. ⌒ In Korea (I'm not speaking of India) the weather (I'm not speaking of, e.g., the roads) is fine.

5. When a subject is mentioned for the first time, the subject particle -가/-이 is usually used. Thereafter the (same) subject is either repeated with -는/-은 added to it or it is omitted altogether. For example : Mr. Kim -가/-이 is a politician. (He -는) was elected to the house of representatives three years ago. (He -는) is going to be sent on a mission to the United States, etc.

6. If -는/-은 is added to the subject or object, the subject and object particles (-가, -를) do not occur. For any other phrases or words, -는/-은 is added to whatever particle would ordinarily be there : For example : 학교에는.

7. The particle -는/-은 occurs in two forms :

a) — 는 after vowels ;

b) — 은 after consonants.

Now look carefully at the following examples.

그 학생은 ˇ요즈음 ˇ학교에서 ˇ한국말을 공부해요. ⌒(not the other student)

요즈음은 ˇ그 학생이 ˇ학교에서 ˇ한국말을 공부해요. ⌒(not formerly)

학교에서는 ˇ그 학생이 ˇ요즈음 ˇ한국말을 공부해요. ⌒(not privately)

한국말은 ˇ그 학생이 ˇ요즈음 ˇ학교에서 공부해요. ⌒(not English)

VIII. The verb 있어요 ; is, exists

Examples :

연필이 ˇ책상 위에 ˇ있어요. ⌒	There is a pencil on the desk.
교실에 ˇ책상이 ˇ있어요. ⌒	There are desks in the classroom.
그 학교는 ˇ정동에 ˇ있어요. ⌒	That school is in Chŏng-dong.
그것은 ˇ학교에 ˇ있어요. ⌒	That is at school.

Notes :

1. This verb refers to existence or location and therefore must be clearly distinguished from the verb of identification -예요/-이에요.(See S.P. No II of this lesson.)

2. It is a free form and therefore can be used alone.

3. Its opposite "is not" is : 없어요.

4. It is also used to express possession or the state of staying.

책이 있어요 :　I have books.=Books exist.

시계가 있어요 : I have a watch.=A watch exists.

집에 있겠어요 : I'll stay home.

IX. The particle 에 : (is) in, at

Examples :

그것은 집에 있어요. ⌒   It's at home.

명도원은 정동에 있어요. ⌒   The Myŏngdo Institute is in Chŏng-

                                           dong.

Notes :

1. This particle denotes static location.

2. Its use is limited to certain verbs like 있어요, 없어요, and a few others.

Text III

X. Negative verb forms.

(A) The verb of identification -예요(-이에요): is, equals

Examples :

1. 이것은 책상이 아니에요. ⌒   This is <u>not</u> a desk.

2. 그것은 의자<u>가</u> 아니에요. ⌒   That is <u>not</u> a chair.

3. 이것이 연필<u>이</u> 아니에요. ⌒   <u>This</u> is not a pencil.

4. 저것이 교과서<u>가</u> 아니에요. ⌒   <u>That</u> is not a textbook.

Notes :

1. We have seen (S.P. No. II of this lesson) that in affirmative sentences of identification, the verb -예요-이에요 is attached directly to the second noun : 이 것이 교과서예요.

2. In negative sentences, however, the second noun is not followed directly by the verb but, rather, by the <u>subject particle</u> (-가/-이) and then by the negative verb 아니에요 : "is not".

3. The first noun is also followed by the subject particle <u>-가/-이</u> or, in order to emphasize the "not", by the topic particle <u>-는/-은</u>.

(B) The verb 있어요 : is, exists

Examples :

그것이 집에 없어요. ⌒   That thing is not in the house.

그분이 교실에 없어요. ⌒   He is not in the classroom.

교실에 의자가 없어요. ⌒   There is no chair in the classroom.

Note :

The negative form of the verb 있어요 is 없어요.

(C) Other verbs

Examples :

제가 공부하지 않아요. ⌒   I don't study.

나는 가르치지 않아요. ⌒   I don't teach.

학생이 많지 않아요. ⌒   There are not many students.

날씨가 좋지 않아요. ⌒   The weather is not good.

Notes :

1. The negative is made by placing the form -지 않아요 directly after the verb stem.

2. Note that in the examples thus far provided, all the verbs are in the present tense.

XI. Independent and dependent nouns

Examples :

Independent nouns (free forms) : Dependent nouns (bound forms) :

연필	pencil	A. -데 (곳)	place	B. 이-
책상	desk	-것	thing	그-
교과서	textbook	-분	person	저-
				어떤-
				어느-
				아무-
				무슨-

Notes :

1. Dependent nouns or bound nouns are nouns that never occur by themselves but must be preceded or followed by some other element (usually another noun but sometimes also an adjective).

2. There are two types of dependent nouns : those that are immediately preceded by another noun (Ex. A), and those that are immediately followed by another noun (Ex. B). Some people call the first category pre-nouns and the second post-nouns.

3. The meaning of these dependent nouns+accompanying element is one, but either side brings in its own connotation.

4. Bound forms when listed by themselves in this text are preceded or followed (or both) by a hypen to indicate that they are bound forms.

이것	this thing	좋은 데(곳)	good place
그것	that thing(or, it)	이분	this person
저것	that thing	그분	that person
좋은 것	a good thing	저분	that person
어느 것	a certain thing	좋은 분	a good person
아무 것	everything	어느 분	a certain person
어떤 것	which thing	어떤 분	what person
일하는 데(곳)	place to work	자는 데(곳)	place to sleep

XII. Cardinal Numbers

There are two sets of cardinal numbers, i.e., the native Korean numbers and the Sino-Korean numbers(e.g. numbers of Chinese origin). Here we introduce the native Korean numbers first.

1	하나(한-)	6	여섯	11	열하나(열한-)
2	둘(두-)	7	일곱	12	열둘(열두-)
3	셋(세-)	8	여덟	13	열셋(열세-)
4	넷(네-)	9	아홉	14	열넷(열네-)
5	다섯	10	열	15	열다섯

16	열여섯	30	서른	80	여든
17	열일곱	40	마흔	90	아흔
18	열여덟	50	쉰	100	백
19	열아홉	60	예순		
20	스물(스무-)	70	일흔		

Note:

Numbers from 하나 "one" to 아흔 아홉 "ninety nine" are of Korean origin, and those from 백 "hundred" to infinity are derived from Chinese numbers.

XIII. Styles of Speech.

Some of the world's languages have developed various styles of speech, each of which is exactly tuned to the social situation for which it was designed. Korean belongs to this group. The situation is not altogether foreign to the speakers of many European languages because something similar can be found in their own linguistic tradition. German, French, Italian, Spanish, Dutch and English, for example, all show certain differences of "style". Korean, however, is one of those languages that has carried this system much further than any of the European languages.

The answer to the question of which various speech styles should be used in a given situation is provided by the social status of both the speaker and the person spoken to as well as by the nature of the situation.

1. The Polite Formal Style (-sŭmnida-style) is used when the social status of the person you are talking to is higher than yours or when his status is equal to or lower than yours but you find yourself talking to him in a formal situation.

2. The Polite Informal Style (-yo-style) is used when you talk informally to people to whom you feel close even though their social status is higher than yours, such as parents, elder brothers and sisters, superiors, and strangers after the initial phase of formality. Remember that this style is not less polite than the polite formal style.

3. The Intimate Style (same as No. 2 with the polite particle -yo dropped) is used with close friends, classmates, younger brothers and sisters, their friends, etc.

It is often mixed with the plain style.

4. The Plain Style (-nŭnda-style) is used with children and sometimes, as mentioned in No. 3, with close friends, younger brothers and sisters, etc.

5. The Familiar Style (-ne-style) is used by students, especially boys, by soldiers and uneducated people.

6. The Authoritative Style (-so-style) is used in situations where the speaker exerts authority of some sort, e.g., a government official or a man in business to his clerks, a policeman to a traffic offender, or anyone in his dealings with servants, etc. Thorough understanding of the Korean social situation is required in order to use this style correctly, otherwise it is better to express oneself in a somewhat more polite style. You will be safe anywhere, in any situation if you use the yo-style. The style of a sentence is determined by the ending of the sentence-final verb. Non-final verb forms are similar in all styles.

XV. The Polite Informal Style.

We have introduced the polite informal or yo-style before any other because it is simple to learn and because it is widely used, especially in the Seoul area. During the Korean War(1950-1953), when the people from Seoul were forced to evacuate the capital, they spread out over the entire country. One of the results of this displacement was the integration of the yo-style of the Seoul dialect into the speech habits of many people in other parts of the country. Women had always used the yo-style while men had resisted it as being feminine. Since the Korean War this has no longer been true.

Examples :

Verb Stem	Ending	Original form	Contraction
a) 좋-	-아요	좋아요	(absent)
많-	-아요	많아요	(absent)
오-	-아요	(오아요)	와요
가-	-아요	(가아요)	가요
b) 재미있-	-어요	재미있어요	(absent)

배우-	-어요	(배우어요)	배워요
주무시-	-어요	주무시어요	주무세요
c) 하-	-여요	하여요	해요
공부하-	-여요	공부하여요	공부해요

Notes :

1. To give the verb its yo-form all you have to do is add the ending -아(-어, -여)요 directly to the stem of the verb.

   a) If the stem of the verb contains either the vowel -아 or the vowel -오, the ending -아요 is added.

   b) If the stem of the verb contains any other vowel, the ending -어요 is added.

   c) The verb stem 하- of the verb 하여요, "does" in both its free and bound form, takes the ending -여요.

2. How to find the stems of verbs ?

   The stem of the great majority of verbs is what remains after removing the present tense negative suffix, -지-. Example : 가/지 (않아요) "does not go". 가- is the stem. However, if the verb contains a sequence of two consonants, the stem is found by removing the -아(-어, -여)요 ending. Example : 읽어요 "reads". 읽- is the stem. The number of verbs belonging to the latter category is small.

3. The ending of the yo-style is the same for the various types of utterances, viz., statement, question, command and proposition. The only tools you are given to set off the one type against the other are the intonation and a feature of length. To master the intonation patterns, therefore, is a matter of great importance. Study the intonation patterns of the yo-style as given below :

Statement	학교에 가요. ⌒	(normal)
Question	학교에 가요? ↗	(often, 학교에 가세요 ?)
Command	학교에 가요. ⌒	(short) (often, 학교에 가세요.)
Proposition	학교에 가요. ⌒	(drawn out a bit)
		(often, 학교에 갑시다)

4. Although the yo-style is used by both sexes, women use it more than men. Men tend to mix it with either the polite formal style or with the intimate style according to the occasion.

5. There are a number of expressions, especially greetings, for which the polite formal style is always used. You have studied some of these in Lesson Three, such as : 고맙습니다, 감사합니다, 실례합니다, 미안합니다.

DRILLS

┌─ [ADDITIONAL VOCABULARY] ─────────────────────────────┐
│ 연필 pencil   교과서 textbook   책상 desk   │
│ 의자 chair   사요(사지-) buys   누가 who   │
│ 언제 when   지우개 eraser   공책 notebook   │
│ 분필 chalk   교실 classroom   방 room   │
│ 집 house   여자 woman   남자 man   │
│ 배워요(배우지-) learns   나빠요(나쁘지-) bad   │
└──┘

Text I

A. Substitution Drill (Attention: Use one of the particle forms given in the parentheses.)

1. 이것이 무엇이에요? ⌢ (이/가)

   What is this?

그것,	저것,	책,
인사,	안부,	날씨

2. 저것이 무슨 학교예요? ⌢ (예요/이에요)

   What (kind of) school is that over there?

책,	연필,	교과서,
책상,	의자	

3. 책을 샀어요. ⌢ (을/를)

   I bought a book.

연필,	책상,	지우개,
교과서,	의자	

4. 학교에서 공부해요. ⌢

   I study at school.

놀아요,	샀어요,	뵙겠어요,
주무세요		

B. Response Drill

1. 학교에서 공부하세요?　　　　예, ⌢ 학교에서 공부해요. ⌢

2. 학교에서 주무세요?　　　　　예, ⌢ 학교에서 자요. ⌢

3. 한국말을 공부하세요?　　　　예, ⌢ 한국말을 공부해요. ⌢

4. 어디에서 공부하세요?　　　　명도원에서 ˇ공부해요. ⌒

5. 학교에서 노세요?　　　　　　예, ⌒ 학교에서 ˇ놀아요. ⌒

6. 아주 바쁘세요?　　　　　　　예, ⌒ 아주 ˇ바빠요. ⌒

C. Intonation Drill

1. 무엇을 공부하세요? ⌒　　　　What are you studying ?

   무엇을 ˇ공부하세요? ↗　　　　Are you studying something ?

2. 누가 공부하세요? ⌒　　　　　Who is studying ?

   누가 ˇ공부하세요? ↗　　　　　Is anyone studying ?

3. 어디 있어요? ⌒　　　　　　　Where is it ?

   어디 ˇ있어요? ↗　　　　　　　Is it somewhere ?

4. 언제 가세요? ⌒　　　　　　　When are you going ?

   언제 ˇ가세요? ↗　　　　　　　Are you going sometime ?

5. 무슨 책을 샀어요? ⌒　　　　What (kind of) book did you buy ?

   무슨 책을 ˇ샀어요? ↗　　　　Did you buy some book ?

D. Expansion Drill

1. 공부해요. ⌒

   한국말을 공부해요. ⌒

   학교에서 ˇ한국말을 공부해요. ⌒

   학생이 ˇ학교에서 ˇ한국말을 공부해요. ⌒

   The student studies Korean at school.

Text II

E. Substitution Drill (Use one of the particle forms given.)

1. 그 학교가 ˇ어때요? ⌒ (이/가)

   How is that school ?

연필,	지우개,	공책,
분필,	교과서,	의자

2. 그런데 ˇ그 책상은 ˇ어디 있어요? ⌒
   (은/는)

   (I see but) where is that desk ?

연필,	지우개,	공책,
분필,	교과서,	의자

3. 그것은 ˇ정˚동에 ˇ있어요. ⌒

That is in Chŏng-dong.

집,	교˚실,	명˚도원,
방,	학˚교,	

4. 한˚국말이 ˇ재˚미있어요? ↗

Is Korean interesting?

나˚빠요,	어˚때요,	아˚니에요,
그˚래요,	좋˚아요,	재˚미없어요

F. Response Drill

1. 그 학˚교가 어때요? 그 학˚교가 ˚좋아요. ⌒

2. 그 학교는 어디 있어요? 그 학교는 ˇ정˚동에 ˇ있어요. ⌒

3. 그 연필은 어디 있어요? 그 연필은 ˚교실에 ˇ있어요. ⌒

4. 그 책상은 어디 있어요? 그 책상은 ˚집에 ˇ있어요. ⌒

5. 저것이 무엇이에요? 저것이 ˚책˚상이에요. ⌒

G. Expansion Drill

ˇ있어요? ⌒

어˚디 있어요? ⌒

그 ˚교˚과서는 ˇ어˚디 있어요? ⌒

김˚ 선생님˚ 그 ˚교˚과서는 ˇ어˚디 있어요? ⌒

그런데˚ 김 선생님˚ 그 ˚교˚과서는 ˇ어˚디 있어요? ⌒

(I see but) Mr. Kim! Where is that textbook?

Text III

H. Substitution Drill (Use one of the particle forms given.)

1. 그 학˚교에 ˚책상이 ˚많아요? ↗ (이/가)

Are there many desks in that school?

책˚,	여˚자,	학˚생,
선˚생,	남˚자,	의˚자

2. 선˚생님은 ˚몇 ˇ분이에요? ⌒ (은/는)

How many teachers are there?

학˚생,	신˚부,	여˚자,
남˚자		

3. 모두 <u>열한</u> 분이에요. ⌒

There are eleven altogether.

I. Pattern Drill

Teacher : 이것이 책이에요. ⌒   This is a book.

Student : 이것이 책이 아니에요. ⌒   This is not a book.

1. 그분이 학생이에요.   그분이 학생이 아니에요. ⌒
2. 이분이 학생이에요.   이분이 학생이 아니에요. ⌒
3. 그것은 의자예요.   그것은 의자가 아니에요. ⌒
4. 저것은 책상이에요.   저것은 책상이 아니에요. ⌒
5. 이것은 교과서예요.   이것은 교과서가 아니에요. ⌒
6. 이것은 공책이에요.   이것은 공책이 아니에요. ⌒

J. Pattern Drill

Teacher : 그것은 교실에 있어요. ⌒   That is in the classroom.

Student : 그것은 교실에 없어요. ⌒   That is not in the classroom.

1. 그것은 학교에 있어요.   그것은 학교에 없어요. ⌒
2. 그것은 명도원에 있어요.   그것은 명도원에 없어요. ⌒
3. 그것은 집에 있어요.   그것은 집에 없어요. ⌒
4. 그 책은 방에 있어요.   그 책은 방에 없어요. ⌒
5. 그 학생은 교실에 있어요.   그 학생은 교실에 없어요. ⌒

K. Pattern Drill

Teacher : 그분은 공부해요. ⌒   He studies.

Student : 그분은 공부하지 않아요. ⌒   He does not study.

1. 그분은 한국말을 가르쳐요.   그분은 한국말을 가르치지 않아요. ⌒
2. 저분은 한국말을 배워요.   저분은 한국말을 배우지 않아요. ⌒
3. 이분은 한국말을 공부해요.   이분은 한국말을 공부하지 않아요. ⌒
4. 그분은 주무세요.   그분은 주무시지 않아요. ⌒
5. 그분은 놀아요.   그분은 놀지 않아요. ⌒
6. 이것은 좋아요.   이것은 좋지 않아요. ⌒

7. 학생이 많아요.   학생이 ^ˇ많지 않아요. ⌒

8. 그 선생님은 바빠요.   그 선생님은 ^ˇ바쁘지 않아요. ⌒

L. Expansion Drill

   1. 가르치지 않아요. ⌒

      한국말을 ^ˇ가르치지 않아요. ⌒

      학교에서 ^ˇ한국말을 ^ˇ가르치지 않아요. ⌒

      김 선생님은 ^ˇ학교에서 ^ˇ한국말을 ^ˇ가르치지 않아요. ⌒

      Mr. Kim does not teach Korean in the school.

   2. 많지 않아요. ⌒

      그리 ^ˇ많지 않아요. ⌒

      학생이 ^ˇ그리 ^ˇ많지 않아요. ⌒

      그 학교에는 ^ˇ학생이 ^ˇ그리 ^ˇ많지 않아요. ⌒

      There are not very many students in that school.

제오과 교통 (Lesson 5 Traffic)

TEXT I

〔VOCABULARY〕

제오 the fifth	저기 over there
교통 traffic	택시 taxi, cab
빨리 quickly, fast	와요(오지-) comes, is coming
갑시다 let's go	스톱 stop
시간 time	-까지 to, up to, as far as
없어요 there is no…, have not	어서 please, quickly
그럽시다 all right(let's do that way)	타요(타지-) gets in, rides
-(으)로 by, by means of	서대문 Sŏdaemun(the West Gate)

1. 김혜경 : 빨리 갑시다. ↘ 시간없어요. ⌢   Let's go quickly. We have no time.

2. 이정석 : 예, ⌢ 그럽시다. ↘ 무엇으로 갈   All right. How shall we go?
   까요? ⌢

3. 김혜경 : 아! ⌢ 저기 택시가 오는군요. ⌢ Ah! Here comes a cab! Let's take it.
   택시로 갑시다. ↘

4. 이정석 : 택시, ⌢ 스톱. ↘   Taxi! Stop.

5. 운전수 : 어서 타세요. ⌢ 어디까지 가세   Please get in. Where are you going?
   요? ⌢

6. 김혜경 : 서대문까지 갑시다. ↘   Let's go as far as Sŏdaemun, please.

TEXT II

〔VOCABULARY〕

여기 here	저분 that person (over there)
늘 always, all the time	수고 trouble, efforts, toil
복잡해요(복잡하지-) is complicated,	누구 who
is crowded.	말이에요 means
광화문 Kwanghwamun.	교통순경 traffic policeman
네거리 crossroads, intersection	

7. 김혜경 : **여기는 늘 복잡해요.** It's always crowded here.

여기가 어디에요? What section is this?

8. 운전수 : **여기는 광화문 네거리예요.** This is the Kwanghwamun intersection.

9. 김혜경 : **저분 참 수고하는데요!** He certainly is working hard!

10. 운전수 : **누구 말이에요?** Whom do you mean?

11. 김혜경 : **저 교통순경 말이에요.** I mean that traffic policeman over there.

12. 운전수 : **그럼요, 수고하고말고요.** He certainly is working hard.

TEXT III

[VOCABULARY]	
집 home, house	그래서 so, therefore
돌아가요(돌아가지-) goes back, returns	일찍 early
	가야겠어요 must go
천천히 slowly	먼저 first, earlier
나는, 난 I	뒤에 later, afterwards
오늘 today	나중에 later, afterwards
피곤해요(피곤하지-) is tired	지하철 subway

13. 김혜경 : **집에 돌아가지 않으시겠어요?** Won't you go back home?

14. 이정석 : **뭐. 천천히 갑시다.** Well! Let's go slowly.

시간이 많은데요, 뭐. We have a lot of time.

15. 김혜경 : **난 오늘 참 피곤해요.** I'm very tired today, so I'll probably

그래서, 일찍 가야겠어요. have to go early.

16. 이정석 : **그러세요?** Is that so?

그럼, 먼저 가세요. Well, why don't you go first?

17. 김혜경 : **뒤에 오시겠어요?** Will you come later?

18. 이정석 : **예, 나중에 지하철로 가겠어요.** Yes, I'll come later by subway.

REMARKS TO THE TEXT

Text I

1. ○ 빨리 is an adverbial meaning (a) "fast, quickly, hastily" (b) "early, soon, instantly". 빠르다 "is fast". Noun modifier : 빠른 "quick". The opposite word is 늦다 "is late". 느리다 "is slow, is tardy."

    빨리 합시다.↘   Let's do (it) quickly. Let's do (it) early.

    기차는 빨라요. ⌒   The train is fast.

    빠른 택시로 갑시다. ↘   Let's take a fast taxi.

2. ○ The verb 가요 "goes" expresses direction away from the speaker, while the verb 와요 "comes" expresses direction towards the speaker. The Koreans are consistent in the use of these two verbs. In some European languages the response to a question like "Why don't you come, too?" could be "All right, I'll come". In Korean you would have to say 가겠어요 "I'll go".

3. ○ 저기 refers to a place "over there" or "over yonder", away from the speaker and the person spoken to, either within sight or out of sight. Compare the following words : 여기 refers to a place close to the speaker, i. e., "this place near me". 거기 refers to (a) a place away from the speaker but close to the person spoken to : "that place near you" ; (b) within sight but slightly away from both speaker and person spoken to : neither "here" nor "over yonder".

5. ○ 어서 depending on the context and intonation, has two different meanings : (a) "please" (b) "quickly, fast".

    어서 오세요. ⌐   Do come, please.

    어서 오세요. ⌒   Come quickly.

6. ○ 서대문 "The Great West Gate" was one of the eight gates in the city wall of Seoul, somewhat less important than either 동대문 "The Great East Gate" or 남대문

"The Great South Gate". It was called 돈의문 "the Gate of Abundant Righteousness", but after its rebuilding (1422) it was better known as 신문 "the New Gate". It stood on the crest of the hill by the former location of the Greek Orthodox Church, from where it was removed by the Japanese in 1915.

Text II

7. ○복잡하다 ; (a) "is complicated", "is intricate ; (b) "is crowded". Noun modifier : 복잡한 "complicated, intricate". Adverbial : 복잡하게 "complicated, intricate". The opposite word is : 간단하다 "is simple". Noun modifier : 간단한 "simple". Adverbial : 간단하게 or 간단히 : "simply".

여기는 복잡해요.	It is crowded here.
한국말은 복잡해요.	Korean is complicated.
이것은 복잡한 일이에요.	This is complicated work.
그분은 복잡하게 말해요.	He speaks in a complicated way.

8. ○광화문 "The Gate of Transformation by Light"

In front of the throne room or main building of the Kyŏngbok Palace in Seoul, there was a series of gates, through which the king's power was conceived as passing out to govern the nation, 광화문 was the outer gate in the series.

10. ○누- "who" always goes together with the subject particle -가. 누가 "who". 누구 "who" always goes together with the object particle -를 : 누구를 "whom".

Text III

14. ○뭐 is a contraction of 무엇. It is an exclamatory expression of meek denial, softening the meaning of what is being said.

15. ○난 is a contraction of 나는.

17. ○뒤에 (a) "after, later, afterwards" ; (b) "behind, back, backward".

뒤에 오세요.	Come later, please.
저분이 책상 뒤에 있어요.	That person is behind the desk.

STRUCTURAL PATTERNS

Text I

I. (A) <u>Verbs</u>

Verbs in Korean are inflected words. Each verb consists of a stem and an ending. Adding various endings to specific verb stems produces changes in either of them or in both. You will gradually learn what those changes are. Before anything else, however, follow your teacher closely when practicing these changes. Being able to use them automatically is of much more value than knowledge of their techniques. The following diagram shows a classification of the Korean verbs:

$$
\text{Verbs}
\begin{cases}
\text{object verbs (transitive)}
\begin{cases}
\text{real object verbs} \\
\text{quasi object verbs}
\end{cases} \text{(all are action verbs)} \\
\\
\text{non-object verbs (intransitive)}
\begin{cases}
\text{action verbs} \\
\text{descriptive verbs}
\end{cases}
\end{cases}
$$

Object verbs are those that are sometimes preceded by a direct object. Non-object verbs are those that are never preceded by a direct object.

(B) <u>Object verbs</u> (or transitive verbs)

Some verbs take only certain direct objects while rejecting others. For this reason they are called quasi-object verbs. They are <u>가요</u> "goes" and <u>와요</u> "comes", used in sentences that express certain situations such as the following:

a) "goal" : <u>학교를 가요</u> "goes to school"

b) "purpose", <u>구경을 가요</u> : "goes to see"

c) "time" : <u>사흘을 가야 해요</u> "must go for three days"

d) "order of time" : <u>첫째 (를) 가요</u> "goes first", "is preeminent"

e) "direction": 강을 건너가요 "goes across the river"

Some other verbs are used with their own substantive form as an objective comple-ment. 잠을 자요 "sleeps"; 춤을 추어요 "dances".

(C) Non-object verbs (or intransitive verbs).

Some non-object verbs are action verbs while others are descriptive verbs. Action verbs are those that tell us SOMETHING HAPPENS or SOMEONE DOES: e.g. 먹어요 "eats". Descriptive verbs are those that tell us SOMEONE OR SOME-THING IS A CERTAIN WAY: e.g. 좋아요 "is good".

A characteristic of descriptive verbs is that they lack some forms common to action verbs, e.g., subjunctive forms (suggestion, command), processive forms(processive modifier, e.g., -는, processive assertive, e.g., -는다).

The verb of identification (copula) -이에요 is a descriptive verb which is never preceded by a pause, as we have seen in Lesson 4, S.P. No. Ⅱ.

The (non-object) verb of existence 있어요 "is"; ∓없어요 "is not", could be called a descriptive verb, but it has all the forms of an action verb except the processive assertive form which in the plain style is not 있는다∓없는다 but 있다 ∓없다.

Some of the information given here is for later reference. Do not be too concerned about it now.

Ⅱ. The propositive form -ㅂ(읍)시다: "Let's"

Examples:

빨리 갑시다. ↘	Let's go quickly.
한국말을 공부합시다. ↘	Let's study Korean.
한국말을 배웁시다. ↘	Let's learn Korean.
여기 있읍시다. ↘	Let's stay here.

Notes:

1. In the propositive form the -ㅂ(읍)시다 form of the polite formal style is used much more than the -아(-어 -여)요 form, although the latter one can occasionally be heard, -가요 or 가세요 (honorific).

2. It is used with action verbs and with the verb of existence 있어요 but not with descriptive verbs or the verb of identification -이에요.

3. It occurs in two shapes, viz., -읍시다 after verb stems ending in a consonant, and -ㅂ시다 after verb stems ending in a vowel, either of which is added directly to the verb stem or to the verb stem plus the honorific infix -시-.

4. With children and sometimes with close friends you use the plain style 가자 "Let's go".

III. Noun + -(으)로 : "by means of"

Examples :

기차로 갑시다. ↘	Let's go by train.
비행기로 가세요? ↗	Do you go by airplane?
지하철로 갑시다. ↘	Let's go by subway.
연필로 씁시다. ↘	Let's write with a pencil.

Notes :

1. The particle -(으)로 attached to a noun denotes the means by which one moves about or does something.

2. -로 is used after nouns ending in a vowel and -으로 is used after nouns ending in all consonants except ㄹ. After ㄹ the shape is -로.

IV. The form -ㄹ(을)까요? : "Shall I⋯?" or "Shall we⋯?"

Examples :

무엇을 할까요? ⌒	What shall I (we) do?
한국말을 공부할까요? ↗	Shall I (we) study Korean?
비행기로 갈까요? ↗	Shall I (we) go by airplane?
영어를 배울까요? ↗	Shall I (we) learn English?
잘까요? ↗	Shall I (we) sleep?
집에 있을까요? ↗	Shall we stay at home?

Notes :

1. When this pattern is used with action verbs :

a) the subject of the sentence is always the first person, singular or plural.

b) it inquires about someone's opinion "You think I should...?", or offers to do something, as the case might be.

2. When used with descriptive verbs, or with 있- "exists" or -이- "is":

a) the subject of the sentence is the <u>third</u> person.

b) it expresses doubt or polite denial. See the following examples:

한국말이 ˇ 재미있을까요? ↗	You say Korean is interesting?
그 책이 ˇ 좋을까요? ↗	You say that book is good?
그분이 ˇ 선생일까요? ↗	You say he is a teacher?

3. The pattern occurs in two shapes: -ㄹ까요? after verb stems ending in a vowel; -을까요? after verb stems ending in a consonant.

4. The intimate style form is obtained by dropping the particle -요.

V. The exclamatory ending: -는군요/-군요

1. This ending occurs in two shapes as indicated in the title of this paragraph. To study the occurrences of either shape you need the following information. The past tense of the Korean verb is formed by inserting the infix -았-/-었- between the verb stem and its ending. The future tense is formed by inserting the infix -겠-. The present tense is signalled by the absence of these infixes. You will soon hear more of these infixes. Now look at the following diagram. A.V.S. stands for action verb stem and D.V.S. stands for descriptive verb stem.

Present	A.V.S. + -는군요
Past	A.V.S. + -었군요 (-았군요, -였군요)
Tentative or probable fact	A.V.S. + -겠군요
Present	D.V.S. + -군요
Past	D.V.S. + -았군요 (-었군요)
Tentative or probable fact	D.V.S. + -겠군요
Present	있- + -군요
Past	있- + -었군요
Tentative or probable fact	있- + -겠군요

Present	이- + -군요
Past	이- + -었군요
Tentative or probable fact	이- + -겠군요

The diagram indicates that the -는군요 shape of this ending occurs in only one case, viz., with action verbs in the present tense. In all other cases the ending takes the -군요 shape.

Examples:

그분이ˇ한국말을ˇ가르치는군요. ⌒	He is teaching Korean!
그분이ˇ한국말을ˇ가르쳤군요. ⌒	He taught Korean!
그분이ˇ한국말을ˇ가르치겠군요. ⌒	I think he is going to teach Korean!
그것이ˇ좋군요. ⌒	That's wonderful (good)!
그것이ˇ좋았군요. ⌒	That was wonderful!
그것이ˇ좋겠군요. ⌒	I definitely think that will be alright!
그것이ˇ여기 있군요. ⌒	That thing is here!
그것이ˇ여기 있었군요. ⌒	That thing was here!
그것이ˇ여기 있겠군요. ⌒	I think that thing is here!
그분이ˇ학생이군요. ⌒	He is a student!
그분이ˇ학생이었군요. ⌒	He was a student!
그분이ˇ학생이겠군요. ⌒	I think he is a student!

2. According to the circumstances this ending expresses delight, surprise, or astonishment.

3. The intimate style form is obtained by dropping the particle -요. 그것이 좋군! 그분이 학생이군! etc.

VI. The particle -까지 : "(all the way up) to"

Examples:

어디까지 가세요? ⌒	How far (lit. as far as what place) are you going?

명도학교까지 가요. ⌒   I am going as far as Myŏngdo school.

서대문까지 갑시다. ↘   Let's go to (as far as) Sŏdaemun.

두 시까지 오세요. ↘   Please come by two o'clock.

Note:

The particle -까지 is attached to nominals of place or time.

Text II

Ⅶ. The exclamatory/inquisitive ending -ㄴ(은)데요/-는데요

   1. This ending also occurs in two shapes. Look at the diagram below:

Present	A.V.S. + -는데요
Past	A.V.S. + -았는데요
Tentative or probable fact	A.V.S. + -겠는데요
Present	D.V.S. + -ㄴ(-은)데요
Past	D.V.S. + -았는데요
Tentative or probable fact	D.V.S. + -겠는데요
Present	있- + -는데요
Past	있- + -었는데요
Tentative or probable fact	있- + -겠는데요
Present	-이 + -ㄴ데요
Past	-이 + -었는데요
Tentative or probable fact	-이 + -겠는데요

The diagram shows that the -ㄴ(은)데요 shape of this ending occurs in two cases: with descriptive verbs in the present tense and with the verb of identification -이- in the present tense. See below: the examples are given in the same order. In all other cases the ending is -는데요. Notice the difference in occurrence with the -군요 ending(No. Ⅴ).

Examples:

그분이 공부하는데요! ↗⌒   He is studying!

그분이 ˇ공부했는데요! ↗⌒	He studied!
그분이 ˇ공부 잘 ˇ하겠는데요! ↗⌒	I think he'll study very well!
날씨가 참 ˇ좋은데요! ↗⌒	The weather is very fine!
그것이 ˇ좋았는데요! ↗⌒	That was wonderful!
그것이 ˇ좋겠는데요! ↗⌒	I think that could be wonderful!
그것이 ˇ여기 있는데요! ↗⌒	That is here!
그것이 ˇ여기 있었는데요! ↗⌒	That was here!
그것이 ˇ여기 있겠는데요! ↗⌒	I think it will be here!
그분이 ˇ학생인데요! ↗⌒	He is a student!
그분이 ˇ학생이었는데요! ↗⌒	He was a student!
그분이 ˇ학생이겠는데요! ↗⌒	I think he will be (quite) a student!

2. This ending, when pronounced with the final contour of the intonation pattern going down⌒, expresses delight, surprise, or astonishment. When pronounced with the final contour going up↗, it tells that the speaker wants to know the opinion or the feelings of the other party. Special care, therefore, should be given to the intonation patterns.

3. -ㄴ(은)데요 has two possible shapes:

   a) -ㄴ데요 after verb stems endning in a vowel;

   b) -은데요 after verb stems ending in a consonant.

4. The intimate style form is obtained by dropping the final particle -요. 날씨가 참 좋은데! etc.

VIII. Verb Stem + -고말고요 : "of course" or "surely"

Examples :

공부하고말고요. ⌒	Of course I study.
재미있고말고요. ⌒	It's certainly interesting.
좋고말고요. ⌒	It surely is good.
그 책이 ˇ있고말고요. ⌒	Of course I have that book.
그분이 학생이고말고요. ⌒	Of course he's a student.

Notes:

1. The ending -고말고요 is used with any verb and means "surely", "of course" or "to say nothing of".

2. The intimate style form is obtained by dropping the final particle -요. 공부하고말고, etc.

Text III

IX. The particle -에 (가요/와요←오아요) : "to" (direction)

Examples:

학교에 가세요? ↗	Are you going to school?
집에 가요. ⌒	I'm going home.
빨리 학교에 오세요. ⌒	Please come to school quickly.
집에 와요. ⌒	Please come home.

Notes:

1. The particle -에 "to" is used after nominals of place and denotes direction when followed by either 가다 or 오다 or similar verbs (compound verbs with 가다≠오다). Therefore it is always used with verbs denoting movement, like 가요≠와요 and their compounds. Some compounds are 걸어오다, 놀러가다.

2. Notice the difference in meaning with the particle -까지 (See this lesson, S.P. No VI).

X. The intentional infix -겠-

Examples:

Statements

집에 가겠어요. ⌒	I intend to go home.
한국말을 공부하겠어요. ⌒	I will study Korean.
한국말을 가르치겠어요. ⌒	I intend to teach Korean.

Questions

무엇을 하시겠어요? ⌒	What do you intend to do?
여기에 오시겠어요? ↗	Will you come here?

한국말을 공부하시겠어요? ↗   Will you study Korean?

Notes :

1. The intentional infix -겠- is inserted between the stem (or the stem plus the
   honorific -시-) and the ending. It states or asks for the subject's intention,
   planning or schedule. It has this meaning, however, in only two cases :
   a) in statements the subject of which is the first person ;
   b) in questions the subject of which is the second person.

2. There is also a suppositional infix -겠-, but this will be studied later.

XI . The pattern -아(-어, -여)야 하다 : "(one) must" or "(one) has to"

Examples :

학교에 가야 해요. ⌢   I have to go to school.

그분은 그것을 빨리 해야 해요. ⌢   He has to do that quickly.

나는 자야 해요. ⌢   I must sleep.

한국말을 공부해야 해요. ⌢   I must study Korean.

나는 여기 있어야 해요. ⌢   I must stay here.

Note :

This pattern may be used with action verbs only and expresses necessity or
obligation.

XII . The Verb Stem + -아(-어, -여)야겠어요 : "will (probably) have to..."

Examples :

빨리 가야겠어요. ⌢   I will (probably) have to go quickly.

한국말을 공부해야겠어요. ⌢   I will (probably) have to study Korean.

기차로 와야겠어요. ⌢   I will (probably) have to come by
                                   train.

그분은 일찍 주무셔야겠어요. ⌢   He will (probably) have to sleep ear-
                                   lier.

Notes :

1. -아(-어, -여)야겠어요 is a contraction of -아(-어, -여)야 하겠어요. The
contracted form is used more often than the full form.

2. The rules for adding this ending to the verb stem are the same as for the -아
(-어, -여)요 ending.

XIII. The Chinese Derived Numbers (or, the Sino-Korean numbers)

1	일	12	십이	23	이십삼	34	삼십사	45	사십오
2	이	13	십삼	24	이십사	35	삼십오	46	사십육
3	삼	14	십사	25	이십오	36	삼십육	47	사십칠
4	사	15	십오	26	이십육	37	삼십칠	48	사십팔
5	오	16	십육	27	이십칠	38	삼십팔	49	사십구
6	육	17	십칠	28	이십팔	39	삼십구	50	오십
7	칠	18	십팔	29	이십구	40	사십	60	육십
8	팔	19	십구	30	삼십	41	사십일	70	칠십
9	구	20	이십	31	삼십일	42	사십이	80	팔십
10	십	21	이십일	32	삼십이	43	사십삼	90	구십
11	십일	22	이십이	33	삼십삼	44	사십사	100	백

200	이백	800	팔백	5,000	오천	20,000	이만	80,000	팔만
300	삼백	900	구백	6,000	육천	30,000	삼만	90,000	구만
400	사백	1,000	천	7,000	칠천	40,000	사만	100,000	십만
500	오백	2,000	이천	8,000	팔천	50,000	오만	1,000,000	백만
600	육백	3,000	삼천	9,000	구천	60,000	육만	10,000,000	천만
700	칠백	4,000	사천	10,000	만	70,000	칠만	100,000,000	억

Note:

As we have seen in Lesson 4, S.P. No XII, Korean uses two sets of numerals, one of which is borrowed from Chinese. For the numerals 1-99 both sets are used; for the numerals 100 and up, only the Chinese set is used.

DRILLS

> ┌─[ADDITIONAL VOCABULARY]─────────────────────────┐
> 기차 train   비행기 airplane   버스 bus
> 지하철 subway   자전거 bicycle   영어 English
> 자동차 automobile   예뻐요(예쁘지-) is pretty   부산 Pusan
> 극장 theatre   식당 restaurant
> └───┘

Text I

A. Substitution Drill

1. 택시로 갑시다. ↘

   Let's go by taxi.

   | 기차, | 비행기, | 자동차, |
   | 버스, | 지하철, | 자전거 |

2. 무엇으로 갈까요? ⌒

   How shall I (we) go?

   | 비행기, | 기차, | 자동차, |
   | 지하철 | | |

B. Substitution Drill

1. 그분이 한국말을 가르치는군요. ⌒   He teaches Korean!
2. 그분이 영어를 공부하는군요. ⌒   He studies English!
3. 저기 택시가 오는군요. ⌒   Here comes a taxi!
4. 그분이 한국말을 배우는군요. ⌒   He learns Korean!
5. 저분이 연필을 사는군요. ⌒   He is buying pencils!

C. Pattern Drill

Teacher : 날씨가 참 좋아요. ⌒   It is very fine weather. (statement)

Student : 날씨가 참 좋군요. ⌒   It is very fine weather! (exclamation)

1. 한국말이 참 재미있어요.   한국말이 참 재미있군요. ⌒
2. 그것이 여기 있어요.   그것이 여기 있군요. ⌒
3. 그분이 학생이에요.   그분이 학생이군요. ⌒

4. 선생님이 참 많아요.　　　　선생님이 참 많군요.

5. 선생님이 참 적어요.　　　　선생님이 참 적군요.

6. 이 책상이 참 좋아요.　　　　이 책상이 참 좋군요.

D. Substitution Drill

1. 서대문까지 갑시다. ↘　　　　Let's go all the way to Sŏdaemun.

2. 서울까지 갑시다. ↘　　　　Let's go all the way to Seoul.

3. 그 교실까지 갑시다. ↘　　　Let's go as far as that classroom.

4. 그 집까지 갑시다. ↘　　　　Let's go as far as that house.

5. 그 방까지 갑시다. ↘　　　　Let's go as far as that room.

E. Response Drill

1. 택시로 갈까요?　　　　예, 택시로 갑시다. ↘

2. 공부할까요?　　　　예, 공부합시다. ↘

3. 무엇으로 갈까요?　　　　기차로 갑시다. ↘

4. 어디까지 가세요?　　　　학교까지 가요.

5. 그 책이 어디에 있어요?　　　그 책이 교실에 있어요.

F. Expansion Drill

1. 갈까요? ↗

　택시로 갈까요? ↗

　서대문까지 택시로 갈까요? ↗

　김 선생님 서대문까지 택시로 갈까요? ↗

　Mr. Kim! Shall we go as far as Sŏdaemun by taxi?

Text II

G. Substitution Drill

1. 누가 가르치세요?

　Who teaches?

| 공부하, | 배우, | 가, |
| 주무, | 바쁘 | |

H. Substitution Drill

1. 저분이 공부하는데요. ↗ (⌢)　　That person over there is studying!

2. 그 책이 ˇ여기 있는데요. ↗(⌢)　　That book is here!

3. 나는 ˇ책이 ˇ없는데요. ↗(⌢)　　I have no book!

4. 한국말이 ˇ재미있는데요. ↗(⌢)　　Korean is interesting!

5. 한국말이 ˇ재미없는데요. ↗(⌢)　　Korean is not interesting!

6. 그분이 ˇ영어를 ˇ가르치는데요. ↗(⌢)　　He is teaching English!

7. 이분이 ˇ한국말을 ˇ배우는데요. ↗(⌢)　　This person is learning Korean!

8. 시간이 ˇ없는데요. ↗(⌢)　　I have no time!

I. Pattern Drill

Teacher : 날씨가 ˇ참 ˇ좋군요. ⌢　　It is very fine weather. (statement)

Student : 날씨가 ˇ참 ˇ좋은데요. ↗(⌢)　　It is very fine weather! (exclamation)

1. 날씨가 참 나쁘군요.　　날씨가 ˇ참 ˇ나쁜데요. ↗(⌢)

2. 시간이 많군요.　　시간이 ˇ많은데요. ↗(⌢)

3. 여기는 늘 복잡하군요.　　여기는 ˇ늘 ˇ복잡한데요. ↗(⌢)

4. 이것은 교실이군요.　　이것은 ˇ교실인데요. ↗(⌢)

5. 저분은 선생이군요.　　저분은 ˇ선생인데요. ↗(⌢)

6. 그분은 바쁘군요.　　그분은 ˇ바쁜데요. ↗(⌢)

7. 그분은 예쁘군요.　　그분은 ˇ예쁜데요. ↗(⌢)

J. Response Drill

Teacher : 한국말이 ˇ재미있어요? ↗　　Is Korean interesting?

Student : 한국말이 ˇ재미있고말고요. ⌢　　Of course Korean is interesting.

1. 그 책이 좋아요?　　그 책이 ˇ좋고말고요. ⌢

2. 그 책이 있어요?　　그 책이 ˇ있고말고요. ⌢

3. 그분이 학생이에요?　　그분이 ˇ학생이고말고요. ⌢

4. 한국말을 가르쳐요?　　한국말을 ˇ가르치고말고요. ⌢

5. 영어를 공부해요?　　영어를 ˇ공부하고말고요. ⌢

6. 여기는 늘 복잡해요?　　여기는 ˇ늘 ˇ복잡하고말고요. ⌢

7. 그분은 늘 바빠요?　　그분은 ˇ늘 ˇ바쁘고말고요. ⌢

K. Pattern Drill

Teacher : 그분이 학생이에요. ⌒   He is a student.

Student : 그분이 학생이 아니에요. ⌒   He is not a student.

1. 선생이 많아요.   선생이 많지 않아요. ⌒

2. 저것은 책이에요.   저것은 책이 아니에요. ⌒

3. 그분은 한국말을 가르쳐요.   그분은 한국말을 가르치지 않아요. ⌒

4. 그분은 기차를 타요.   그분은 기차를 타지 않아요. ⌒

5. 그분은 공부해요   그분은 공부하지 않아요. ⌒

6. 그분은 예뻐요.   그분은 예쁘지 않아요. ⌒

L. Response Drill

1. 빨리 갈까요?   예, ⌒ 빨리 갑시다. ↘

2. 택시로 갈까요?   예, ⌒ 택시로 갑시다. ↘

3. 여기가 어디예요?   여기가 광화문 네거리예요. ⌒

4. 누가 수고해요?   한 선생님이 수고해요. ⌒

5. 저분이 누구예요?   저분이 교통순경이에요. ⌒

6. 어디까지 가세요?   학교까지 가요. ⌒

M. Response Drill

1. 누구 말이에요?   저 교통순경 말이에요. ⌒

2. 무엇 말이에요?   저 책 말이에요. ⌒

3. 무슨 연필 말이에요?   이 연필 말이에요. ⌒

4. 저 자동차 말이에요?   예, ⌒ 저 자동차 말이에요. ⌒

5. 서대문 말이에요?   예, ⌒ 서대문 말이에요. ⌒

6. 광화문 네거리 말이에요?   예, ⌒ 광화문 네거리 말이에요. ⌒

Text III

N. Substitution Drill

1. 집에 갑시다. ↘

   Let's go home.

부산,	학교,	극장,
방,	식당,	서대문

O. Substitution Drill

1. **가**지 않으시겠어요? ↗   Won't you go?
2. **주무시**지 않으시겠어요? ↗   Won't you sleep?
3. **공부하**지 않으시겠어요? ↗   Won't you study?
4. **기차를 타**지 않으시겠어요? ↗   Won't you take a train?
5. **집에 오**지 않으시겠어요? ↗   Won't you come to my home?
6. **그 책상을 사**지 않으시겠어요? ↗   Won't you buy that desk?
7. **한국말을 배우**지 않으시겠어요? ↗   Won't you learn Korean?
8. **집에 돌아가**지 않으시겠어요? ↗   Won't you go back home?

P. Pattern Drill

Teacher : **학교**에 **가**요. ⌒   I go to school.

Student : **학교**에 **가**겠어요. ⌒   I intend to go to school.

1. 한국말을 가르쳐요.   **한국말을 가르치**겠어요. ⌒
2. 영어를 배워요.   **영어를 배우**겠어요. ⌒
3. 한국말을 공부해요.   **한국말을 공부하**겠어요. ⌒
4. 집에 와요.   **집에 오**겠어요. ⌒
5. 집에 돌아가요.   **집에 돌아가**겠어요. ⌒
6. 비행기를 타요.   **비행기를 타**겠어요. ⌒
7. 책을 사요.   **책을 사**겠어요. ⌒
8. 학교에서 놀아요.   **학교에서 놀**겠어요. ⌒

Q. Pattern Drill

Teacher : **학교**에 **가**요. ⌒   I go to school.

Student : **학교**에 **가**야 해요. ⌒   I have to go to school.

1. 한국말을 가르쳐요.   **한국말을 가르쳐**야 해요. ⌒
2. 영어를 배워요.   **영어를 배워**야 해요. ⌒
3. 한국말을 공부해요.   **한국말을 공부해**야 해요. ⌒
4. 집에 와요.   **집에 와**야 해요. ⌒
5. 집에 돌아가요.   **집에 돌아가**야 해요. ⌒
6. 비행기를 타요.   **비행기를 타**야 해요. ⌒

7. 한국말 책을 사요.　　　　　　　한국말 책을 ˇ사야 해요. ⌒

8. 학교에서 놀아요.　　　　　　　학교에서 ˇ놀아야 해요. ⌒

R. Pattern Drill

Teacher : 학교에 ˇ가야 해요. ⌒　　　I have to go to school.

Student : 학교에 ˇ가야겠어요. ⌒　　　I will (probably) have to go to school.

1. 학교에 와야 해요.　　　　　　학교에 ˇ와야겠어요. ⌒

2. 한국말을 가르쳐야 해요.　　　한국말을 ˇ가르쳐야겠어요. ⌒

3. 영어를 배워야 해요.　　　　　영어를 ˇ배워야겠어요. ⌒

4. 한국말을 공부해야 해요.　　　한국말을 ˇ공부해야겠어요. ⌒

5. 집에 돌아가야 해요.　　　　　집에 ˇ돌아가야겠어요. ⌒

6. 비행기를 타야 해요.　　　　　비행기를 ˇ타야겠어요. ⌒

S. Response Drill

1. 무엇으로 가시겠어요 ?　　　　지하철로 ˇ가겠어요. ⌒

2. 무엇을 사시겠어요 ?　　　　　자동차를 ˇ사겠어요. ⌒

3. 뒤에 오시겠어요 ?　　　　　　예, ⌒ 뒤에 ˇ가겠어요. ⌒

4. 일찍 가시겠어요 ?　　　　　　예, ⌒ 일찍 ˇ가겠어요. ⌒

5. 나중에 배우시겠어요 ?　　　　예, ⌒ 나중에 ˇ배우겠어요. ⌒

6. 무엇을 가르치시겠어요 ?　　　한국말을 ˇ가르치겠어요. ⌒

T. Expansion Drill

1. 가야겠어요. ⌒

　집에 ˇ가야겠어요. ⌒

　일찍 ˇ집에 ˇ가야겠어요. ⌒

　택시로 ˇ일찍 ˇ집에 ˇ가야겠어요. ⌒

　나는 ˇ택시로 ˇ일찍 ˇ집에 ˇ가야겠어요. ⌒

　I'll have to go home early by taxi.

제육과 물건사기 I (Lesson 6 Shopping I)

TEXT I

┌─ 〔VOCABULARY〕 ─────────────────────────────────┐

어서 please   사천 four thousand
점원 clerk, shop-man   원 wŏn
물건 goods, thing, article   좀 for a moment, please
만년필 fountain pen   보여요(보이지-) shows
얼마예요 how much is (it)   주어요(주지-) gives
어느 which   드려요(드리지-) gives(honorific)
말이에요 means   돈 money
까만 black

└───┘

1. 점 원 : **어서** 오십시오. ⌐   Welcome ! (Do come, please.)

2. 한만일 : 저 **만년필**(이) **얼마예요**? ⌒   How much is that fountain pen over
                                          there ?

3. 점 원 : **어느** 것 말이에요? ⌒   Which one do you mean ?

4. 한만일 : 저 **까만** 것 말이에요. ⌒   I mean that black one over there.

5. 점 원 : 예, ⌒ **사천** 원이에요. ⌒   I see. That one is four thousand wŏn.

6. 한만일 : 좀 **보여** 주시겠어요? ↗   May I look at it? (Show me, please.)

7. 점 원 : 예, ⌒ **보여** 드리지요. ⌒   Please do! (I'll show it to you.)

8. 한만일 : 돈, **여기** 있어요. ⌒   Here is the money.

9. 점 원 : **감사합니다**. ⌐ 또 오세요. ⌐   Thank you. Come again.

TEXT II

〔VOCABULARY〕

예쁜 것 beautiful thing
인형 doll
어때요 how is it, how about
커요(크지-) is big
너무 too (much)
없어요 there is no..., have not
작은 것 small thing
빨간 red
마음 mind, spirit, mentality

들어요(들지-) is satisfied with, suits, catches
괜찮아요(괜찮지-) is pretty good
같아요(같지-) is the same
얼마 how much
오천 five thousand
이백 two hundred
비싸요(비싸지-) is expensive
싸요(싸지-) is cheap

10. 한만일 : 한국 인형 예쁜 것 있어요? ↗   Do you have any beautiful Korean dolls?

11. 점 원 : 예, ⌒ 있어요. ⌒ 이것(은) 어떠세요? ⌒   Yes, we do. How about this one?

12. 한만일 : 너무 크군요. ⌒ 좀 작은 것 없어요? ↗   It's too big. Don't you have a smaller one?

13. 점 원 : 그럼, 이 빨간 것은 어떠세요? ⌒   Well, then, how about this red one?

14. 한만일 : 예, ⌒ 마음에 들어요. ⌒ 괜찮을 것 같군요. ⌒ 얼마지요? ↗   Yes, I like it. It's pretty good. How much is it?

15. 점 원 : 오천 이백 원이에요. ⌒   It's five thousand two hundred wŏn.

16. 한만일 : 너무 비싼데요. ↗ 좀 싸게 합시다. ↘   It's too expensive. Let's make it a little cheaper.

TEXT III

〔VOCABULARY〕

담배 cigarette
한 갑 a pack of (cigarettes)
아리랑 Arirang
자 well!
받아요(받지-) receivces

-짜리 worth, price, value, bill
잔돈 change, small money
잠깐 for a moment, for a while
기다려요(기다리지-) wait

17. 한만일 :	담배 한 갑 주세요. ⌒	Give me a pack of cigarettes, please.
18. 점 원 :	무슨 담배 드릴까요? ⌒	What kind of cigarettes do you want?
19. 한만일 :	아리랑 한 갑 주세요. ⌒	Give me a pack of Arirang, please.
20. 점 원 :	예, ⌒ 여기 있어요. ⌒	Here it is.
21. 한만일 :	자, ⌒ 돈 받으세요. ⌒	Well, here is the money. It's a thou-
	천 원짜리예요. ⌒	sand wŏn bill.
22. 점 원 :	잔돈이 없는데요. ↗	I have no change. Do you have any
	잔돈 없으세요? ↗	change ?
23. 한만일 :	잠깐 기다려 보세요. ⌒	Just a moment. I'll check. Ah! Here
	아, ⌒ 여기 있군요. ⌒	it is.
24. 점 원 :	감사합니다. ⌐	Thank you.

REMARKS TO THE TEXT

Text I

1. ○어서 오십시오. "Do come, please ; Welcome!" is regularly used for greeting a customer entering a store, restaurant, hotel, etc., and also for welcoming a guest to one's home.

2. ○만년필(萬年筆) is a fountain pen. Its literal meaning is "ten thousand years brush." 저 만년필(이) 얼마예요? Here the subject particle -이 is omitted.

3. 4. ○The object particle -을 is omitted. See Lesson 4, S. P. No. IV.

5. ○-원 is a Korean money classifier. It must be used with the Chinese derived numerals. About 700 wŏn equals one U.S. dollar according to the currency exchange rate in effect at the time of revision of this text.

9. ○It is customary to say 감사합니다, not 감사해요, which is considered impolite and used to children by adults.

Text II

10. ○인형. Korean dolls are comparatively famous and popular with foreigners because of their dress. Nowadays they are exported in quantity to foreign countries.

   ○있다, depending on the context, has several meanings, e.g., "is located", "exists", "has", "stays". See Lesson 4, S.P. No. VIII. See the following examples :

   a) 책 있어요? ↗   Do you have a book ?

   　담배 있어요? ↗   Do you have cigarettes ?

   　돈 있어요? ↗   Do you have money ?

   b) 여기 있어요. ⌢   It is here.

   　책상이 교실에 있어요. ⌢   There is a desk in the classroom.

   　사람이 많이 있어요. ⌢   There are many people.

c) **두 시까지 여기 있겠어요. ⌒**   I will stay here until two.

14. ○**마음에 들어요** : **마음** is "mind, spirit, mentality" and **들어요** "is satisfied with, takes one's fancy, takes a fancy". Therefore, its literal meaning is "I take a fancy to it", or "it appeals to me". Notice the following examples :

저분은 마음이 좋아요. ⌒   He is a good-hearted person.

그분은 마음이 나빠요. ⌒   He is an evil-minded person.

내 마음에 드는 집이 있어요. ⌒   There is a house to my taste.

내 마음에 드는 여자가 있어요. ⌒   There is a woman after my own heart.

Text III

17. ○**담배** "cigarette" is being distinguished from other things to smoke, e.g., pipes, cigars, etc. Cigar is **여송연** or **입담배**. See the cultural notes below.

18. ○**드리다** is the honorific verb for "gives". The non-honorific verb would be **주다**.

19. ○**아리랑** : The name Arirang is used here to denote a certain brand of Korean cigarettes. It is taken from the folk song of the same name. See the cultural notes below.

○**-갑** is a classifier meaning "a pack of". It must be used with the Korean numerals, not with the Chinese numerals.

21. ○**자** is an exclamatory expression to arouse one to action or attention.

23. ○**아** "Ah" is an exclamatory expression of astonishment, surprise or delight.

Cultural Note :

Korean people indicate "money" by making a circle with the thumb and index finger, whereas the equivalent gesture in the West might be holding the hand up and rubbing the thumb and index finger quickly and lightly across one another. In Korea, it's not polite for a young person to smoke cigarettes in front of older people, superiors, etc. Smoking is strictly prohibited for middle and high school students. Arirang is an extremely popular folk song of Korea. Its origin seems to go back to the earliest beginnings of Korea, and it is thought that its sad tune and at least the words of its refrain have come down unchanged. The word "Arirang" seems to stand for the Arirang Pass which is supposedly none other than the Tongsŏn Pass on Chabi mountain at the extreme north of Hwanghae Province. The song expresses the sadness and melancholy of the pastoral people as they crossed the fatal Pass that gave access to a new country after having been displaced by invaders from the North. There are several kinds of Arirang; "Miryang Arirang", "Kangwŏn Arirang", "Chŏngsŏn Arirang", etc.

STRUCTURAL PATTERNS

Text I

I. The noun modifier marker -ㄴ (-은) with descriptive verbs

Many languages use adjectives and relative clauses to modify nouns. Korean does not. To modify nouns Korean uses nouns and verbs, which functionally correspond to the adjectives or relative clauses found in other languages. In English you say "A big school" or "The man who came yesterday". In Korean you say "An is big school" or "The yesterday came man".

1. Modifier pre-nouns that are non-conjugating :

Samples of pre-nouns modifying other nouns are the following :

새 —— in 새 세계   new world

온 —— in 온 세계   whole world

학교 — in 학교 선생   a school teacher

The modifying pre-noun is simply put in front of the noun it modifies.

2. Modifier verbs

By far the majority of the noun modifiers in Korean are verbs. Verbs when used as modifiers take special suffixes which differ in shape according to the nature of the verb (action verbs, descriptive verbs) and its relation to time (present, past, future).

At this point we will study the marker -ㄴ (-은) used with descriptive verbs. It also occurs with action verbs but that use will be treated later.

The noun modifier marker -ㄴ (-은) used with descriptive verbs :

a) always refers to the present tense ;

b) its meaning is "...that is..." (Descriptive verbs, as you remember, always mean "is a certain way", while action verbs mean "does something").

c) it occurs in two shapes : -ㄴ after stems ending in a vowel ;

-은 after stems ending in a consonant.

Descriptive Verbs		D. V. Stem+Marker		Noun Modifiers	

Its place is directly after the verb stem.

복잡해요	is complicated	복잡하-	-ㄴ	복잡한	(is) complicated
작아요	is small	작-	-은	작은	(is) small
예뻐요	is beautiful	예쁘-	-ㄴ	예쁜	(is) beautiful
싸요	is cheap	싸-	-ㄴ	싼	(is) cheap
좋아요	is good	좋-	-은	좋은	(is) good

Among those descriptive verbs whose stem ends with -ㅎ-, a few drop the -ㅎ- before the noun modifier marker -ㄴ. Most of them you will find listed below :

Stems		Modifiers	Stems		Modifiers
이렇-	is this way	이런	노랗-	is yellow	노란
그렇-	is that way	그런	하얗-	is white	하얀
저렇-	is that way	저런	파랗-	is blue	파란
아무렇-	is any way	아무런	보얗-	is whitish	보얀
빨갛-	is red	빨간	뽀얗-	is grey	뽀얀
까맣-	is black	까만	말갛-	is clear	말간

II. Action Verb Stem+-아(-어, -여) { 주다 / 드리다

Examples :

a) 그것 좀 보여 주세요. ⌒   Show me that, please.

거기 좀 가 주세요. ⌒   Go there, please (for me).

여기 좀 와 주세요. ⌒   Come here, please (for me).

한국말을 좀 가르쳐 주세요. ⌒   Teach me Korean, please.

b) 보여 드리겠어요. ⌒   I'll show you.

가 드리겠어요. ⌒   I'll go (for you).

한국말을 가르쳐 드리지요. ⌒   I'll teach you Korean.

Notes :

1. This pattern is a combination of two verbs, a main verb (가, goes) and another one called the auxiliary verb.(주다, 드리다).

2. In structures like this the main verb is usually in the infinitive form, sometimes in the gerund form (V. S. + -고).

3. The infinitive form of the verb is what remains after dropping the final particle -요 of the polite informal style : 보여요 "shows", 가(아)요 "goes "(-아- is always dropped after the -아- of the stem). This is one way. Another way to arrive at the infinitive form is by adding either of the vowels -아, -어 to the verb stem ; -아 if the vowel of the preceding syllable is either -아- or -오-, otherwise -어. 하-, the stem of the verb 하다 "does", takes -여. The infinitive is used in a great many patterns. The name "infinitive" is not very indicative. It has little to do with the infinitive of some European languages.

4. In the pattern we are presently studying the auxiliary verb -주다 signals that the action of the main verb is requested in favor of the speaker and it can be roughly translated with the English "please". The auxiliary verb -드리다 signals that the action of the main verb is being done in favor of the person spoken to or spoken about : "for you, for him, for them". 좀 means "please" also. It literally means "a little".

5. Some auxiliary verbs occur as independent verbs as well, in which case their meaning is slightly different. 주다 "gives" 드리다 "gives to someone honored". Ex. 책을 주었어요. 책을 드렸어요. "I gave (him) a book".

III. The polite informal ending -지요

Examples :

1. 프랑스도 날씨가 춥지요. ⌒   In France we also have cold weather. (information)

2. 집에 가시지요. ⌒   Go home. (imperative)

3. 그것도 참 좋지요. ⌒   That's also very good. (declarative)

4. 같이 가시지요. ⌒   Shall we go together? (propositive)

5. 그것은 ˇ교실에 ˇ있지요. ⌒	It's in the classroom. (declarative)
6. 그분은 ˇ학생이지요. ⌒	He is a student. (declarative)
7. 한국말은 ˇ어렵지요? ↗	The Korean language is difficult, isn't it?
8. 그분도 ˇ가시지요? ↗	He also goes, I suppose.
9. 그 ˇ책은 ˇ교실에 있지요? ↗	That book is in the classroom, I suppose.
10. 그분은 ˇ선생이지요? ↗	He's a teacher, isn't he?

Notes :

1. The polite informal style can be given a nuance of casualness by replacing the infinitive ending -아(-어, -여) before -요 with the marker -지 :

좋아요 ; 가(아)요, (-아- is dropped)

좋지요 ; 가지요

2. -지요 is a sentence final ending and can be used with action verbs as well as with descriptive verbs, 있어요 and -이에요 included.

3. It can be used in statements, commands, propositions and questions.

   a) In statements it is often used for giving information. (Ex. No. 1)

   b) In commands and propositions the marker -지 sounds especially casual and therefore humble when the verb is honorific. (Ex. Nos. 2 and 4)

   c) In questions -지 sometimes signals a faint doubt or conjecture. (Ex. Nos. 7-10)

   d) Answering questions about oneself is usually done by employing the -아(etc.) 요 form, not the -지요 form. 참 ˇ좋지요? ↗ 예, 좋아요. ⌒

4. Since the ending -지요 is the same for all types of sentences, the intonation and especially the final contour are of great importance.

Text II

IV. (A) <u>Verb Stem+ -ㄹ(-을) 것 같아요</u> : "It looks like...", "It seems to be...",
"I think that...", or "It looks like it will..."

Examples :

참 재미있을 것 같아요. ⌒   It looks very interesting.

좋을 것 같아요. ⌒   It seems to be good.

아주 클 것 같아요. ⌒   I think it is very big.

좀 복잡할 것 같아요. ⌒   I think it is a little complicated.

비가 올 것 같아요. ⌒   It looks like it will rain.

그것이 여기 있을 것 같아요. ⌒ I think it is here.

Notes :

1. The pattern -ㄹ(을) 것 같아요 can be used with any verb and brings out an idea of likelihood : "looks" or "seems like".

2. -ㄹ 것 같아요 is used after verb stems ending in a vowel, and -을 것 같아요 is used after verb stems ending in a consonant.

(B) Noun+같아요 : "It looks like…" or "It seems to be…"

Examples :

저것이 학교 같아요. ⌒   That over there looks like a school.

그분은 학생 같아요. ⌒   He seems to be a student.

이것은 교실 같아요. ⌒   This seems to be a classroom.

Notes :

1. 같아요 attached to nouns shows similarity.

2. The descriptive verb 같아요 means "is the same".

Ⅴ. Adverbs and Adverbials

Examples :

한국말을 재미있게 공부합시다. ↘ Let's study Korean in an interesting way.

그렇게 합시다. ↘   Let's do it that way.

어떻게 한국말을 공부하세요? ⌒ How do you study Korean ?

한국말은 참 재미있어요. ⌒   Korean is really interesting.

Notes :

1. Korean adverbs are uninflected words which modify verbs, noun modifiers,

other adverbs, phrases, or whole sentences.

잘	well	퍽	quite	아주	extremely
다	all	참	really	못	can't,

2. This function, however, can also be performed by descriptive verbs. The signalling device or pattern for this is D.V.S.+ -게. In other words, by adding the adverbial marker -게 to the stems of descriptive verbs, you get adverbials.

3. Some descriptive verbs functioning as adverbs take suffixes other than -게. There is no rule governing the choice; each must be learned as a separate item. Fortunately there are not too many of these suffixes, viz., only -이, -히, and -리.

어떻게	how	다행히	fortunately
그렇게	that way	많이	many ; much
재미있게	interesting	높이	high ; highly
복잡하게	complicated	빨리	quick ; quickly
예쁘게	beautifully	깊이	deep ; deeply

VI. The Ordinal Numbers

(A) Korean Ordinal Numbers : Examples

첫째	first	다섯째	fifth	여덟째	eighth
둘째	second	여섯째	sixth	아홉째	ninth
셋째	third	일곱째	seventh	열째	tenth
넷째	fourth				

(B) Chinese Ordinal Numbers : Examples

제일	first	제오	fifth	제팔	eighth
제이	second	제육	sixth	제구	ninth
제삼	third	제칠	seventh	제십	tenth
제사	fourth				

Notes :

1. There are two sets of ordinal numbers, Korean and Sino-Korean (e.g. of Chinese origin).

2. The Korean ordinal numbers are made by adding the suffix -째 to the Korean cardinal numbers with the exception of the word "first". See the examples (A).

3. Because the suffix -째 originally means "turn" or "place in line", it can be used with the meaning of what place (in line, or in the order of doing something, or in evaluation). See the following example :

그분이 몇째입니까? What place is he in line ? Or : Which place did he receive ? (in evaluation or competition)

4. The Chinese ordinal numbers are made by prefixing 제- to the cardinal numbers as shown in the above examples (B).

Text III

VII. Classifiers :

In the English expressions "four sheets of paper", "two head of cattle", and "a pitcher of milk", the words "sheets", "head" and "pitcher" tell us something about the nature of the things being counted and the unit used for measuring. These words are classifiers. In Korean there are many of them. Most are used with the Korean numerals, only a few with the Chinese numerals. In the list given below notice the shape some numerals take when occurring before certain classifiers.

Used with Korean numerals :

한 시	두 시	세 시	네 시	o'clock
한 시간	두 시간	세 시간	네 시간	hours
한 번	두 번	세 번	네 번	times
한 살	두 살	세 살	네 살	years old
한 갑	두 갑	세 갑	네 갑	pack (of cigarettes, etc.)
한 사람	두 사람	세 사람	네 사람	people (plain)
한 분	두 분	세 분	네 분	people (honorific)
한 마리	두 마리	세 마리	네 마리	animals, fish
한 권	두 권	세 권	네 권	bound volumes
한 채	두 채	세 채	네 채	houses

한 대	두 대	세 대	네 대	vehicles, machines
한 병	두 병	세 병	네 병	bottles
한 개	두 개	세 개	네 개	items, units, objects
한 자루	두 자루	세 자루	네 자루	small stick (pencil, brush, etc.)
한 달	두 달	석 달 *	넉 달 *	months
한 장	두 장	석 장 *	넉 장 *	sheet
한 자	두 자	석 자 *	넉 자 *	measure of about 33.3 cm
한 말	두 말	서 말 *	너 말 *	measure of about 18 litres

Used with Chinese numerals :

일 분	이 분	삼 분	사 분	minutes
일 년	이 년	삼 년	사 년	years
일 원	이 원	삼 원	사 원	wŏn
일층	이층	삼층	사층	floor
일월	이월	삼월	사월	January, etc.

A very general rule is that in counting a small number of items, e.g., no larger than a dozen or so in our daily life, the Korean numerals are used with classifiers while in counting items that are larger than a hundred or so, the Sino-Korean numerals are used. Also, modern mechanization tends to favor the use of the Sino-Korean numerals, thus, this tendency giving rise to regularization at the unconscious level of the speaker.

---

* There is an alternative way of counting these items. Instead of 석 장, 넉 장, for example, 세 장, 네 장 is just often used. So are 세 자, 네 자 and 세 말, 네 말. Also, 세 달, 네 달 is used but much less frequently than the other three. The Korean numerals that change the form when used with classifiers are only five : 하나 → 한(개), 둘→두(개), 셋→세(개), 넷→네(개), 스물→스무(개) including compound numerals, 열하나 → 열한(개), 열둘 → 열두(개), 스물하나 → 스물한(개), etc.

VIII. The suffix -짜리

The suffix -짜리 is preceded by a figure and the name of the monetary unit. The English equivalent is "a thing worth...". 오 원짜리, 십 원짜리, 백 원짜리, 천 원짜리, 만 원짜리, 십만 원짜리, 백만 원짜리.

The above form is often followed by the name of the thing whose price or value it is expressing.

오 원짜리 연필	5 wŏn pencil
십 원짜리 공책	10 wŏn notebook
백 원짜리 책	100 wŏn book
천 원짜리 만년필	1,000 wŏn fountain pen
세 살짜리 어린애	3 year old child
열 장짜리 공책	10 sheet notebook

IX. The pattern A.V.S.+-아(-어, -여) 봐요(보다)

Examples :

한국말을 공부해 보겠어요. ⌒	I will try studying Korean.
이것을 잡숴 보세요. ⌒	Please try this (food).
잠깐 기다려 보세요. ⌒	Please wait a minute and see.
학교에 가 보세요. ⌒	Please go to school and see.

Notes :

1. This is another main verb+auxiliary verb pattern. See this lesson, S.P. No. II, 2, 3, 5.

2. As an independent verb 봐요 means "looks", "sees", or "reads". As an auxiliary verb it means "tries doing", "doing and then seeing what it is like", "exploring something by doing", but not "tries to do".

3. This pattern is often used with the main verbs 가요 "goes" and 와요 "comes".

DRILLS

Text I

A. Substitution Drill

1. 저 만년필 얼마에요? ⌒

   How much is that fountain pen over there?

연필,	의자,	공책,
사전,	책상,	교과서

2. 어느 것 말이에요? ⌒

   Which one do you mean?

연필,	의자,	교과서,
공책,	책상,	책가방

3. 저 까만 것 말이에요. ⌒

   I mean that black one over there.

하얀 책,	노란 연필,	파란 사전,
좋은 것,	까만 자동차,	빨간 책상

4. 그것은 이백 원이에요. ⌒

   That is two hundred wŏn.

삼백,	사백,	오백,	육백,
칠백,	팔백,	천	

B. Response Drill

Teacher : 좀 보여 주시겠어요? ↗   Show me that one, please.

Student : 예, ⌒ 보여 드리지요. ⌒   All right! (Yes, I'll show you that.)

1. 좀 가 주시겠어요?   예, ⌒ 가 드리지요. ⌒

2. 한국말을 가르쳐 주시겠어요?   예, ⌒ 가르쳐 드리지요. ⌒

3. 그 만년필 사 주시겠어요?   예, ⌒ 사 드리지요. ⌒

4. 여기 와 주시겠어요?   예, ⌒ 가 드리지요. ⌒

5. 집에 돌아가 주시겠어요?   예, ⌒ 돌아가 드리지요. ⌒

6. 버스로 가 주시겠어요?   예, ⌒ 버스로 ˅가 드리지요. ⌒

7. 그 만년필 보여 주시겠어요?   예, ⌒ 보여 드리지요. ⌒

C. Response Drill

Teacher : 그분이 ˅공부하시지요? ↗   He is studying, isn't he ?

Student : 예, ⌒ 그분이 ˅공부해요. ⌒   Yes, he is studying.

1. 그것이 참 좋지요?   예, ⌒ 그것이 ˅참 좋아요. ⌒

2. 한국말이 재미있지요?   예, ⌒ 한국말이 ˅재미있어요. ⌒

3. 그 책이 교실에 있지요?   예, ⌒ 그 책이 ˅교실에 있어요. ⌒

4. 여기는 늘 복잡하지요?   예, ⌒ 여기는 늘 복잡해요. ⌒

5. 그분이 한국말을 가르치시지요?   예, ⌒ 그분이 ˅한국말을 가르쳐요. ⌒

6. 그분이 선생님이시지요?   예, ⌒ 그분이 ˅선생님이에요. ⌒

7. 이 학교에 책이 많지요?   예, ⌒ 이 학교에 ˅책이 ˅많아요. ⌒

D. Expansion Drill

1. 주시겠어요? ↗

   보여 주시겠어요? ↗

   좀 ˅보여 주시겠어요? ↗

   책 좀 ˅보여 주시겠어요? ↗

   한국말 책 좀 ˅보여 주시겠어요? ↗

   김 선생님 ˅한국말 책 좀 ˅보여 주시겠어요? ↗

   Mr. Kim ! Will you please show me that Korean book ?

Text II

E. Substitution Drill (Use one of the particle forms given.)

1. 이 ˅사전은 ˅어떠세요? ⌒ (은/는)

   How about this dictionary ?

저 교과서,	이 공책,	그 책상,
노란 것,	하얀 것,	빨간 것

2. 그 연필이 ˇ마음에 들어요. ⌒ (이/가)

I like that pencil.

저 의자,	그 교과서,	저 자동차,
그 공책,	저 학교,	이 책상

3. 그것이 ˇ책 같아요. ⌒

That looks like a book.

연필,	만년필,	지우개,
책상,	책가방,	교과서

F. Pattern Drill

Teacher : 그분이 ˇ학교에 가요. ⌒ He is going to school.

Student : 그분이 ˇ학교에 ˇ갈 것 같아요. ⌒ I think he'll go to school.

1. 참 재미있어요. 참 ˇ재미있을 것 같아요. ⌒

2. 좋아요. 좋을 것 같아요. ⌒

3. 나빠요. 나쁠 것 같아요. ⌒

4. 사람이 많아요. 사람이 ˇ많을 것 같아요. ⌒

5. 사람이 적어요. 사람이 ˇ적을 것 같아요. ⌒

6. 그것은 너무 커요. 그것은 ˇ너무 ˇ클 것 같아요. ⌒

7. 그것은 너무 작아요. 그것은 ˇ너무 ˇ작을 것 같아요. ⌒

8. 그것이 여기 있어요. 그것이 ˇ여기 있을 것 같아요. ⌒

G. Response Drill

Teacher : 빨갛게 ˇ할까요? ↗ Shall we make it red ?

Student : 예, ⌒ 빨갛게 ˇ합시다. ↘ Yes, let's make it red.

1. 재미있게 공부할까요? 예, ⌒ 재미있게 ˇ공부합시다. ↘

2. 크게 할까요? 예, ⌒ 크게 ˇ합시다. ↘

3. 작게 할까요? 예, ⌒ 작게 ˇ합시다. ↘

4. 예쁘게 할까요? 예, ⌒ 예쁘게 ˇ합시다. ↘

5. 좋게 할까요? 예, ⌒ 좋게 ˇ합시다. ↘

6. 저렇게 할까요? 예, ⌒ 저렇게 ˇ합시다. ↘

7. 노랗게 할까요? 예, ⌒ 노랗게 ˇ합시다. ↘

8. 하얗게 할까요? 예, ⌒ 하얗게 ˇ합시다. ↘

H. Expansion Drill

1. 좋을 것 같아요. ⌒

   만년필은 ˇ좋을 것 같아요. ⌒

   저 ˇ빨간 만년필은 ˇ좋을 것 같아요. ⌒

   한 선생님 ˇ저 ˇ빨간 만년필은 ˇ좋을 것 같아요. ⌒

   Mr. Han! That red fountain pen over there seems to be good.

Text III

I. Substitution Drill

1. 담배 ˇ한 갑 주세요. ⌒

   Give me a pack of cigarettes, please.

두 갑,	다섯 갑,	여덟 갑,
세 갑,	일곱 갑,	여섯 갑

2. 종이 ˇ열 장 ˇ주시겠어요? ↗

   Would you please give me ten sheets of paper ?

서른 장,	스무 장,	마흔 장,
쉰 장,	일흔 장,	예순 장,
여든 장,	아흔 장,	백 장

3. 삼천 원짜리 ˇ만년필을 ˇ샀어요. ⌒

   (을/를)

   I bought a fountain pen for 3,000 wŏn.

천삼백 — 책,	이천팔백 — 사전,
칠백 — 공책,	사천 — 인형,
이백 — 지우개,	만 — 칠판

J. Pattern Drill

Teacher : 한국말을 ˇ공부하세요. ⌒   Study Korean, please.

Student : 한국말을 ˇ공부해 보세요. ⌒   Try studying Korean, please.

1. 집에 가세요.   집에 ˇ가 보세요. ⌒
2. 여기 오세요.   여기 ˇ와 보세요. ⌒
3. 잠깐 기다리세요.   잠깐 ˇ기다려 보세요. ⌒
4. 한국말을 가르치세요.   한국말을 ˇ가르쳐 보세요. ⌒
5. 영어를 배우세요.   영어를 ˇ배워 보세요. ⌒

6. 한국말로 하세요.　　　　　　　한국말로 해˅ 보세요. ⌒

7. 이것을 받으세요.　　　　　　　이것을 받˅아 보세요. ⌒

K. Response Drill

1. 무슨 담배(를) 드릴까요?　　　　아리랑 한 갑˅ 주세요. ⌒

2. 이 책(을) 드릴까요?　　　　　　예, ⌒ 그 책 주세요. ⌒

3. 무얼 드릴까요?　　　　　　　　책˅ 두 권 주세요. ⌒

4. 이 연필(을) 드릴까요?　　　　　예, ⌒ 그 연필 주세요. ⌒

5. 오백 원짜리(를) 드릴까요?　　　예, ⌒ 오백 원짜리 주세요. ⌒

6. 잔돈 드릴까요?　　　　　　　　예, ⌒ 잔돈 주세요. ⌒

7. 하얀 것 드릴까요?　　　　　　　예, ⌒ 하얀 것 주세요. ⌒

L. Expansion Drill

1. 기다려 보세요. ⌒

　　잠깐˅ 기다려 보세요. ⌒

　　학교에서˅ 잠깐˅ 기다려 보세요. ⌒

　　김 선생님˅ 학교에서˅ 잠깐˅ 기다려 보세요. ⌒

Mr. Kim! Wait in the school for a while, please.

제칠과 물건사기 II (Lesson 7 Shopping II)

TEXT I

[VOCABULARY]

계속 continuance, continuation	밖에 except, outside
종이 paper	연필 pencil
장 unit classifier for sheets of paper	어떤 what kind of
십 원 ten wǒn	여러 가지 many kinds, various kinds
석 장 three sheets of (paper)	제일 the first, the best, the most
-씩 distributive suffix	자루 unit classifier for pencils, chalk,
더 more	etc.
좋은 good	백 원 100 wǒn

1. 한만일 : **이 종이 한 장에 얼마예요? ⌒** — How much per sheet is this paper?
2. 점 원 : **십 원에 석 장씩이에요. ⌒** — It's ten wǒn for three sheets.
3. 한만일 : **더 좋은 것 없어요? ↗** — Do you have anything better?
4. 점 원 : **이런 종이밖에 없어요. ⌒** — This is the only kind of paper I have.
   미안합니다. ⌐ — I am sorry.
5. 한만일 : **연필은 어떤 것이 있지요? ↗** — What kind of pencils do you have?
6. 점 원 : **여러 가지가 있어요. ⌒** — There are many kinds.
7. 한만일 : **제일 좋은 것은 얼마지요? ↗** — How much are the most expensive ones?
8. 점 원 : **한 자루에 백 원씩이에요. ⌒** — 100 wǒn per pencil.

TEXT II

[VOCABULARY]

공책 notebook	자꾸 continually
권 unit classifier for books,	올라요(오르지-) goes up
notebook, etc.	큰 big
잉크 ink	일 thing, affairs, work
병 bottle	나요(나지-) happens
사백 400	다섯 five
값 price	-만 only

9. 한만일 : 이 공책은 얼마에요?	How much are these notebooks?
10. 점 원 : 한 권에 삼백 원이에요.	300 wŏn apiece.
11. 한만일 : 저 잉크는요?	How much is the ink over there?
12. 점 원 : 한 병에 사백 원이구요.	It's 400 wŏn per bottle.
13. 한만일 : 물건 값이 자꾸 오르는군요.	The price of things is continually going up!
14. 점 원 : 예, 큰일났어요.	Yes, it's terrible.
15. 한만일 : 연필 열 자루하고 공책 다섯 권(을) 주세요. 그리고 잉크는 한 병만 사겠어요.	Give me ten pencils and five notebooks and a bottle of ink, please.
16. 점 원 : 고맙습니다.	Thank you.

TEXT III

┌─[VOCABULARY]─────────────────────────┐
│ 문방구점 stationery store   시장 market   │
│ 뭘(무엇을) what   길이에요 is on the road(way) │
│ 지금 now, presently   │
└──────────────────────────────────────┘

17. 김선자 : 어디 갔다가 오세요? 한 선생님.	Where have you been, Mr. Han?
18. 한만일 : 예, 안녕하세요? 김 선생님. 문방구점에 좀 갔다 와요.	How are you, Mr. Kim? I'm coming from the stationery store.
19. 김선자 : 뭘 많이 사셨군요.	You certainly bought a lot!
20. 한만일 : 예, 이것저것 좀 샀어요.	Yes, I bought quite a few things.
21. 김선자 : 저도 지금 시장에 가는 길이에요.	I'm on my way to the market now myself.
22. 한만일 : 그러세요? 어서 다녀오세요.	Is that right? Well, see you later.
23. 김선자 : 예, 빨리 갔다 와야겠어요. 그럼 또 뵙겠어요.	I must hurry. Well, see you again.

REMARKS TO THE TEXT

Text I

3. ○더 "more" is an adverbial modifying the words it precedes and expressing comparison. See the following sentences :

더 주무세요. ⌒   Please sleep longer.

더 사겠어요. ⌒   I'll buy more.

더 공부하세요. ⌒   Study more, please.

더 기다려 보세요. ⌒   Please wait a little more and see.

4. ○이런 means "like this", "this kind (sort) of". The verbs 이렇다 and 이러하다 mean "is like this". See Lesson 6, S.P. No. I.

이런 책 있어요? ↗   Do you have books like this?

이런 연필은 좋지 않아요. ⌒   This kind of pencil is not good.

이런 것은 괜찮아요. ⌒   This kind of thing is all right.

8. ○-자루 is a classifier used for pencils, fountain pens, and pieces of chalk. It goes with the Korean numerals. See Lesson 6, S.P. No. VI.

Text II

11. ○잉크 "ink" is derived from English. Pay attention to the difference between the Korean and the English pronunciations.

12. ○사백 원이구요 is an informal speech form of 사백 원이고요. -고 is the gerund conjunctive ending and -요 is the polite particle. We will study this ending in Lesson 8.

13. ○(물건)값 "the price of things" is a pure Korean word ; 물가 has the same meaning but is derived from Chinese.

○자꾸 : Depending on the context, its meaning is "repeatedly" or "continually".

14. ○큰일났어요 : 큰일 means "a problem", "a serious matter" and 나다 "happens" or "takes place". Therefore, its literal meaning is "have a problem" or "Things have come to a pretty pass". It is used when you meet a problem.

Text III

17. ○한 선생 : 한 is a family name. See the Cultural Note below.

19. ○뭘 is a contraction of 무엇을. It is used here as an indefinite pronoun, meaning "something".

20. ○이것 저것 "this thing and that thing" is used to avoid mentioning specifically what was bought.

22. ○다녀 오세요 : 다니다 means "goes and comes", "goes back and forth". The expression is used to address someone when he is going somewhere and is expected to return soon. The person addressed answers saying : 다녀 오겠어요.

Cultural Note :

Korean Names : Korean names usually consist of three syllables corresponding to the three Chinese characters used for writing them. The family name is written first and the given name last. For instance : 김정희. The two syllables of the given name can never be separated. Surnames in Korea number approximately two hundred ninety. The most common surnames are : 김, 이, 박, 최, 조, 한, 장, 민, 오, 홍, 전, 윤, 황, 안, 정, 서, etc. A few people have two-syllable family names and one-syllable given names.

According to custom, adults use the given name only among intimate friends. In the family and outside the home, children's given names are used by parents and adults. It is customary for adults to call teenagers by their given names.

A Korean woman keeps her maiden name as well as her given name even after marriage. It is also customary for a husband not to address his wife by name. He calls her attention by saying 여보 "hello darling" without the use of her name. Since this expression is used between husband and wife you have to be careful. The general address term for "hello" when calling others' attention is 여보세요, as on the telephone, etc.

STRUCTURAL PATTERNS

Text I

Ⅰ. The particle -에 : "per" or "for"

Examples :

이 종이 한 장에 얼마예요? ⌒　　　　How much per sheet is this paper?

이 책은 한 권에 천 오백 원이에요. ⌒　　This book is 1,500 wŏn (per volume).

저 연필은 세 자루에 이백 원이에요. ⌒　Those pencils are three for 200 wŏn.

이 공책은 한 권에 사백 원이에요. ⌒　These notebooks are 400 wŏn apiece.

이 담배는 한 갑에 오백 원이에요. ⌒　These cigarettes are 500 wŏn per
　　　　　　　　　　　　　　　　　　　pack.

Note :

The particle -에 is added to nouns whenever the price of the objects they refer to is mentioned.

Review :

You have already studied (1) the particle -에 "at", "in" denoting static location and used with the verbs 있다, 없다, 많다(See Lesson 4, S.P. Ⅸ) (2) the particle -에 "to", indicating destination and used with either 가다 or 오다 or similar verbs (compound verbs with 가다/오다) (See Lesson 5, S.P. Ⅸ). Let's review them.

(1) 그 책은 집에 있어요. ⌒　　　That book is at home.

　　그 학교는 정동에 있어요. ⌒　That school is in Chŏng-dong.

　　내 공책이 교실에 없어요. ⌒　My notebook is not in the classroom.

　　서울에 사람이 많아요. ⌒　　There are many people in Seoul.

(2) 집에 갑시다. ↘　　　　　　Let's go home.

　　학교에 가겠어요. ⌒　　　　I'll go to school.

이 학생이 교실에 가요. ⌒   This student is going to the classroom.

빨리 학교에 오세요. ⌒   Please come to school quickly.

II. The suffix -씩 : "(so much) at a time", or "(so much) per (person)"

Examples :

하나씩 주세요. ⌒   Please give them to me one by one (one at a time).

두 개씩 잡수세요. ⌒   Please eat two each.

한 사람한테 둘씩 주세요. ⌒   Please give two to each person.

네 시간에 한 개씩 잡수세요. ⌒   Take one every four hours.

Note :

The suffix -씩 is always attached to a numeral or a numeral plus classifier and denotes distribution.

III. Noun + -밖에 없다, or Verb Stem + -지 않다 (Negative Predicate)

(A) Noun + -밖에 없다 : "There is no one(nothing, no other) but..."

Examples :

교실에 김 선생밖에 없어요. ⌒   There is no one but Mr. Kim in the classroom.

그분은 이 책밖에 없어요. ⌒   He has no other book besides this.

이런 종이밖에 없어요. ⌒   This is the only kind of paper I have.

(B) Noun + -밖에 Verb Stem + -지 않다 : "one does nothing but..."

Examples :

김 선생밖에 크지 않아요. ⌒   Mr. Kim is the only tall one.

이 책밖에 사지 않겠어요. ⌒   The only thing I'll buy is this book.

그분밖에 예쁘지 않아요. ⌒   She is the only beautiful person.

Notes :

1. The pattern "Noun + -밖에" is always followed by a negative predicate.

2. The noun before "-밖에" can be either the subject or the object of the sentence.

IV. The superlative marker 제일 or 가장 : "Number one" or "most" or "the first".

Examples :

이것이 제일(가장) 좋아요. ⌒	This is the best one.
저것이 제일(가장) 커요. ⌒	That over there is the largest.
이것이 제일(가장) 싼 만년필이에요. ⌒	This is the cheapest fountain pen.
제일 비싼 것은 그것이에요. ⌒	That one is the most expensive.
그분이 공부를 제일 잘 해요. ⌒	He studies best of all.

Notes :

1. The superlative marker 제일 "to the greatest degree" goes with descriptive verbs, noun modifiers, and adverbials.

2. 제일 may be replaced by 가장.

3. Notice that in Korean there is no modifying suffix expressing superlative or comparative degree. To express the superlative you use 제일 or 가장 ; to express comparison -보다...(더). (See this lesson, Remarks to the Text No. 3. -보다 will be studied later.)

Text II

V. The past tense formation : V.S. + -았-(-었-, -였-)+ending(−어요, etc.)

To make the past tense forms of any verb, you need only insert the past tense infix -았-(-었-, -였-) between the verb stem(or verb stem plus the honorific infix -시-) and the ending.

Examples :

Verb Stem		Past Infix	Ending	Past Form	Contraction
(A) -았- :	좋-	-았-	-어요	좋았어요	...
	많-	-았-	-어요	많았어요	...
	보-	-았-	-어요	보았어요	봤어요
	가-	-았-	-어요	(가았어요)	갔어요
	오-	-았-	-어요	(오았어요)	왔어요
(B) -었- :	가르치-	-었-	-어요	(가르치었어요)	가르쳤어요
	배우-	-었-	-어요	(배우었어요)	배웠어요

주무시-	-었-	-어요	(주무시었어요)	주무셨어요	
있-	-었-	-어요	있었어요	…	
재미있-	-었-	-어요	재미있었어요	…	
⒞ -였- : 하-	-였-	-어요	하였어요	했어요	
공부하-	-였-	-어요	공부하였어요	공부했어요	
좋아하-	-였-	-어요	좋아하였어요	좋아했어요	
감사하-	-였-	-어요	감사하였어요	감사했어요	

Notes :

1. The vowel changes of the past tense marker, as you have noticed, follow the same rules as those given for the infinitive mood ending (See Lesson 6, S.P.No. II).

   -았- after -아- and -오- ;

   -었- after any other vowel ;

   -였- after 하-, the stem of the verb 하다 "does".

2. The forms given in the column "Contraction" are more frequently heard than the regular ones.

3. The vowel of the -어요 ending of the polite informal style never changes.

4. The meaning of the past tense marker is completed, definite action or state and so usually past.

VI. The conjunctive particle -하고 : "and" or "with"

   Examples :

   연필하고 교과서를 샀어요. ⌒ I bought a pencil and a textbook.

   교실에 책상하고 의자가 있어요. ⌒ There are desks and chairs in the classroom.

   만년필하고 사전은 비싸요. ⌒ Fountain pens and dictionaries are expensive.

   잉크 한 병하고 책 두 권이 있어요. ⌒ I have a bottle of ink and two books.

   Note :

   The conjunctive particle -하고 "and" is used between nouns or nominals. In pronunciation there is no pause between -하고 and the preceding noun.

Ⅶ. The particle -만 : "only"

Examples :

1. Replacing subject particles :

김 선생만 공부해요. ⌒　　　　Only Mr. Kim studies.

그분만 교실에 계세요. ⌒　　　Only he is in the classroom.

그 학교만 좋아요. ⌒　　　　 Only that school is good.

2. Replacing subject particles :

우리는 한국말만 공부해요. ⌒　 We study only Korean.

그분은 영어만 가르쳐요. ⌒　　 He teaches only English.

그분은 그 책상만 좋아해요. ⌒　He likes only that desk.

3. With other particles :

그분은 학교에서만 공부해요. ⌒　He studies only at school.

칠판은 교실에만 있어요. ⌒　　 Blackboards are (found) only in the

　　　　　　　　　　　　　　　　classrooms.

서울에만 사람이 많아요. ⌒　　 Only in Seoul are there many people.

학교까지만 오세요. ⌒　　　　 Please just come to school.

Note :

The particle -만 "only" replaces the subject and object particles and can be used with other particles. (Compare this particle -만 with -밖에 in S.P. No. Ⅲ of this lesson.)

Text III

Ⅷ. The transferentive mood marker -다(가) : A.V.S. + -다(가), A.V.S. + -았-+ -다(가)

(A) A.V.S. + -다(가)

Examples :

학교에 가다(가) 와요. ⌒　　　I was on my way to school but am

　　　　　　　　　　　　　　　　coming back.

학교에 가다(가) 왔어요. ⌒

I was on my way to school but came back.

공부하다(가) 왔어요. ⌒

I came before finishing my studies.

한국말을 가르치다(가) 와요. ⌒

I was teaching Korean but (stopped the class and) am on my way back (home).

여기 있다(가) ⌒ 가겠어요. ⌒

I'll stay here a while and then go.

조금 있다(가) ⌒ 오세요. ⌒

Come after a little while.

(B) <u>A.V.S. + -았- + -다(가)</u>

Examples :

서울에 갔다(가) 와요. ⌒

I went to Seoul and am on my way back.

서울에 갔다(가) 왔어요. ⌒

I went to Seoul (and came back).

자동차를 샀다(가) ⌒ 팔았어요. ⌒

I bought a car and sold it again.

옷을 입었다(가) ⌒ 벗었어요. ⌒

I put on my clothes and took them off again.

Notes :

1. The transferentive marker -다(가) indicates the change of one action into another. When it is used without the past tense infix, it expresses the interruption or suspension of an action. The verb is generally either 가다 or 오다.

2. But, when it is attached to the past tense infix, it expresses the succession of one action by another, after the first action has been completed, or nullification of an action. In both cases -다(가) can be translated : "but then (something else happened)".

3. This pattern is mostly used with action verbs and the verb 있-.

4. The marker appears in two shapes -다가 and -다.

5. When two past transferentives are followed by a form of 하다, they indicate alternation. The alternatives are mostly contrastives. This structural pattern was

not used in the text of Lesson 7, but it is an extended structure of A.V.S. + -다가. See the examples below.

1) 그분이 왔다 갔다 해요.   He is going to and fro.

그분이 앉았다 섰다 해요.   He is sitting and then standing up again (and so forth).

그분이 웃었다 울었다 해요.   He is laughing and crying all the time.

그분이 들어왔다 나갔다 해요.   He keeps coming in and going out.

그분이 불을 껐다 켰다 해요.   He is turning the lights on and off all the time.

그분이 올라갔다 내려왔다 해요. He keeps going up and down.

그분이 신을 신었다 벗었다 해요. He puts his shoes on and then takes them off again (all the time).

2) 내가 잡지를 읽었다 라디오를 들었다 했어요.

I was reading magazines and listening to the radio off and on.

내가 한국말을 공부했다 영어를 공부했다 했어요.

I was studying Korean and English in turns.

선생이 읽었다 내가 읽었다 했어요.

Sometimes the teacher read, and at other times I read.

한국에 있었다 미국에 있었다 했어요.

I was going back and forth between Korea and America.

이가 아팠다 머리가 아팠다 했어요.

I had a toothache and a headache alternately.

IX. The particle -도 : "too", "also", "indeed", or "even"

Examples :

1. Replacing subject particles :

김 선생님도 가요.   Mr. Kim is also going.

저도 학생이에요.   I am a student, too.

그분도 한국말을 가르쳐요.   He also teaches Korean.

2. Replacing object particles :

저는 ˇ한국말도 ˇ가르쳐요. ⌒   I teach Korean, too.

저는 ˇ공부도 해요. ⌒   I study, too.

저는 ˇ그분도 ˇ좋아해요. ⌒   I like him, too

3. With other particles :

그분은 ˇ학교에서도 ˇ공부해요. ⌒   He studies at school, too.

부산에도 ˇ사람이 ˇ많아요. ⌒   There are many people in Pusan, too.

4. With adverbials :

그분은 ˇ아직도 ˇ공부해요. ⌒   He is still studying.

그분은 ˇ공부를 ˇ잘도 해요. ⌒   He studies very well.

서울에는 ˇ사람이 ˇ너무도 많아요. ⌒   There are too many people in Seoul.

5. With negative forms :

그분은 ˇ그 책을 ˇ보지도 않아요. ⌒   He does not even look at that book.

물건 값이 ˇ그리 ˇ비싸지도 않아요. ⌒   The prices of things are not so expen-
                                       sive.

그분은 ˇ학교에 ˇ가지도 않았어요. ⌒   He did not even go to school.

Notes :

1. The particle -도 "also" replaces the subject and object particles, and can also be used with other particles.

2. When the particle -도 is used with adverbials, it expresses admiration or emphasizes the quality of the adverbials.

3. When it is used with negative forms, it has the meaning of "even" or emphasizes the negative form itself.

4. The particle -도 always refers to the word preceding it.

DRILLS

[ADDITIONAL VOCABULARY]

성냥 match	상점 shop	미국 America
영국 England	독일 Germany	프랑스 France
일본 Japan	중국 China	소련 the Soviet Union
이탈리아 Italy	읽어요(읽지-) reads	먹어요(먹지-) eats
봐요(보지-) sees	밥 cooked rice	영화 movie
아직 still, yet		

Text I

A. Substitution Drill

1. 이 종이 한 장에 얼마에요? ⌒

   How much per sheet is this paper?

잉크 한 병,	담배 한 갑,
의자 한 개,	공책 한 권,
책 한 권,	연필 한 자루

2. 십 원에 석 장씩이에요. ⌒

   Three sheets for ten wŏn.

십 원 — 넉 장,	이백 원 — 세 권,
백 원 — 세 병,	오십 원 — 네 자루,
백 원 — 일곱 장,	삼십원 — 네 갑

3. 이런 종이밖에 없어요. ⌒

   This is the only kind of paper I have.

책상,	칠판,	교과서,
사전,	연필,	만년필

4. 책은 어떤 것이 있지요? ↗ (은/는)

   What kind of books do you have?

책상,	의자,	교과서,
칠판,	만년필,	지우개

B. Pattern Drill

Teacher : 한국말을 가르쳐요. ⌒   I teach Korean.

Student : 한국말밖에 가르치지 않아요. ⌒   I don't teach any language but Korean.

1. 영어를 공부해요. 영어밖에 **공**부하지 않아요. ⌒
2. 기차를 타요. 기차밖에 **타**지 않아요. ⌒
3. 김 선생이 커요. 김 선생밖에 **크**지 않아요. ⌒
4. 이 책을 사겠어요. 이 책밖에 **사**지 않겠어요. ⌒
5. 그 여자가 예뻐요. 그 여자밖에 **예쁘**지 않아요. ⌒
6. 이것이 좋아요. 이것밖에 **좋**지 않아요. ⌒
7. 저는 피곤해요. 저밖에 **피곤**하지 않아요. ⌒
8. 그것이 작아요. 그것밖에 **작**지 않아요. ⌒

C. Response Drill

1. 제일 좋은 것은 얼마지요? 제일 좋은 것은 **삼백** 원이에요. ⌒
2. 제일 큰 것은 얼마지요? 제일 큰 것은 **사십** 원이에요. ⌒
3. 제일 작은 것은 얼마지요? 제일 작은 것은 **칠십** 원이에요. ⌒
4. 제일 예쁜 것은 얼마지요? 제일 예쁜 것은 **천** 원이에요. ⌒
5. 제일 비싼 것은 얼마지요? 제일 비싼 것은 **만** 원이에요. ⌒
6. 가장 많은 것은 얼마지요? 가장 많은 것은 **사천** 원이에요. ⌒
7. 가장 적은 것은 얼마지요? 가장 적은 것은 **삼백** 원이에요. ⌒
8. 가장 나쁜 것은 얼마지요? 가장 나쁜 것은 **백팔십** 원이에요. ⌒

D. Expansion Drill

1. **오** 원이에요. ⌒

   칠십오 원이에요. ⌒

   사백칠십오 원이에요. ⌒

   오천사백칠십오 원이에요. ⌒

   이만 오천사백칠십오 원이에요. ⌒

   한 개에 **이만** 오천사백칠십오 원이에요. ⌒

   좋은 것이 **한** 개에 **이만** 오천사백칠십오 원이에요. ⌒

   제일 좋은 것이 **한** 개에 **이만** 오천사백칠십오 원이에요. ⌒

   The very best one costs 25, 475 wŏn.

Text II

E. Substitution Drill

1. **연필 열** 자루하고 **책 다섯 권** 주세요. ⌒

   Give me ten pencils and five books.

2. **책 두 권**하고 **잉크 한 병** 주세요. ⌒

   Give me two books and one bottle of ink.

3. **잉크 세 병**하고 **공책 두 권** 주세요. ⌒

   Give me three bottles of ink and two notebooks.

4. **담배 두 갑**하고 **성냥 한 갑** 주세요. ⌒

   Give me two packs of cigarettes and one box of matches.

5. **종이 스무 장**하고 **공책 서른 권** 주세요. ⌒

   Give me twenty pieces of paper and thirty notebooks.

6. **십 원짜리 연필**하고 **백 원짜리 공책** 주세요. ⌒

   Give me a ten wŏn pencil and a hundred wŏn notebook.

F. Substitution Drill

1. 잉크는 **한 병만 사겠어요.** ⌒

   I'll buy only one bottle of ink.

2. 종이는 **마흔 장만 사겠어요.** ⌒

   I'll buy only forty sheets of paper.

3. 담배는 **쉰 갑만 사겠어요.** ⌒

   I'll buy only fifty packs of cigarettes.

4. 연필은 **한 자루만 사겠어요.** ⌒

   I'll buy only one pencil.

5. 의자는 **두 개만 사겠어요.** ⌒

   I'll buy only two chairs.

6. 공책은 **세 권만 사겠어요.** ⌒

   I'll buy only three notebooks.

7. 칠판은 **한 개만 사겠어요.** ⌒

   I'll buy only one blackboard.

G. Pattern Drill

Teacher : 그분은 **학교에 가요.** ⌒   He goes to school.

Student : 그분은 **학교에 갔어요.** ⌒   He went to school.

1. 나는 공부해요.   **나는 공부했어요.** ⌒

2. 한국말을 가르쳐요.   **한국말을 가르쳤어요.** ⌒

3. 영어를 배워요.   **영어를 배웠어요.** ⌒

4. 그분은 주무셔요.   **그분은 주무셨어요.** ⌒

5. 나는 그분을 기다려요.　　　나는 그분을 기다렸어요. ⌒
6. 한국말이 재미있어요.　　　한국말이 재미있었어요. ⌒
7. 그 책이 교실에 있어요.　　　그 책이 교실에 있었어요. ⌒
8. 책상이 많아요.　　　책상이 많았어요. ⌒

H. Pattern Drill

Teacher : 그분이 학교에 갔어요. ⌒　　　He went to school.

Student : 그분이 학교에 가지 않았어　　　He didn't go to school.
　　　　　요. ⌒

1. 그 책이 좋았어요.　　　그 책이 좋지 않았어요. ⌒
2. 학생이 많았어요.　　　학생이 많지 않았어요. ⌒
3. 여기서 그분을 기다렸어요.　　　여기서 그분을 기다리지 않았어요. ⌒
4. 그분이 비행기를 탔어요.　　　그분이 비행기를 타지 않았어요. ⌒
5. 그분은 집에 돌아갔어요.　　　그분은 집에 돌아가지 않았어요. ⌒
6. 그분은 바빴어요.　　　그분은 바쁘지 않았어요. ⌒
7. 책 세 권을 샀어요.　　　책 세 권을 사지 않았어요. ⌒

I. Pattern Drill

Teacher : 학교에 가겠어요. ⌒　　　I intend to go to school.

Student : 학교에 가지 않겠어요. ⌒　　　I don't intend to go to school.

1. 한국말을 공부하겠어요.　　　한국말을 공부하지 않겠어요. ⌒
2. 그분을 기다리겠어요.　　　그분을 기다리지 않겠어요. ⌒
3. 집에 돌아가겠어요.　　　집에 돌아가지 않겠어요. ⌒
4. 영어를 배우겠어요.　　　영어를 배우지 않겠어요. ⌒
5. 여기서 자겠어요.　　　여기서 자지 않겠어요. ⌒
6. 안부 전해 드리겠어요.　　　안부 전해 드리지 않겠어요. ⌒
7. 그 돈을 받겠어요.　　　그 돈을 받지 않겠어요. ⌒
8. 한국말을 가르치겠어요.　　　한국말을 가르치지 않겠어요. ⌒

J. Pattern Drill

Teacher : 김 선생님이 가르쳐요. ⌒　　　Mr. Kim teaches.

Student : 김 선생님만 가르쳐요.   Only Mr. Kim teaches.

1. 그분이 교실에 계세요.   그분만 교실에 계세요.

2. 한국말이 재미있어요.   한국말만 재미있어요.

3. 그분이 집에 돌아갔어요.   그분만 집에 돌아갔어요.

4. 물건 값이 자꾸 오르는군요.   물건 값만 자꾸 오르는군요.

5. 여기가 늘 복잡해요.   여기만 늘 복잡해요.

6. 그분이 아주 바빠요.   그분만 아주 바빠요.

7. 신부님이 이곳에 오셨어요.   신부님만 이곳에 오셨어요.

8. 나는 가겠어요.   나만 가겠어요.

K. Expansion Drill

1. 샀어요.

   서른 권만 샀어요.

   공책 서른 권만 샀어요.

   열 자루하고 공책 서른 권만 샀어요.

   연필 열 자루하고 공책 서른 권만 샀어요.

   저 상점에서 연필 열 자루하고 공책 서른 권만 샀어요.

   I bought only ten pencils and thirty notebooks in that shop over there.

Text III

L. Substitution Drill

   1. 서울에 갔다(가) 와요.

   I went to Seoul and am coming back.

미국,	영국,	일본,
중국,	소련,	독일

   2. 지금 시장에 가는 길이에요.

   I am on the way to the market now.

미국,	영국,	프랑스,
중국,	일본,	이탈리아

M. Pattern Drill

   Teacher : 학교에 가요.   I go to school.

Student : 학교에 가다가 와요. ⌒   I was on the way to school but am coming back.

1. 밥을 먹어요.   밥을 먹다가 와요. ⌒
2. 책을 읽어요.   책을 읽다가 와요. ⌒
3. 한국말을 배워요.   한국말을 배우다가 와요. ⌒
4. 영어를 가르쳐요.   영어를 가르치다가 와요. ⌒
5. 학교에서 공부해요.   학교에서 공부하다가 와요. ⌒
6. 그분을 기다려요.   그분을 기다리다가 와요. ⌒
7. 집에서 놀아요.   집에서 놀다가 와요. ⌒
8. 영화를 봐요.   영화를 보다가 와요. ⌒

N. Pattern Drill

Teacher : 학교에 가요. ⌒   I go to school.

Student : 학교에 가다가 왔어요. ⌒   I was on the way to school but came back.

1. 밥을 먹어요.   밥을 먹다가 왔어요. ⌒
2. 학교에서 공부해요.   학교에서 공부하다가 왔어요. ⌒
3. 나는 책을 읽어요.   나는 책을 읽다가 왔어요. ⌒
4. 한국말을 가르쳐요.   한국말을 가르치다가 왔어요. ⌒
5. 그분을 기다려요.   그분을 기다리다가 왔어요. ⌒
6. 집에서 놀아요.   집에서 놀다가 왔어요. ⌒
7. 영어를 배워요.   영어를 배우다가 왔어요. ⌒

O. Substitution Drill

1. 미국에 갔다⌒ 왔어요. ⌒

I went to America (and came back).

시장,	영국,	일본,
중국,	소련,	독일

P. Response Drill

1. 저분도 선생님이에요?   예, ⌒ 저분도 선생님이에요. ⌒
2. 그분도 한국말을 가르쳐요?   예, ⌒ 그분도 한국말을 가르쳐요. ⌒
3. 그분이 영어도 공부해요?   예, ⌒ 그분이 영어도 공부해요. ⌒

4. 그 집에도 자동차가 있어요?   예, 그 집에도 자동차가 있어요.

5. 아직도 공부하세요?   예, 아직도 공부해요.

6. 학교에 가지도 않았어요?   예, 학교에 가지도 않았어요.

7. 그 책을 읽지도 않았어요?   예, 그 책을 읽지도 않았어요.

8. 공부하다가 오셨어요?   예, 공부하다가 왔어요.

9. 어디에 갔다 오세요?   학교에 갔다 와요.

10. 어디에 가는 길이에요?   미국에 가는 길이에요.

Q. Expansion Drill

1. 와야겠어요.

    갔다 와야겠어요.

    영국에 갔다 와야겠어요.

    빨리 영국에 갔다 와야겠어요.

    비행기로 빨리 영국에 갔다 와야겠어요.

    I must visit England by airplane quickly.

    (Lit. I must go to England and come back by airplane quickly.)

제팔과 계절과 날씨 (Lesson 8 Seasons and Climate)

TEXT I

[VOCABULARY]

계절	season	욕심	greediness, avarice
기후	climate, weather	말씀	words, speech
매우	very, greatly, exceedingly	-보다	(more) than
어느	which, what	겨울	winter
철	season	여름	summer
봄	spring	-중	between, among
가을	fall	-지만	but

1. 존 : 한국의 기후는 어때요?   How is the weather in Korea?

2. 차정자 : 예, 매우 좋아요.   It is very good.

3. 존 : 어느 철을 제일 좋아하세요?   Which season do you like best?

4. 차정자 : 저는 봄과 가을이 좋아요.   I like spring and fall.

5. 존 : 욕심도 많군요. 하나만 말씀   That's too much (you are greedy). Tell
    하세요.   me only one.

6. 차정자 : 글쎄요. 가을보다는 봄이 더   Well, I like spring better than fall.
    좋아요.

7. 존 : 여름과 겨울 중에서는요?   And between summer and winter
         (which do you prefer)?

8. 차정자 : 겨울도 좋지만 여름이 더 좋   I like winter, but I like summer more.
    아요.

TEXT II

[VOCABULARY]

따뜻해요(따뜻하지-)	is warm	돼요(되지-)	becomes
비	rain	몹시	very much, awfully, heavily
더워요(덥지-)	is hot	추워요(춥지-)	is cold
선선해요(선선하지-)	is cool	눈	snow

9. 존   : 봄에는 날씨가 어때요?

How is the weather in spring?

10. 차정자 : 봄에는 날씨가 따뜻해요.

In spring, the weather is warm.

11. 존   : 여름에는요?

And in summer?

12. 차정자 : 여름에는 비가 많이 오고 더
          워요.

In summer, it rains a lot and it's hot.

13. 존   : 가을엔 덥지 않아요?

Isn't it hot in the fall?

14. 차정자 : 예, 가을엔 덥지 않아요.
          선선해요.

It's not hot. It's cool.

15. 존   : 겨울이 되면 날씨가 어때
          요?

When winter comes, how is the weather?

16. 차정자 : 겨울엔 몹시 춥고 눈이
          와요.

In winter, it's very cold and it snows.

TEXT III

[VOCABULARY]

흐려요(흐리지-) is cloudy
또 again, once more, and, moreover
걱정 worry, anxiety, concern
바람 wind
불어요(불지-) blows
시작해요(시작하지-) begins

어쩌면 perhaps, possible, by any possibility
개요(개지-) clears up, becomes clear
볕 sunshine, sunlight, sunbeam
나요(나지-) comes out

17. 존   : 날씨가 흐렸군요. 비가 또
          올것 같지요?

The weather is cloudy! It looks like it is going to rain.

18. 차정자 : 예, 비가 너무 오기 때문에
          걱정이에요.

We have had too much rain (so I am worried).

19. 존   : 바람이 불기 시작하는데요.
          어쩌면 개일 것 같지요?

The wind is beginning to blow.
Perhaps the weather will clear up.

20. 차정자 : 글쎄요, 볕이 났으면 좋겠는
          데.

Well, I wish the sun would shine.

REMARKS TO THE TEXT

Text I

1. ○기후 "climate" or "weather" is derived from Chinese, and 날씨 "weather" is a pure Korean word. See the following sentences :

한국의 기후는 어때요? ⌒	How is the weather in Korea ?
한국의 기후는 참 좋아요. ⌒	The weather in Korea is very good.
날씨가 참 좋지요? ↗	The weather is very good, isn't it ?
예, ⌒ 날씨가 참 좋아요. ⌒	Yes, it's certainly good.

2. ○매우 "very", "greatly", or "exceedingly" is an adverb regularly occurring as a modifier of the following adjectivals, verbals, or adverbials. It is similar to and interchangeable with 참 and 아주.

    참 is much more used than 아주 and 매우 in colloquial language.

3. ○어느 "which" is a noun modifier.

4. ○저 "I" is regularly used with the contrast particle -는, whereas 제 "I" must always be used with the subject particle -가. 저(는) and 제(가) are polite pronouns expressing reverence for the hearer. Therefore, they are used when the speaker wishes to refer to himself in an unpretentious way. 나 "I" is regularly used with the contrast particle -는, whereas 내 "I" must always be used with the subject particle -가. 나(는) and 내(가) are used when the hearer's supposed social status is lower than or equal to that of the speaker. But this custom is gradually changing so that 나는 or 내가 are often used without any discrimination.

    Examples :

저는 하겠어요. ⌒	I will do that.
제가 학교에 가겠어요. ⌒	I will go to school.
나는 한국말을 가르치겠어요. ⌒	I will teach Korean.

내가 ˇ그분을 ˇ만나겠어요. ⌒   I will meet him.

○좋다 "is good" is a descriptive verb used without an object and 좋아하다 "likes" is an action verb used with an object. But depending on the context, 좋다 also has the meaning of "likes". For example, 나는 ˇ그분이 ˇ좋아요. ⌒ "I like him".

5. ○욕심도 ˇ많군요. ⌒ : 욕심 "greediness", "covetousness", or "avarice". -도 means "also". Therefore, its literal meaning is "You(he, she) are (also) greedy". It is used when one is selfish or wants to have more than what is feasible. 욕심꾸러기(욕심쟁이) ; "a grasping fellow" or "a greedy man". Compare with 깍쟁이 "a miser".

○말씀하다 is the honorific verb of 말하다. 말씀 is a noun meaning "words", "speech", or "language". There are nouns, especially those of Chinese origin, that can be made into verbs by adding the dependent verb -하다 to them.

Examples :

말씀을 ˇ하세요. ⌒   Please tell me.

말씀하세요. ⌒   Please tell me.

집에서 ˇ공부를 ˇ해요. ⌒   I study at home.

집에서 ˇ공부해요. ⌒   I study at home.

6. ○글쎄요 "well" is an exclamatory expression of uncertainty.

7. ○여름과 ˇ겨울 중에서는요? ⌒ is an unfinished sentence standing for 여름과 ˇ겨울 중에서는 ˇ어느 철을 ˇ더 ˇ좋아하세요? ⌒ -는 is the contrast particle, and the particle -요 is used here to make this sentence polite.

Text II

10. ○따뜻하다 "is warm" is the descriptive verb. 따뜻한 "warm"(noun modifier). 따뜻하게 "warm"(adverb).

Examples :

봄은 ˇ따뜻해요. ⌒   Spring is warm.

나는 ˇ따뜻한 봄이 ˇ더 ˇ좋아요. ⌒   I like warm spring better.

몸을 ˇ따뜻하게 하세요. ⌒   Keep yourself warm, please.

11. ○**여름에는요?**⌢ is an unfinished sentence standing for **여름에는** ˅ **날씨가** ˅ **어때요?**⌢

13. ○**가을엔** is a contraction of **가을에는**.

16. ○**겨울엔** is a contraction of **겨울에는**.

Text III

17. ○흐렸군요 is a contraction of 흐리었군요. Note that to say "it is cloudy" in Korean, you use the past tense.

   ○또 has different meanings depending on the context. See the following sentences :

또 오세요.⌐	Come again (See you again).
또 한번 말씀해 주세요. ⌢	Please say it once more.
그분은 선생이며⌢ 또 학생이에요. ⌢	He is both a teacher and a student.

18. ○걱정 is a noun meaning "worry", "anxiety", and 걱정하다 is a descriptive verb meaning "is anxious", "is worried about".

19. ○개요 "clear up". Notice that to say "The sky is clear", in Korean you say "The sky has become clear"(past tense).

STRUCTURAL PATTERNS

Text I

Ⅰ. The particle of subordination and modification -의

Examples :

한국의 기후는 어때요?	How is the weather in Korea ?
이것은 그분의 책이에요.	This is his book.
그것은 선생님의 사전이에요.	That is your dictionary.
교실에 그 학생의 책이 있어요.	That student's book is in the class-room.

Notes :

1. The particle -의 expresses a relation of subordination or modification between two nouns. It signals origin, location, possession, etc. There is no single word in English which is exactly equivalent to -의 ; "of" is about the closest.

2. In careful pronunciation, -의 is pronounced ŭi. But in casual speech, it is pronounced in three different ways depending on its position. In initial position as in 의자 'chair', 의사 'doctor', etc. it is pronounced ŭ; in other positions, it is pronounced i, as in 회의 'conference', 내의 'under wear', etc. ; when 의 is used as the possessive, it is pronounced 에[e], for example, the 의 in 한국의 기후, 그분의 책, 선생님의 사전, etc. is read 에.

Ⅱ. The conjunctive particle -과/와 : "and"

Examples :

분필과 칠판	chalk and blackboard
책과 공책	book and notebook
선생과 학생	teacher and student
의자와 책상	chair and desk

교과서와 연필   textbook and pencil

Notes:

1. The particle -과/와 "and" occurs between nominals to connect them. It does not regularly connect verbals or adjectivals.

2. The conjunctive particle occurs in two shapes: -와 after a word ending in a vowel and -과 after a word ending in a consonant.

3. It is less colloquial than -하고, which means also 'and' or 'with'.

III. The particle of comparison -보다…(더) : "more than"

Examples:

이 책보다 그 책이 (더) 커요. ⌒   That book is larger than this book.

김 선생보다 이 선생이 (더) 재미있어   Mr. Lee is more interesting than Mr.
요. ⌒   Kim.

연필보다 만년필이 (더) 비싸요. ⌒   The fountain pen is more expensive
                                             than the pencil.

자동차보다 비행기가 (더) 빨라요. ⌒   The airplane is faster than the auto-
                                             mobile.

Notes:

1. The particle -보다 "more than" added to a noun expresses a relation of comparison. The noun to which it is added may be preceded by any kind of noun modifier.

2. 더- is sometimes added for more emphasis.

3. The phrase ending with -보다 may occur either immediately before the predicate or before the subject of the main sentence. See the examples below:

이 책보다 그 책이 더 커요. ⌒   That book is larger than this book.

그 책이 이 책보다 더 커요. ⌒   That book is larger than this book.

4. Comparison in questions, which in some other languages begin with an interrogative pronoun, is handled somewhat differently.

김 선생과 이 선생은 누가 더 커요? ⌒

   Who is bigger—Mr. Kim or Mr. Lee?

연필과 ˅ 만년필은 ˅ 어느 것이 ˅ 더 ˅ 비싸요? ⌒

Which is more expensive—the pencil or the fountain pen ?

IV. The contrastive ending -지만 : "but"

Examples :

나는 ˅ 학교에 ˅ 가지만, ⌒ 그분은 ˅ 가지 않아요. ⌒

I go to school, but he does not go.

이것은 ˅ 좋지만, ⌒ 그것은 ˅ 좋지 않아요. ⌒

This is good, but that is bad.

나는 ˅ 영어를 ˅ 공부했지만, ⌒ 그분은 ˅ 불어를 ˅ 공부했어요. ⌒

I studied English, but he studied French.

Notes :

1. The position of the marker of contrast -지만 is as follows :

   - for the present tense : V.S. + -지만

   - for the past tense : V.S. + -았- + -지만

   - for the future tense : V.S. + -겠- + -지만 (This has not been introduced yet.)

2. The verb to which it is added can be either a descriptive verb, an action verb, 있- or -이-.

3. Its function being to bring out a contrast between two verbs, a second verb usually follows. In lively conversation, however, this second verb is sometimes not expressed. Ex. 저는 가지만, … "I am going but…"

Text II

V. The gerund form of the verb V.S. + -고 : "is and" (descriptive verb) "does and" (action verb)

Examples :

그분은 ˅ 한국말을 ˅ 공부하고, ⌒ 저는 ˅ 영어를 ˅ 공부해요. ⌒

He is studying Korean, and I'm studying English.

이 책상은 ˅ 싸고, ⌒ 저 책상은 ˅ 비싸요. ⌒

This desk is cheap, and that one over there is expensive.

이 만년필은 ˇ 싸고 ⌢ 좋아요. ⌢

This fountain pen is cheap and good.

비행기는 ˇ 빠르고, ⌢ 자동차는 ˇ 느려요. ⌢

The airplane is fast, and the automobile is slow.

Notes :

1. V.S. + -고 is the gerund form of the verb. It is used in a number of constructions of which we will presently study only one.

2. The gerund as used in the above examples serves to link two clauses with the meaning "and". Remember the gerund merely links the two clauses ; it does not show any specific relation between them.

3. The subjects of the two clauses can be either the same or different.

4. Any verb (descriptive verbs, etc.) can be given its gerund form.

VI. The use of 예 and 아니오

Compare very carefully the following Korean sentences with English and you will find that the use of 예 and 아니오 is quite different from the English "yes" and "no", especially when used in response to negative questions.

Examples :

1. Answers to affirmative questions

a) 학교에 가세요? ↗   Are you going to school?

예, ⌢ 학교에 가요. ⌢   Yes, I am going to school.

아니오, ↗ 학교에 가지 않아요. ⌢   No, I am not going to school.

b) 그것은 좋아요. ↗   Is that good?

예, ⌢ (그것은) 좋아요. ⌢   Yes, that is good.

아니오, ↗ (그것은) 좋지 않아요. ⌢   No, that is not good.

2. Answers to negative questions

a) 학교에 가지 않아요? ↗   Aren't you going to school?

예, ⌢ 학교에 가지 않아요. ⌢   No, I am not going to school.

(Yes, what you said is true : I'm not going to school.)

아니오, ↗ 학교에 ˇ가요. ⌒

Yes, I am going to school.

(No, what you said is not true : I am going to school.)

b) 그것은 ˇ좋지 않아요? ↗

Isn't that good?

예, ⌒ 그것은 ˇ좋지 않아요. ⌒

No, that is not good. (Yes, what you said is true : it's not good.)

아니오, ↗ 그것은 ˇ좋아요. ⌒

Yes, that is good. (No, what you said is not true ; it is good.)

Notes :

1. 예 usually means "what you just said is right". In answer to affirmative questions it corresponds to English "yes", but in answer to negative questions anticipating a negative answer, it usually confirms the negative and corresponds to the English "no".

2. 아니오, the opposite of 예, means "what you just said is wrong" and behaves in a parallel way. In answer to affirmative questions, it corresponds to the English "no" but in answer to negative questions anticipating a negative answer, it usually contradicts the negative and corresponds to the English "yes".

Ⅶ. The conditional conjunctive ending <u>V.S. + -(으)면</u> : "if"

Examples :

선생님이 ˇ가면, ⌒ 저도 ˇ가겠어요. ⌒

If the teacher goes, I will go too.

그것이 ˇ좋으면, ⌒ 삽시다. ↘

If it is good, let's buy it.

그분이 ˇ시계를 사면, ⌒ 나는 ˇ자동차를 사겠어요. ⌒

If he buys a watch, I'll buy a car.

돈이 있으면, ⌒ 좀 ˇ주세요. ⌒

If you have money, give me a little bit.

그분이 ˇ한국 사람이면, ⌒ 한국말로 ˇ말하세요. ⌒

If he is Korean, speak to him in Korean.

Notes:

1. The conditional form -(으)면 corresponds to the English "if", but it is never equivalent to "whenever". It regularly refers to a single instance. It may be used with any verb and any form.

2. The subject of the if-clause, if different from that of the main clause, usually takes the particle -이/-가.   If both subjects are the same, the particle added to the subject of the if-clause is -은/-는. See the examples below.

그분이 오시면, ⌒ 가세요. ⌒   If he comes, please go.

나는 그분을 만나면, ⌒ 가겠어요. ⌒   If I meet him, I will go.

3. In Korean the dependent clause precedes the main clause, while in English the order can be either way.

Text III

Ⅷ. The causal conjunctive ending -(기)때문에

(A) V.S. + 기 때문에 : "because"

Examples:

그분이 가기 때문에, ⌒ 나도 가요. ⌒

Because he is going, I am going too.

사람이 너무 많기 때문에, ⌒ 좋지 않아요. ⌒

Because there are too many people, it's not good.

그것이 좋지 않기 때문에, ⌒ 사지 않겠어요. ⌒

Because that is not good, I'll not buy it.

Notes:

1. The causal conjunctive ending -기 때문에 expresses "reason" or "cause". It corresponds to the English "because", "therefore", or "so".

2. It may be used with any verb, and the tense infixes(-았-, -겠-) can be used if necessary (in most other constructions in Korean the tense is expressed only in the main clause).

3. In this pattern, -기 때문에 usually ends with comma intonation.

(B) Noun + -때문에 : "because of...", "on account of..."

Examples :

그분 때문에 가지 않았어요. ⌢

I did not go because of him.

숙제 때문에 자지 못했어요. ⌢ (못- means "cannot", cf. Lesson 10 S.P. Ⅷ)

I could not sleep because of the homework.

Note :

-때문에 can be added to any noun and indicates reason.

Ⅸ. Verb stem + -았(-었, -였)으면 좋겠다 : "I hope something will happen" or "I wish something would happen".

Examples :

한국말을 공부했으면⌢ 좋겠어요. ⌢

I wish I could study Korean. (Lit. If I could study Korean, it would be good.)

집에 갔으면⌢ 좋겠어요. ⌢

I hope I can go home. (Lit. If I could go home, it would be good.)

사람이 많았으면⌢ 좋겠어요. ⌢

I hope there will be many people. (Lit. If there would be many people, it would be good.)

볕이 났으면⌢ 좋겠어요. ⌢

I wish the sun would shine. (Lit. If the sun would shine, it would be good.)

Notes :

1. This pattern -았(-었, -였)으면 좋겠다 may be used with any verb and expresses the hope of the speaker. It is equivalent to the English "I wish so-and-so would happen".

2. Although the past infix -았- etc. is used in this pattern, the meaning is that of the present tense. The use of the past infix makes the expression more polite. The present tense -(으)면 좋겠다 can also be used.

X. Verbal noun formation

There are several ways of making (verbal) nouns out of verbs. You will find the most important ones treated below.

(A) V.S. + -기

Verb		V.S.	Suffix	Verbal Noun	Meaning
가다	goes	가-	-기	가기	the going
가르치다	teaches	가르치-	-기	가르치기	the teaching
공부하다	studies	공부하-	-기	공부하기	studying
좋다	is good	좋-	-기	좋기	good

Notes :

1. In order to make a verb into a noun, the nominalizing suffix -기 is attached to the verb stem. -기 may be attached directly to any verb stem, but it is not a sentence nominalizer.

2. The verbal noun so made indicates the activity or the state of being as a concrete thing. It corresponds to English "ing" or to infinitive to(do)", etc.

3. Verbal nouns made with the suffix -기 are used in many ways : as a subject or object, in adverbial and idiomatic phrases. See the following examples : (Later we will study "-기" verbal nouns used in adverbial and idiomatic phrases.)

Examples :

1. "-기" verbal nouns with the subject particle -가/-이

   한국말을 공부하기가 재미있어요. ⌒

   It is interesting to study Korean. or : Studying Korean is interesting.

   물건을 사기가 쉬워요. ⌒

   It is easy to buy things(goods). or : Buying things(goods) is easy.

2. "-기" verbal nouns with the object particle -를/-을

   그분은 공부하기를 좋아해요. ⌒   He likes to study.

   나는 가르치기를 싫어해요. ⌒   I don't like to teach.

(B) <u>V.S. + -ㅁ/-음.</u>

Verb		V.S.	Suffix	Verbal Noun	Meaning
일하다	works	일하-	-ㅁ	일함	working
자다	sleeps	자-	-ㅁ	잠	sleeping
추다	dances	추-	-ㅁ	춤	dancing
꾸다	dreams	꾸-	-ㅁ	꿈	dreaming
그리다	draws	그리-	-ㅁ	그림	drawing
살다	lives	살-	-ㅁ	삶	living
걷다	walks	걸-	-음	걸음	walking

Notes:

1. Another way of making verbal nouns out of verbs is by attaching the nominalizing suffix -ㅁ/-음 to the verb stem: -ㅁ after verb stems ending in a vowel, -음 after verb stems ending in a consonant.

2. **The verbal noun made by adding -ㅁ/-음 to the stem, rather than indicating the concrete activity as -기 does, refers to the activity more as an abstract matter. As with any rule, however, exceptions do exist.**

3. Not a few -ㅁ/-음 nouns are used overlappingly with their own verbs:

잠자다	sleeps	꿈꾸다	dreams
숨쉬다	breathes	뜀뛰다	jumps
춤추다	dances	그림그리다	draws

(C) Other ways of verbal noun formation

Verb		V.S.	Suffix	Verbal Noun	Meanning
높다	is high	높-	-이	높이	height
깊다	is deep	깊-	-이	깊이	depth
길다	is long	길-	-이	길이	length
넓다	is wide	넓-	-이	넓이	width
춥다	is cold	춥-(ㅂ 우)	-이	추위	cold
덥다	is hot	덥-(ㅂ 우)	-이	더위	heat
지다	carries	지-	-게	지게	A-frame

집다	picks up	집-	-게	집게	pincers
무겁다	is heavy		-게	무게	weight
두껍다	is thick		-게	두께	thickness
날다	flies	날-	-개	날개	wing
쓰다	puts on	쓰-	-개	쓰개	veil

Notes :

1. As you have noticed when reading the examples, there are many more ways of verbal noun formation. The most important ones are those which take either of the suffixes -이, -게 or 개. The formation is not always regular just as with any language. Some English nominalizers, for example, are -ness, -tion, -sion, -y, -ity, -er, etc.

2. The number of the verbs that can be changed into verbal nouns by the use of these and other suffixes is very limited. The best way to handle them is learning them as single vocabulary items.

DRILLS

[ADDITIONAL VOCABULARY]

일본말(일어) Japanese	프랑스말(불어) French	이태리말(이태리어) Italian
소련말(노어) Russian	독일말(독어) German	중국말(중국어) Chinese
스페인말(스페인어) Spanish	어려워요(어렵지-) is difficult	쉬워요(쉽지-)is easy
		온화해요(온화하지-) is mild
시원해요(시원하지-) is refreshing	무더워요(무덥지-) is sultry	쌀쌀해요(쌀쌀하지-) is chilly
서늘해요(서늘하지-)is cool	구름 cloud	끼어요(끼지-) is cloudy
태풍 typhoon	폭풍우 rainstorm	번개가 쳐요(치지-) lightning
장마철 the rainy season	가물어요(가물지-)droughty	소나기 shower

Text I

A. Substitution Drill

1. 한국의 기후는 어때요? ⌒

   How is the weather in Korea?

미국,	프랑스,	이태리
일본,	중국,	독일

2. 어느 철을 제일 좋아하세요? ⌒ (을/를)

   Which season do you like best?

만년필,	의자,	책상,
연필,	인형,	사전

3. 저는 봄과 가을이 좋아요. ⌒

   (와/과—이/가)

   I like spring and fall.

여름—겨울,	한국말—영어,
한국—독일,	프랑스—이태리,
이 만년필—그 책	

4. 가을보다 봄이 더 좋아요. ⌒

   I like spring better than fall.

겨울—여름,	일본말—프랑스말,
독일말—중국말,	이태리말—소련말

B. Integration Drill

Teacher : 이것은 좋아요. 그것은 나빠요.　　This is good. That is bad.

Student : 이것은 좋지만. 그것은 나빠요.　　This is good, but that is bad.

1. 그분은 가요. 나는 가지 않아요.

   그분은 가지만 나는 가지 않아요.

2. 불어는 재미있어요, 독어는 재미없어요.

   불어는 재미있지만 독어는 재미없어요.

3. 한국말은 가르쳐요. 영어는 가르치지 않아요.

   한국말은 가르치지만 영어는 가르치지 않아요.

4. 날씨가 좋아요. 가지 않겠어요.

   날씨가 좋지만 가지 않겠어요.

5. 그분은 택시로 가요. 저는 버스로 가요.

   그분은 택시로 가지만 저는 버스로 가요.

6. 그분은 선생이에요. 이분은 학생이에요.

   그분은 선생이지만 이분은 학생이에요.

7. 저는 책이 있어요. 그분은 책이 없어요.

   저는 책이 있지만 그분은 책이 없어요.

C. Response Drill

Teacher : 김 선생과 이 선생은 누가 더 커요?

　　　　　Who is taller — Mr. Kim or Mr. Lee?

Student : 김 선생보다 이 선생이 더 커요.

　　　　　Mr. Lee is taller than Mr. Kim.

1. 한국말과 영어는 어느 것이 더 어려워요?

   한국말보다 영어가 더 어려워요.

2. 버스와 택시는 어느 것이 더 빨라요?

   버스보다 택시가 더 빨라요.

3. 한국말과 불어는 어느 것이 더 복잡해요?

   한국말보다 불어가 더 복잡해요.

4. 독일말과 이태리말은 어느 것이 더 재미있어요?

독일말보다 이태리말이 더 재미있어요. ⌒

5. 소련말과 일본말은 어느 것이 더 쉬워요?
   소련말보다 일본말이 더 쉬워요. ⌒

D. Expansion Drill

1. 더 좋아요. ⌒
   여름이 더 좋아요. ⌒
   겨울보다 여름이 더 좋아요. ⌒
   겨울도 좋지만⌒ 겨울보다 여름이 더 좋아요. ⌒
   저는 겨울도 좋지만⌒ 겨울보다 여름이 더 좋아요. ⌒
   I like winter, but I like summer better than winter.

Text II

E. Substitution Drill

1. 날씨가 따뜻해요. ⌒
   The weather is warm.

선선해요,	시원해요,	무더워요
온화해요,	쌀쌀해요,	서늘해요

2. 날씨가 덥지 않군요. ⌒
   The weather is not hot.

무덥지,	선선하지,	시원하지,
온화하지,	쌀쌀하지,	서늘하지

F. Integration Drill

Teacher : 이것은 책이에요. ⌒ 저것은 공책이에요. ⌒

This is a book. That over there is a notebook.

Student : 이것은 책이고⌒ 저것은 공책이에요. ⌒

This is a book, and that over there is a notebook.

1. 나는 학교에 가요. 그분은 집에 가요.
   나는 학교에 가고⌒ 그분은 집에 가요. ⌒

2. 나는 한국말을 공부해요. 그분은 영어를 공부해요.
   나는 한국말을 공부하고⌒ 그분은 영어를 공부해요. ⌒

3. 비행기는 빨라요. 자동차는 느려요.

비행기는 ˅빠르고⌒ 자동차는 ˅느려요. ⌒

4. 그것은 교실에 있어요. 책은 여기 있어요.

   그것은 ˅교실에 있고⌒ 책은 ˘여기 있어요. ⌒

5. 그분은 선생이에요. 저는 학생이에요.

   그분은 ˅선생이고⌒ 저는 ˅학생이에요. ⌒

6. 여름에는 비가 많이 와요. 더워요.

   여름에는 ˅비가 ˘많이 오고⌒ 더워요. ⌒

G. Integration Drill

   Teacher : 영어가 ˅어려워요. ⌒ 공부하지 않겠어요.

   English is difficult. I'll not study (it).

   Student : 영어가 ˅어려우면, ⌒ 공부하지 않겠어요. ⌒

   If English is difficult, I'll not study it.

1. 일본말이 재미있어요. 공부하겠어요.

   일본말이 ˅재미있으면⌒ 공부하겠어요. ⌒

2. 독일말이 재미없어요. 배우지 않겠어요.

   독일말이 ˅재미없으면⌒ 배우지 않겠어요. ⌒

3. 시간이 없어요. 가지 않겠어요.

   시간이 ˅없으면⌒ 가지 않겠어요. ⌒

4. 그분이 와요, 가야겠어요.

   그분이 ˅오면⌒ 가야겠어요. ⌒

5. 그분이 자동차를 사요. 나는 비행기를 사겠어요.

   그분이 ˅자동차를 ˅사면⌒ 나는 ˅비행기를 ˘사겠어요. ⌒

6. 날씨가 무더워요. 집에 있겠어요.

   날씨가 ˅무더우면⌒ 집에 있겠어요. ⌒

H. Response Drill

   Teacher : 그것이 ˅좋지 않아요? ↗

   Isn't that good?

   Student : 예, ⌒ 그것이 ˅좋지 않아요. ⌒ 아니오, ↗ 그것이 ˅좋아요. ⌒

   No, that is not good. Yes, that is good.

1. 한국말이 어렵지 않아요?

   예,⌒ 한국말이˅ 어렵�‌지 않아요.⌒ 아니오,↗ 한국말이˅ 어려워요.⌒

2. 그분이 한국말을 가르치지 않아요?

   예,⌒ 그분이˅ 한국말을˅ 가르치지 않아요.⌒ 아니오,↗ 그분이˅ 한국말을˅ 가르쳐요.⌒

3. 그분이 학생이 아니에요?

   예,⌒ 그분이˅ 학생이˅ 아니에요.⌒ 아니오,↗ 그분이˅ 학생이에요.⌒

4. 집에 돌아가지 않겠어요?

   예,⌒ 집에˅ 돌아가지 않겠어요.⌒ 아니오,↗ 집에˅ 돌아가겠어요.⌒

5. 날씨가 덥지 않아요?

   예,⌒ 날씨가˅ 덥지 않아요.⌒ 아니오,↗ 날씨가˅ 더워요.⌒

I. Response Drill

1. 그분이 가시면 가시겠어요?   예,⌒ 그분이˅ 가시면⌒가겠어요.⌒

2. 봄에는 날씨가 어때요?   봄에는˅ 날씨가˅ 따뜻해요.⌒

3. 겨울이 되면 날씨가 어때요?   겨울이 되면⌒ 날씨가˅ 추워요.⌒

4. 이것은 좋지만 저것은 나쁘지요?   예,⌒ 이것은˅ 좋지만⌒ 저것은˅ 나빠요.

5. 겨울엔 덥지 않아요?   예,⌒ 겨울엔˅ 덥지 않아요.⌒

J. Expansion Drill

1. 더워요.⌒

   비가˅ 많이˅ 오고⌒ 더워요.⌒

   여름이 되면⌒ 비가˅ 많이 오고⌒ 더워요.⌒

   눈이 오고⌒ 춥지만⌒ 여름이 되면⌒ 비가˅ 많이˅ 오고⌒ 더워요.⌒

   겨울에는˅ 눈이˅ 오고⌒ 춥지만⌒ 여름이 되면⌒ 비가˅ 많이˅ 오고⌒ 더워요.⌒

   In winter it snows and it's cold, but in summer it rains a lot and it's hot.

Text III

K. Substitution Drill

1. 바람이˅ 불기˅ 시작하는데요.⌒(↗)

   The wind is beginning to blow!

구름이˅ 끼,	태풍이˅ 불,
번개가˅ 치,	폭풍우가˅ 불

2. 태풍이 불 것 같아요. ⌒

It seems that the typhoon will blow.

폭풍우가 불,   번개가 칠,
소나기가 올,   날씨가 가물

3. 영어는 가르치기 어려워요. ⌒

It is difficult to teach English.

중국어는 공부하기,
스페인어는 배우기,
프랑스어는 배우기

L. Integration Drill

Teacher : 그분이 가요. ⌒ 나도 가요. ⌒   He is going. I am going too.

Student : 그분이 가기 때문에⌒ 나도   Because he is going, I am going too.

       가요.

1. 돈이 없었어요. 사지 않았어요.

    돈이 없었기 때문에⌒ 사지 않았어요. ⌒

2. 사람이 너무 많아요. 좋지 않아요.

    사람이 너무 많기 때문에⌒ 좋지 않아요. ⌒

3. 그것이 좋지 않아요. 사지 않겠어요.

    그것이 좋지 않기 때문에⌒ 사지 않겠어요.

4. 너무 더워요. 집에 있겠어요.

    너무 덥기 때문에⌒ 집에 있겠어요. ⌒

5. 저는 학생이에요. 공부해야 해요.

    저는 학생이기 때문에⌒ 공부해야 해요. ⌒

6. 가물어요. 큰일났어요.

    가물기 때문에⌒ 큰일났어요. ⌒

M. Pattern Drill

Teacher : 한국말을 공부해요. ⌒   I study Korean.

Student : 한국말을 공부했으면⌒ 좋겠   I wish I could study Korean.

       어요. ⌒

1. 집에 가요.   집에 갔으면⌒좋겠어요. ⌒

2. 사람이 많아요.　　　　　　　　사람이 많았으면⌒ 좋겠어요. ⌒

3. 볕이 나요.　　　　　　　　　　볕이 났으면⌒ 좋겠어요. ⌒

4. 불어를 공부해요.　　　　　　　불어를 공부했으면⌒ 좋겠어요. ⌒

5. 구름이 끼어요.　　　　　　　　구름이 끼었으면⌒ 좋겠어요. ⌒

6. 소나기가 와요.　　　　　　　　소나기가 왔으면⌒ 좋겠어요. ⌒

N. Response Drill

1. 왜 학교에 가지 않겠어요?　　　날씨가 춥기 때문에⌒ 가지 않겠어요. ⌒

2. 무엇이 불기 시작해요?　　　　바람이 불기 시작해요. ⌒

3. 무엇이 올 것 같아요?　　　　　비가 올것 같아요. ⌒

4. 무엇을 공부했으면 좋겠어요?　한국말을 공부했으면⌒ 좋겠어요. ⌒

5. 한국말을 공부하기 어렵지요?　예, ⌒ 한국말을 공부하기 어려워요. ⌒

6. 무엇을 가르치기를 좋아하세요?　불어를 가르치기를 좋아해요. ⌒

O. Expansion Drill

1. 좋겠어요. ⌒

　　볕이 났으면⌒ 좋겠어요. ⌒

　　비가 많이 왔기 때문에⌒ 볕이 났으면⌒ 좋겠어요. ⌒

　Because it has rained a lot, I wish the sun would shine.

제구과 시간 (Lesson 9 Time)

TEXT I

[VOCABULARY]

시간 time	떠나요(떠나지-) leaves
날마다 every day	항상 always
몇 시 what time	여덟 eight
-경 about	십 ten
일어나요(일어나지-) gets up	도착해요(도착하지-) arrives at
대개 usually, mostly, mainly	아홉 nine
일곱 seven	부터 from
-분 minute	수업 lesson, school, class
전 before	정각 just, sharp
아침 morning	

1. 박성희 : 날마다 몇 시경에 일어나세요? — About what time do you get up every day?

2. 임상빈 : 대개 일곱시 오분 전에 일어나요. — Usually I get up at five minutes to seven.

3. 박성희 : 아침 몇 시에 집에서 떠나세요? — What time do you leave the house in the morning?

4. 임상빈 : 항상 여덟시 십분에 떠나지요. — I always leave at ten minutes after eight.

5. 박성희 : 그럼 학교에 몇 시에 도착하세요? — What time then do you arrive at school?

6. 임상빈 : 아홉시 십분 전에 도착해요. — I arrive at ten minutes to nine.

7. 박성희 : 몇 시부터 수업을 시작해요? — When does class begin? (From what time does class begin?)

8. 임상빈 : **정각** **아홉**시에 **수업**을 **시작해**   Class begins exactly at nine o'clock.
　　　　요.

<table>
<tr><td colspan="2">TEXT II</td><td colspan="2">〔VOCABULARY〕</td></tr>
</table>

TEXT II

〔VOCABULARY〕

하루 a day	토요일 Saturday
끝나요(끝나지-) ends, comes to an end	일요일 Sunday
	금요일 Friday
두시 two o'clock	-까지 till, until, to
반 half	월요일 Monday
매일 every day	

9. 박성희 : **하루**에 **몇** 시간씩 **공부하시지**   How many hours a day do you study?
　　　　요?

10. 임상빈 : **하루**에 **여섯** 시간씩 **공부해요.**   I study six hours a day.

11. 박성희 : 그럼 **몇** 시에 **수업**이 **끝나세**   What time then does class end?
　　　　요?

12. 임상빈 : 날마다 **두시** 반에 **수업**이 **끝**   Class ends every day at two thirty.
　　　　나요.

13. 박성희 : **매일** **공부하세요?**   Do you study every day?

14. 임상빈 : **아니오,** **토요일**과 **일요일**엔   No, I don't study on Saturday or
　　　　공부하지 **않아요.** **월요일**부   Sunday. I study from Monday through
　　　　터 **금요일까지** **공부해요.**   Friday.

15. 박성희 : **몇** 시에 **집**으로 **돌아가세요?**   At what time do you go home?

16. 임상빈 : **세시**에 **집**으로 **돌아가요.**   I go home at three o'clock.

TEXT III

〔VOCABULARY〕

언제 when	걸려요(걸리지-) takes (time)
작년 last year	약 about
비행기 airplane	오래 long time
배 boat, ship	죽어요(죽지-) dies
-쯤 about, around	

17. 박성희 : 언제˘ 한국에˘ 오셨어요? ⌒	When did you come to Korea?
18. 임상빈 : 작년에˘ 한국에˘ 왔어요. ⌒	I came to Korea last year.
19. 박성희 : 한국에˘ 오실 때⌒ 비행기로˘ 오셨어요? ↗	Did you come to Korea by airplane? (When you come to Korea, did you come by airplane?)
20. 임상빈 : 아니오, ↗ 배로 왔어요. ⌒	No, I came by boat.
21. 박성희 : 얼마쯤 걸렸어요? ⌒	About how long did it take?
22. 임상빈 : 약˘ 이 주일 걸렸어요. ⌒	It took about two weeks.
23. 박성희 : 한국에˘ 오래 계시겠어요? ⌒	Will you be in Korea for a long time?
24. 임상빈 : 그럼요, ⌒ 죽을 때까지⌒ 있겠어요. ⌒	Of course, I will be here till I die.

REMARKS TO THE TEXT

Text I

1. ○시간 : As an independent noun 시간 means "time" ; as a bound form with the native Korean numerals it means "hour". See Lesson 6, S.P. No. VII.

2. ○-시, -분 : See Lesson 6, S.P. No. VII. Notice that -분 "minute" is used with the Sino-Korean numerals, while -분 "honored people" is used with the Korean numerals. 이분 means "two minutes" ; 두분 means "two honored people". One more tricky thing to notice is that 이분 can also mean "this honored person" 초 is "second".

   ○ 전- is added to time expressions to indicate the time before the hour. See the following examples :

   네시 십분 전이에요.   It's ten minutes to four.

   아홉시 십오분 전이에요.   It's a quarter to nine.

3. ○아침 always takes the particle -에. 아침 is the period of time from daybreak till about ten o'clock in the morning.

   ○The names for the various parts of the day are as follows :

새벽	dawn	깊은 밤	midnight
아침	morning	저녁	evening
낮	day	밤	night
오전	forenoon	오후	afternoon
정오	noontime	자정	midnight

   ○떠나다 "leaves"(pure Korean), 출발하다 "leaves"(from Chinese). Both verbs are used with either of the two particles -을/-를 and -에서. See the examples below :

   집을 떠나요(출발해요).   I leave the house.

집에서 ˅떠나요(출발해요). ⌒   I leave the house.

4. ○항상 "always"(from Chinese) ; 늘 "always"(pure Korean).

5. ○도착하다 "arrives, reaches" (from Chinese) ; 닿다 "arrives, reaches"(pure Korean).

7. ○수업. "gives classes" is 수업을 하다 ; "takes classes" is 수업을 받다. 시작하다 "begins" is an object verb (-를) ; its non-object counterpart is 시작되다 "(something) begins."

Text II

11. ○끝나다 "ends, finishes" is a non-object verb(intransitive) ; 끝내다 "ends, completes" is an object verb(transitive) ; 마치다 "ends, completes" is an object verb (transitive). See the examples below :

두시 반에 ˅수업이 ˅끝나요. ⌒   Class ends at two thirty.
세시에 ˅공부를 끝내겠어요. ⌒   I'll finish studying at three.
한시까지 ˅그 일을 ˅마치세요. ⌒   Finish that work before one o'clock.

13. ○매일 : 매- stands for the Chinese character meaning "every". Study the following compounds : 매일 "every day" ; 매주 "every week" ; 매월 "every month" ; 매년 "every year". All are time nominals and all occur without the particle -에 "at" (time).

14. ○일요일엔 is a contraction of 일요일에는.

Text III

18. ○작년에 "last year". Study the following expressions :

Chinese expressions used with the particle -에 :	Pure Korean expressions used with or without the particle -에 :
작년에 last year	지난해(에) last year
금년에 this year	올해(에) this year
내년에 next year	다음해(에) next year

21. ○걸리다 : This verb has several meanings, some of which are illustrated in the following examples :

여기서 두 시간 걸려요. ⌒   It takes two hours from here.

그것은 벽에 걸려 있어요. ⌒   It hangs on the wall.

그분이 순경한테 걸렸어요. ⌒   He was caught by a policeman.

그분이 감기에 걸렸어요. ⌒   He caught a cold.

그것이 마음에 걸려요. ⌒   That weighs heavy on my mind.

As shown in Ex. No. 1, when used with the meaning of "takes time" 걸리다 is a non-object verb (intransitive).

22. ○약 "approximate quantity" occurs before time and quantity expressions which answer the questions "how much?", "how long?", "how many?", or "how far?"

◎ -주일 "week" : -주일, -개월, -년 are classifiers meaning respectively "week", "month", "year". They are all used with the Sino-Korean numerals.

STRUCTURAL PATTENS

Text I

I. Noun + 마다 : "every"

Examples :

저는 날마다 공부해요.　　　　　　　　I study every day.

집집마다 사람이 있어요.　　　　　　　There are people in every house.

책상마다 달라요.　　　　　　　　　　Every desk is different.

삼십 분마다 와요.　　　　　　　　　　It comes every thirty minutes.

Note :

The particle -마다 can be added to any nominal. It corresponds to the English "every".

II. The suffix -경 : "about"

Examples :

몇 시경(에) 일어나세요?　　　　　　About what time do you get up?

다섯 시경(에) 일어나요.　　　　　　I get up about five o'clock.

삼일경(에) 오세요.　　　　　　　　Please come about the third of the month.

Note :

The suffix -경 is added to time expressions which answer the question "when?". It means "approximate point of time." It occurs both with or without the particle -에 indicating time when something happens.

III. The particle -에 : "at, on, in"

Examples :

일곱시 십오분에 왔어요.　　　　　　I came at 7 : 15.

목요일에 가겠어요.　　　　　　　　I will go on Thursday.

그분이 사월에 가요.　　　　　　　He goes in April.

Notes :

1. The particle -에 is suffixed to time expressions to indicate the time at which something happens.(Compare the English use of "at" with hours of the day, "on" with days of the week, and "in" with months and years.)

2. Time words which occur without the particle -에 are 지금 "now", 어제 "yesterday", 오늘 "today", 내일 "tomorrow", etc.

3. Some time expressions, for example those ending with -경, occur both with or without -에.

4. In time expressions containing the names of the days of the week, the final -일 "day" is usually reinforced by the word 날 "day". The same way, the final -월 "month" is reinforced by -달 "month". See the following examples :

일요일날에 가겠어요. ⌒	I'll go on Sunday.
삼일날 오세요. ⌒	Please come on the third of the month.
오월달에 가겠어요. ⌒	I will go in May.

Review of the particle -에 :

1. -에 meaning "in, at"(static location). See Lesson 4, S.P. No. IX.

2. -에 meaning "to"(direction). See Lesson 5, S.P. No. IX.

3. -에 meaning "per". See Lesson S.P. No. I.

IV. The particle -에서 : "from"

Examples :

그분은 미국에서 왔어요. ⌒	He came from America.
서울에서 부산까지 멀어요? ↗	Is it far from Seoul to Pusan?
이태리에서 가지고 왔어요. ⌒	I brought (it) from Italy.

Note :

The particle -에서 is added to nominals of place and indicates a starting point of movement.

Review :

You have studied the particle -에서 denoting dynamic location in the S.P. No. VI of Lesson 4. If some one does something at a certain place, the particle designating the location is -에서. Let's review it.

Examples :

학교에서 공부해요. ⌒   I study at school.

그분은 교실에서 자요. ⌒   He is sleeping in the classroom.

그분은 한국에서 한국말을 배웠어요. ⌒   He learned Korean in Korea.

Ⅴ. The particle -부터 : "from" (when)

Examples :

1. 아홉시부터 두시 반까지 공부해요. ⌒   We study from nine to two thirty.

   몇 시부터 수업을 시작하세요 ? ⌒   What time does class begin? (From
                                        what time do you begin class?)

   언제부터 가르치기 시작했어요 ? ⌒   When did you begin to teach?.

2. 이것부터 하세요. ⌒   Do this first.

   여기서부터 읽겠어요. ⌒   I'll read from here.

   선생님부터 공부하세요. ⌒   Study yourself first.

Note :

The particle -부터 indicates a movement away from a certain place or time.
However, practically it is much more used for time than for place.

Text II

Ⅵ. Counting ("how many?") and naming ("what day?") the days of the month.

1. For counting and naming the days of the month, two sets of terms are used, one
   set being pure Korean and the other Sino-Korean. Neither set, however, is used for
   the entire month. To avoid confusion, the following generalization may be helpful :

   The first 20 days : for naming the days ("what day?"), the Sino-Korean set of terms
                       is used (but see Note 2) ; for counting the days ("how many?"),
                       the pure Korean set of terms is used.

   Over 20 days : for both naming and counting the days, the Sino-Korean set is used
                  exclusively.

2. For naming the days under 20 you will also occasionally hear the pure Korean set being used, especially by older people and by people in the countryside. To avoid ambiguity between naming, and counting: in the case of counting one sometimes uses the word 동안 "-long" after the counting expression. See the examples below:

부산에 이틀 동안 있었어요. ⌒   I stayed in Pusan for two days.

닷새 동안 공부했어요. ⌒   I studied for five days.

3. The expressions of the Sino-Korean set are made up of the Sino-Korean numerals plus the classifier -일 "day". For the pure Korean set see below.

Now let's look at counting and naming the days of the month separately and in detail.

(A) Counting the days of the month

하루	one day	열하루	11 days	이십일 일간	21 days
이틀	two days	열이틀	12 days	이십이 일간	22 days
사흘	three days	열사흘	13 days	이십삼 일간	23 days
나흘	four days	열나흘	14 days	이십사 일간	24 days
닷새	five days	열닷새	15 days	이십오 일간	25 days
엿새	six days	열엿새	16 days	이십육 일간	26 days
이레	seven days	열이레	17 days	이십칠 일간	27 days
여드레	eight days	열여드레	18 days	이십팔 일간	28 days
아흐레	nine days	열아흐레	19 days	이십구 일간	29 days
열흘	ten days	스무날	20 days	삼십 일간	30 days
				삽십일 일간	31 days

Notes:

1. From 21 days up, the suffix -간 "-long" is usually added to -일. See the following examples:

사흘 (동안) 일했어요.   I worked three days.

삼십 일간 공부했어요.   I studied 30 days.

2. A counting expression belonging to the lunar calendar which you should

remember is 보름 "fifteen days" (hence, 보름 동안 "for fifteen days"). See the following examples :

보름 동안 부산에 있었어요.　　　　　I stayed in Pusan for 15 days.

보름 후에 가겠어요.　　　　　　　I'll go 15 days later.

(B) Naming the days of the month

일일 the first	십 일일 the eleventh	이십 일일 the twenty-first
이일 the second	십 이일 the twelfth	이십 이일 the twenty-second
삼일 the third	십 삼일 the thirteenth	이십 삼일 the twenty-third
사일 the fourth	십 사일 the fourteenth	이십 사일 the twenty-fourth
오일 the fifth	십 오일 the fifteenth	이십 오일 the twenty-fifth
육일 the sixth	십 육일 the sixteenth	이십 육일 the twenty-sixth
칠일 the seventh	십 칠일 the seventeenth	이십 칠일 the twenty-seventh
팔일 the eighth	십 팔일 the eighteenth	이십 팔일 the twenty-eighth
구일 the ninth	십 구일 the nineteenth	이십 구일 the twenty-ninth
십일 the tenth	이십일 the twentieth	삼십일 the thirtieth
		삼십 일일 the thirty-first

Notes :

1. For the first several days of the month (approximately from 1 to 5), you will SOMETIMES hear the prefix 초- "first" or "beginning" pronounced in front of the COUNTING expression. Also, the fifteenth day and the last day of the month are named 보름(날) and 그믐(날) respectively. (Don't worry because no change of meaning is involved. Most young people, especially in the cities, do not use this prefix.) See the following examples :

오늘은 초하루예요.　　　　　　Today is the first day (of the month).

오늘은 초이틀이에요.　　　　　Today is the second day.

오늘은 초사흘이에요.　　　　　Today is the third.

오늘은 보름(날)이에요.　　　　Today is the fifteenth.

오늘은 그믐(날)이에요.　　　　Today is the last day (of the month).

2. To give any complete date, Koreans give the year first, the month next, and the

day last. Example : "September 30, 1988" becomes 천 구백 팔십 팔년 구월 삼십일.

3. Nowadays, Koreans use the international A. D. system. (Before the 1961 military revolution, Koreans used both A.D. and 단기 in official documents.) In old official documents, diplomas, citations, etc., however, you will frequently find the traditional Korean system. This counts the years beginning with the year of the foundation of the country. The 단기 year can be calculated by adding 2333 years to the A. D. year. For example, the 단기 year for 1988 is 4321.

VII. Time expression + -까지 : "until" or "surely not after"

Examples :

어제 몇 시까지 저를 기다렸어요?	Until what time did you wait for me yesterday?
아홉시까지 기다렸어요.	I waited for you until nine o'clock.
몇 시부터 몇 시까지 공부하세요?	From and to what time do you study?
아홉시부터 두시 반까지 공부해요	I study from nine to two thirty.

Note :

The particle -까지 after a time expression means "until" or "surely not after".

Review :

Compare the pattern : place + -까지 studied in Lesson 5, S.P. No VI.

어디까지 가세요?	How far are you going?
서대문까지 갑시다.	Let's go as far as Sŏdaemun.
여기까지 읽었어요.	I read up to here.

VIII. The particle -(으)로 : "to"

Examples :

어디로 가세요?	Where are you going?
집으로 가요.	I am going home.
학교로 갑시다.	Let's go to school.
교실로 가요.	I am going to the classroom.
이리로 오세요.	Come here, please.

Notes :

1. The particle -(으)로 "to" has the same meaning as the direction particle -에. It is used after nominals of place and denotes direction, i.e., when either 가다 or 오다 or similar verbs(compound verbs with 가다/오다) follow. It always goes together, therefore, with verbs denoting movement, like 가요, 와요 and their compounds.

2. -로 after a nominal ending in a vowel (Ex. 1, 3, 5) and nominals ending with the consonant ㄹ(Ex. 4). -으로 after a nominal ending in a consonant except the consonant ㄹ (Ex. 2).

3. The particle -에 may be replaced by the particle -(으)로 without changing the meaning of the sentence. See the following examples :

학교에 가요. ⌒	I am going to school.
학교로 가요. ⌒	
서울에 갑시다. ↘	Let's go to Seoul.
서울로 갑시다. ↘	

Review :

You have studied the particle -(으)로 "by means of" (instrumental) in the S. P. No. III of Lesson 5. It is attached to nouns and denotes the means by which one moves about or does something.

무엇으로 돌아오시겠어요? ⌒	How (by means of what) will you come back?
비행기로 돌아오겠어요. ⌒	I'll come back by airplane.
연필로 씁시다. ⌒	Let's write with a pencil.
한국말로 말합시다. ⌒	Let's talk in Korean.

Text III

Ⅸ. V.S+the conjunctive ending -ㄹ(을) 때 : "when" or "while"

Examples :

학교에 올 때, ⌒ 그분을 만났어요. ⌒   On the way to school, I met him.

시간이 ˇ있을 때,⌢ 오세요.⌢   When you have time, please come
                                   here.

내가 공부할 때,⌢ 그분이 ˇ나갔어요.⌢   While I was studying, he went out.

날씨가 좋을 때,⌢ 갑시다.↘   When the weather is fine, let's go.

Notes :

1. The pattern -ㄹ(을) 때   may be used with any verb. It corresponds to the
English "when" or "while".

2. The pattern -ㄹ(을) 때   forming the dependent clause always precedes the
main clause.

3. The past infix (-았-)   is not usually used in this pattern when the actions of
the two clauses are concurrent.

4. But the past infix can be used in this pattern when the action or the state of the
main clause had already begun when the action of the dependent clause was
concluded. See the following examples :

    내가 ˇ교실에 ˇ들어갔을 때,⌢ 그분이 ˇ공부하고 있었어요.⌢

    When I entered the classroom, he was studying.

    그분을 ˇ만났을 때,⌢ 그분의 얼굴이 ˇ참 ˇ좋았어요.⌢

    When I met him, he looked well.

5. -ㄹ 때   after verbals ending in a vowel ; -을 때   after verbals ending in a consonant.

6. This pattern -ㄹ(을) 때   may be followed by any of the particles -에,   -부터,
-도, etc. See the following examples :

학교에 올 때에,⌢ 그분을 ˇ만났어요.⌢   On the way to school, I met him.

내가 ˇ어렸을 때부터⌢ 그분을 ˇ좋아했   I've liked him since I was a child.

어요.⌢

내가 ˇ갈 때는⌢ ˇ두 시간 걸렸어요.⌢   When I went, it took two hours.

집에 갈 때도⌢ ˇ그분을 ˇ만나지 않았어   Even when I went home, I didn't see

요.⌢   him.

X. The suffix -쯤 : "about" or "approximately"

Examples :

몇 시쯤 오시겠어요? ⌒   About what time will you come?

열 사람쯤 왔어요. ⌒   About ten people came.

언제쯤 가시겠어요? ⌒   About when will you go?

Notes :

1. The suffix -쯤 is attached to nominals and means "about" or "approximately".

2. Depending on the context, the suffix -쯤 can also be used to belittle something. See the following examples :

한국말쯤 문제 없어요. ⌒   Korean is no problem.

그 사람쯤 문제 없어요. ⌒   He is no problem.

XI. The conjunctive ending A.V.S. + -ㄹ(을) 때까지 : "until"

Examples :

그분이 올 때까지⌒ 기다리세요. ⌒   Please wait until he comes.

나는 죽을 때까지⌒ 한국에 있겠어요. ⌒   I'll be in Korea till I die.

Notes :

1. To say "something is done or has to be done until something else happens," we use the pattern A.V.S. + -ㄹ(을) 때까지.

2. The dependent clause always precedes the main clause.

3. -ㄹ 때까지 after verbals ending in a vowel ; -을 때까지 after verbals ending in a consonant.

DRILLS

──〔ADDITIONAL VOCABULARY〕──

닿아요(닿지-) arrives	목요일 Thursday	늦게 late
끝내어요(끝내지-) finishes	달라요(다르지-) is different	매년 every year
매월 every month	매주 every week	지금 now
금년 this year	마쳐요(마치지-) finishes	지난해 last year
내년 next year	올해 this year	살아요(살지-)
화요일 Tuesday	다음해 next year	lives
수요일 Wednesday		

Text I

A. Substitution Drill

1. 대개 **다섯 시**경에 일어나요.
   I usually get up about five o'clock.

여섯 시,	여섯 시 사십오 분,
일곱 시,	일곱 시 반

2. **한 시 오 분** 전에 시작하세요.
   Start at five minutes to one, please.

네 시 십오 분,	일곱 시 팔 분,
두 시 삼 분,	열한 시 사 분

3. 그분은 **미국**에서 왔어요.
   He(She) came from America.

영국,	일본,	중국

4. 정각 **아홉 시**에 수업을 시작해요.
   Class begins exactly at nine o'clock.

두 시,	여섯 시,	여덟 시,
열 시,	열한 시,	열두 시

B. Pattern Drill

Teacher : 아홉시에 수업을 시작해요. Class begins at nine o'clock.

Student : 아홉시부터 수업을 시작해요. Class begins from nine o'clock.

1. 두시에 공부를 시작해요. 두시부터 공부를 시작해요.

2. 세시에 일을 시작해요. 세시부터 일을 시작해요.

3. 일곱 시에 공부하기 시작해요.　　일곱 시부터 공부하기 시작해요.

4. 아홉 시에 자기 시작해요.　　아홉 시부터 자기 시작해요.

5. 열한 시에 가르쳐요.　　열한 시부터 가르쳐요.

6. 두 시에 배워요.　　두 시부터 배워요.

C. Response Drill

1. 몇 시경에 일어나세요?　　여섯 시경에 일어나요.

2. 몇 시에 집에서 떠나세요?　　여덟 시 반에 집에서 떠나요.

3. 몇 시에 학교에 도착하세요?　　아홉 시 십 분 전에 학교에 도착해요.

4. 몇 시부터 수업을 시작하세요?　　정각 아홉 시부터 수업을 시작해요.

5. 날마다 공부하세요?　　아니오, 날마다 공부하지 않아요.

6. 선생마다 다르지요?　　예, 선생마다 달라요.

7. 어느 것부터 할까요?　　이것부터 하세요.

8. 어디부터 읽을까요?　　여기부터 읽으세요.

D. Expansion Drill

떠났어요.

일곱 시 반에 떠났어요.

늦게 일어났기 때문에, 일곱 시 반에 떠났어요.

오늘 아침에는 늦게 일어났기 때문에, 일곱 시 반에 떠났어요.

대개 일찍 집에서 떠나지만, 오늘 아침에는 늦게 일어났기 때문에 일곱 시 반에 떠났어요.

Usually I leave the house early, but this morning I left at seven thirty, because I got up late.

Text II

E. Substitution Drill

1. 하루에 몇 시간씩 주무세요?

   How many hours a day do you sleep?

노세요,	일하세요,	배우세요,
읽으세요,	가르치세요	

2. **그분은** ˇ**부산에** ˇ 하루 있었어요. ⌢

   He(She) stayed in Pusan one day.

이틀,	사흘,	나흘,	닷새,
엿새,	이레,	여드레,	아흐레

3. 수요일부터 ˇ금요일까지 ˇ일해요. ⌢

   I(We) work from Wednesday to

   Friday.

화요일 — 목요일,	아침 — 저녁,
봄 — 가을,	오늘 — 내일

F. Pattern Drill

Teacher : **저는** ˇ**지금** **집에** 가요. ⌢ I am going home now.

Student : **저는** ˇ**지금** **집으로** 가요. ⌢ I am going home now.

1. 저는 지금 이태리에 가요. 저는 ˇ지금 ˇ이태리로 가요. ⌢

2. 저는 지금 부산에 가요. 저는 ˇ지금 ˇ부산으로 가요. ⌢

3. 저는 지금 서울에 가요. 저는 ˇ지금 ˇ서울로 가요. ⌢

4. 저는 지금 일본에 가요. 저는 ˇ지금 ˇ일본으로 가요. ⌢

5. 저는 지금 교실에 가요. 저는 ˇ지금 ˇ교실로 가요. ⌢

G. Response Drill

1. 부산에 ˇ며칠 동안 계셨어요? 부산에 ˇ이틀 동안 ˇ있었어요. ⌢

2. 오늘 아침에 무엇으로 학교에 왔어요? 오늘 아침에 ˇ버스로 ˇ학교에 왔어요. ⌢

3. 몇 시부터 몇 시까지 공부하세요? 아홉 시부터 ˇ두 시 반까지 ˇ공부해요. ⌢

4. 무엇으로 쓰겠어요? 만년필로 쓰겠어요. ⌢

5. 날마다 몇 시에 수업을 끝내세요? 날마다 ˇ두 시 반에 ˇ수업을 끝내요. ⌢

H. Expansion Drill

마치지 못했어요. ⌢

그 일을 ˇ마치지 못했어요. ⌢

이틀 동안 ˇ있었지만, ⌢ 그 일을 ˇ마치지 못했어요. ⌢

육일부터 ˇ칠일까지 ˇ이틀 동안 ˇ있었지만, ⌢ 그 일을 ˇ마치지 못했어요. ⌢

부산에 ˇ육일부터 ˇ칠일까지 ˇ이틀 동안 ˇ있었지만, ⌢ 그 일을 ˇ마치지 못했어요. ⌢

I stayed in Pusan for two days from the sixth until the seventh, but I could not finish

   that work.

Text III

I. Substitution Drill

1. 약 <u>삼 주일간</u> 걸려요. ⌒

   It takes about three weeks.

한 시간,	세 시간,	이틀,
이십 분,	한 달,	일 년

2. <u>그분이 갈</u> 때까지⌒ 기다리세요. ⌒

   Please wait until he goes.

내가 떠날,	내가 도착할,
그분이 잘,	그분이 일어날

3. <u>내일</u>쯤 오세요. ⌒

   Please come about tomorrow.

두시, 내년, 일요일, 월요일, 토요일

J. Integration Drill

Teacher : 사람이 많아요. ⌒ 가겠어요. ⌒

　　　　　There are many people. I will go.

Student : 사람이 많을 때, ⌒ 가겠어요. ⌒

　　　　　I will go when there are many people.

1. 날씨가 좋아요. 갑시다.　　　　　날씨가 좋을 때, ⌒ 갑시다. ⌉

2. 그분이 공부해요. 나도 공부하겠어　　그분이 공부할 때⌒ 나도 공부하겠어
   요.　　　　　　　　　　　　　　　　요. ⌒

3. 시간이 있어요. 가야겠어요.　　　　시간이 있을 때⌒ 가야겠어요. ⌒

4. 학교에 가세요. 버스로 가세요.　　학교에 갈 때⌒ 버스로 가세요. ⌒

5. 날씨가 더워요. 좀 쉬세요.　　　　날씨가 더울 때⌒ 좀 쉬세요.

6. 물건 값이 싸요. 삽시다.　　　　　물건 값이 쌀 때, ⌒ 삽시다. ⌉

K. Pattern Drill

Teacher : 약 한 시간 걸려요. ⌒　　　It takes about one hour.

Student : 한 시간쯤 걸려요. ⌒　　　　It takes about one hour.

1. 약 이틀 걸려요.　　　　　　　　이틀쯤 걸려요. ⌒

2. 약 사흘 걸려요.　　　　　　　　사흘쯤 걸려요. ⌒

3. 약 닷새 가르쳤어요.　　　　　　닷새쯤 가르쳤어요. ⌒

4. 약 다섯 권 샀어요.　　　　　　　다섯 권쯤 샀어요.

5. 약 네 사람 왔어요.　　　　　　　네 사람쯤 왔어요.

6. 약 일 주일 잤으면 좋겠어요.　　　일주일쯤 잤으면, 좋겠어요.

L. Response Drill

1. 약 몇 시간 걸려요?　　　　　　　약 두 시간 걸려요.

2. 언제까지 한국에 계시겠어요?　　　죽을 때까지 한국에 있겠어요.

3. 언제쯤 오시겠어요?　　　　　　　토요일쯤 오겠어요.

4. 몇 시까지 공부하시겠어요?　　　　여섯 시까지 공부하겠어요.

5. 몇 시경에 주무세요?　　　　　　　열 시 경에 자요.

6. 하루에 몇 시간씩 공부하세요?　　　하루에 여섯 시간씩 공부해요.

M. Pattern Drill

Teacher : 일요일에 가겠어요.　　　　I'll go on Sunday.

Student : 일요일날 가겠어요.　　　　I'll go on Sunday.

1. 토요일에 오세요.　　　　　　　　토요일날 오세요.

2. 금요일에 갑시다.　　　　　　　　금요일날 갑시다.

3. 화요일에 공부하지 않아요.　　　　화요일날 공부하지 않아요.

4. 목요일에 가르치겠어요.　　　　　목요일날 가르치겠어요.

N. Expansion Drill

가야 해요.

미국에 가야 해요.

내년쯤 미국에 가야 해요.

한국에 있었으면 했지만, 내년쯤 미국에 가야 해요.

죽을 때까지 한국에 있었으면 했지만, 내년쯤 미국에 가야 해요.

I had in mind to stay in Korea until I die, but I'll have to go to America about next
　　year.

제십과 방문 (Lesson 10 Visiting)

TEXT I

[VOCABULARY]

방문 visiting	후(에) after, afterwards
방금 just now	돌아와요(돌아오지-) returns
잠깐 for a while	미국 America
들어와요(들어오지-) comes in	석달 three months
멀리 far away, in the distance	

1. 손 님 : 김 선생님 계세요? ↗
   Is Mr. Kim in?

2. 비 서 : 방금 계셨는데, ⌒ 잠깐 나가셨어요. 좀 들어오시지요. ⌒
   He was here a moment ago but he just stepped out for a moment. Please come in.

3. 손 님 : 그럽시다. ↘ 그런데 멀리 나가셨어요? ↗
   All right. Did he go far?

4. 비 서 : 아니오, ↗ 멀리 나가지 않았어요. ⌒ 한 십 분 후에 돌아오실거예요. ⌒
   No, he didn't go far. He will be back in about ten minutes.

5. 손 님 : 언제 그분이 미국에서 돌아오셨지요? ↗
   When did he come back from America?

6. 비 서 : 약 석달 전에 돌아오셨어요. ⌒
   He came back about three months ago.

TEXT II

[VOCABULARY]

웬 what	시월 October
-동안 during, for (time)	벌써 already
유월 June	내년(다음해) next year
금년 this year	이젠 now, any more

7. 손　님 : 참 오래간만이군요. ⌒　　　　It certainly has been a long time.

8. 김일두 : 이거 웬일이세요? ↗ 자, ⌒ 내　　Oh! You're here! Let's go to my room.
　　　　　 방으로 들어갑시다. ↘

9. 손　님 : 미국에 얼마동안 계셨지요? ↗　How long were you in America?

10. 김일두 : 작년 유월부터 금년 시월까　From June of last year to October of
　　　　　 지 있었어요. ⌒ 그러니까⌒　　 this year. So, I was there a year and
　　　　　 일 년 오 개월간 있었어요. ⌒　five months.

11. 손　님 : 벌써 그렇게 되었군요. ⌒ 내년　It's already been that long! Are you
　　　　　 에 또 가시나요? ↗　　　　　 going again next year?

12. 김일두 : 아니오, ↗ 이젠 안 가겠어요. ⌒　No, I am not going any more.

TEXT III

[VOCABULARY]

놀아요(놀지-) relaxes, plays,　　　　오후　afternoon
　　　　amuses oneself　　　　　　　모레　the day after tomorrow
바쁘기 때문에 because (one) is　　　글피　two days after tomorrow
　　　　busy　　　　　　　　　　　틈　leisure, spare time
오전 the forenoon, the morning　　같이　together
---

13. 손　님 : 좀 놀러 가시지 않겠어요? ↗　Would you like to go out for a while?

14. 김일두 : 지금 바쁘기 때문에, ⌒ 못 가겠　I am busy now, so I can't go.
　　　　　 어요. ⌒

15. 손　님 : 그럼 저녁때쯤 시간 있으세요? ↗　Then, will you have time this evening?

16. 김일두 : 요즘은 오전보다 오후가 더 바　These days I am busier in the afternoon
　　　　　 빠요. ⌒　　　　　　　　　　　 than in the morning.

17. 손　님 : 내일이나 모레는 어때요? ⌒　　How about tomorrow or the day after
　　　　　　　　　　　　　　　　　　　 tomorrow?

18. 김일두 : 글피쯤은 틈이 있을 것 같은데　I think I will have some free time three
　　　　　 요. ⌒　　　　　　　　　　　 days from now.

19. 손　님 : 그럼, 그때 같이 놀러 갑시다. ↘　Well, let's go out together then.

20. 김일두 : 감사합니다. ⌐　　　　　　　　 Thank you.

REMARKS TO THE TEXT

Text I

2. ○방금 meaning "just now" or "a moment ago" is different from 지금 "now". 방금 with a past verbal refers to the immediate past, whereas 지금 with a non-past verbal refers to the immediate future, and with a past verbal to the immediate past. See the following examples:

그분이 방금 나갔어요.	He went out just now.
그분이 방금 왔어요.	He came just now.
지금 해야 해요.	We must do (it) now.
지금 왔어요.	I just came.

○잠깐 is a time word corresponding to English "for a while" or "for some time". It is used not only as an adverbial but also as a nominal. See the following examples:

잠깐 기다려 주세요.	Wait a moment, please. (adverbial)
잠깐 갔다 오겠어요.	I shall be out for just a short while. (adverbial)
세월은 잠깐이에요.	Time passes quickly (lit. Time is short). (nominal)

○나가다 refers to a person's <u>going out</u> from a room, classroom, or building, etc. 나오다 refers to a person's <u>coming out</u> from a room, classroom, or building, etc. 들어오다 refers to a person's <u>coming in</u>(into) a room, or building, etc. 들어가다 refers to a person's <u>going into</u> a room, or building, etc. It also refers to a student entering school, an employee beginning work for a company, a patient being hospitalized, etc. See the following examples:

들어가세요.	Go in, please.

들어오세요. ⌒	Come in, please.
나가세요. ⌒	Go out, please.
나오세요. ⌒	Come out, please.

3. ○ <u>멀리</u> is an adverbial meaning "far away" or "in the distance"; <u>멀다</u> is a descriptive verb meaning "is far"; <u>먼</u> is its noun modifier; <u>멀리</u>≠<u>가까이</u> or <u>가깝게</u> "far away≠near, close". See the following examples:

멀리 나가셨어요? ↗	Did he go far (away)?
아니오, ↗ 멀리 나가지 않았어요. ⌒	No, he didn't go far (away).
여기서 학교까지 멀어요? ↗	Is it far from here to the school?
아니오, ↗ 멀지 않아요. ⌒	No, it isn't far.
그분은 먼 곳에서 왔어요. ⌒	He came from a distance.

4. ○ <u>한-</u> "approximate quantity" occurs before time and/or quantity expressions which ask or answer the questions "how much ?", "how long?", "how many?", or "how far?" It is frequently reinforced by the suffix <u>-쯤</u> "about" to emphasize the statement. See the following examples :

한 십 분(쯤) 걸려요. ⌒	It takes about ten minutes.
한 스무 개(쯤) 사세요. ⌒	Buy approximately twenty.
한 십 미터(쯤) 돼요. ⌒	It is about ten meters.

○돌아오다 means "comes back" or "returns" to a place where one habitually spends time, e.g., one's own home, office, native land, etc. <u>돌아가다</u> means "goes back," or makes a detour but since this verb is also frequently used to say that somebody died, it has to be handled with care.

6. ○석달 means "three months". To <u>count</u> the months of the year, i.e., "how many months" you use either the classifier <u>-달</u> "month" preceded by the native Korean numerals or the classifier <u>-개월</u> "month" preceded by the Sino-Korean numerals. To <u>name</u> the months, i.e., "which month", you use the classifier <u>-월</u> preceded by the Sino-Korean numerals. See the examples below :

일월 (정월) January	한 달 or 일 개월	1 month

이월	February	두 달 or 이 개월	2 months
삼월	March	석 달 or 삼 개월	3 months
사월	April	넉 달 or 사 개월	4 months
오월	May	다섯 달 or 오 개월	5 months
유월	June	여섯 달 or 육 개월	6 months
칠월	July (chi-rwol)	일곱 달 or 칠 개월	7 months
팔월	August (pha-rwol)	여덟 달 or 팔 개월	8 months
구월	September	아홉 달 or 구 개월	9 months
시월	October	열 달 or 십 개월	10months
십일월	November (sibi-rwol)	열한 달 or 십일 개월	11months
십이월	December (sibi-wol)	열두 달 or 십이 개월	12months
		몇 달 or 몇 개월	how many months?

Note:

Some numerals take a different shape when occurring before certain classifiers. Notice 유월 "June", 시월 "October", 석 달 "three months", and 넉 달 "four months".

Text II

8. ○이거 웬일이세요? ↗ : 이거 is a contraction of 이것 ; 웬 means "what" ; 일 means "a matter", "an affair", or "work", etc. Therefore, it means "What is the matter (with you)?"

   a) It is used when one meets a friend or a well-known person unexpectedly.

   b) When one is astonished (웬일이냐?).

   c) When someone you are waiting for doesn't come (웬일일까? or 웬일이냐?).

   ○내 is a contraction of 나의 "my". The contracted form is used more often than the full form.

9. ○동안 is a nominal indicating length of time. It corresponds to English "for" or "during". It is modified by the preceding modifiers and/or time expressions. It may be replaced by the suffix -간. See the following examples :

삼 주일 동안 or 삼 주일간	for three weeks
삼 개월 동안 or 삼 개월간	for three months
삼 년 동안 or 삼 년간	for three years

10. ○그러니까 is a conjunctive word meaning "so", "therefore", or "for that reason".

11. ○벌써 used with an affirmative means "already", "yet", or "now already". The opposite "not yet" is 아직도 + negative verb form. 아직도 occurs in the 아니오 answer to a 벌써 question, and 벌써 occurs in the 아니오 answer to an 아직도 question. See the following examples :

   a) 김 선생이 벌써 공부했어요? ↗   Has Mr. Kim studied already?

   예, ⌒ 벌써 공부했어요. ⌒   Yes, he has (studied already).

   아니오, ↗ 아직도 공부하지 않았어   No, he hasn't studied yet.
   요. ⌒

   b) 김 선생이 아직도 공부하지 않았어   Hasn't Mr. Kim studied yet ?
   요? ↗

   예, ⌒ 아직도 공부하지 않았어요. ⌒   That's right. He hasn't studied yet.

   아니오, ↗ 벌써 공부했어요. ⌒   That's not right. He has studied already.

   아직도 + affirmative verb form means "still". See the examples below :

   아직도 나빠요? ↗   Is it still bad?

   예, ⌒ 아직도 나빠요. ⌒   Yes, it is still bad.

   아니오, ↗ 이젠 나쁘지 않아요. ⌒   No, it is not bad any more.

12. ○이젠 is a contraction of 이제는. 이제 means "now" or "this occasion" and -는 is the contrast particle. But when 이젠 is used with a negative, it means "(not) any more". 이젠 occurs in the 아니오 answer to an 아직도 question, and 아직도 occurs in the 아니오 answer to an 이젠 question. See the following examples :

   a) 아직도 한국말을 공부하세요? ↗   Are you still studying Korean?

   예, ⌒ 아직도 공부해요. ⌒   Yes, I am (still studying).

   아니오, ↗ 이젠 공부하지 않아요. ⌒   No, I'm not studying any more.

   b) 이젠 한국말을 공부하지 않아요? ↗   Aren't you studying Korean any more?

   예, ⌒ 이젠 공부하지 않아요. ⌒   That's right. I'm not studying any more.

아니오, ↗ 아직도 공부해요. ⌒   That's not right. I'm still studying.

Text III

13. ○좀, depending on the context, can mean (1) "for a while" or "just a moment",
(2) "a bit", "a little", or "slightly".

   ○놀다 is the opposite of 일하다 "works". Depending on the context, it can mean
"plays", "has a good time", "is at leisure", "visits (for pleasure)", "is unemployed",
"loafs", etc.

15. ○저녁 followed by the particle -에 means "evening". Depending on the context.
it also means "supper". In the same manner, 아침 means "morning" or "breakfast".
낮 "daytime"; 밤 "night". All occur with a following particle -에. See the following examples:

   아침에 무엇을 하셨어요? ⌒   What did you do in the morning?
   아침 잡수셨어요? ↗   Did you take breakfast?
   낮에 무엇을 하셨어요? ⌒   What did you do during the day?
   저녁에 무엇을 하세요? ⌒   What do you do in the evening?
   저녁 잡수셨어요? ↗   Did you take supper?
   밤에 몇 시에 주무세요? ⌒   At what time do you go to bed at night?

   ○요즘 is a contraction of 요즈음 "lately" or "these days".

16. ○오전 is used both as a conversational term of "morning" and as a technical
term corresponding to English "a.m." The opposite word is 오후, which is also
used both as a conversational term for "afternoon" and as a technical term corresponding to English "p.m." 오전 and 오후 occur with a following particle -에 indicating time when something happens. In the newspapers 상오 "a.m." and 하오 p.
m." are used as technical terms.

17. ○내일 tomorrow   오늘 today
     모레 the day after tomorrow   어제 yesterday
     글피 two days after tomorrow   그저께 the day before yesterday

그글피 three days after tomorrow   그끄저께 two days before yesterday

All these are time words which occur without particles.

18. ○틈, depending on the context, can mean (1) "spare time" or "time to spare", (2) "a gap" or "crack", (3) "chance", (4) "an unguarded moment", etc. See the following examples :

저는 틈이 없어요. ⌒   I have no leisure. (or : I am pressed for time.)

문 틈에서 바람이 들어와요. ⌒   The wind is coming through a chink in the door.

도망갈 틈이 없어요. ⌒   I have no chance of escape.

그분은 빈틈이 없어요. ⌒   He is always on the alert.

19. ○같이 is pronounced [가치]. ㅌ is palatalized ㅊ before the following 이 in Korean. So is ㄷ palatalized ㅈ followed by 이(굳이→[구지]). ㅌ followed by all other vowels retains its own sound value as in 같은데요→[가튼데요].

STRUCTURAL PATTERNS

Text I

Ⅰ. <u>V.S. + -는데 / -ㄴ(은)데</u> : conjunctive introduction

Examples :

그것이 좋은데, ⌒ 사지 않으시겠어요? ↗

That's good (so) why don't you buy it?

그분이 한국말 선생인데, ⌒ 왜 여기 왔어요? ⌒

He is a Korean teacher (so) why did he come here?

그분은 공부하는데, ⌒ 왜 공부하지 않아요? ⌒

He is studying (so) why don't you study?

저는 학교에 가는데, ⌒ 그분은 가지 않아요. ⌒

I go to school, but he isn't going.

나는 시계가 없는데, ⌒ 하나 살까요? ↗

I don't have a watch (so) shall I buy one?

그분이 미국에 갔는데, ⌒ 내년에 와요. ⌒

He went to America, and he will come back next year.

그것이 여기 있는데, ⌒ 쓰세요. ⌒

It's here (so) use it.

그때 그분이 학생이었는데, ⌒ 지금은 선생이에요. ⌒

He was a student at that time, but now he is a teacher.

Notes :

1. For the technique of this pattern see Lesson 5, S.P. No. Ⅶ.

2. The ending -는데 / -ㄴ(은)데, attached to the verb of a non-final sentence, serves as an introduction to the sentence which follows.

3. -ㄴ(은)데 is used with D.V.S. and the verb -이다. -는데 is used with all

other stems, e.g., A.V.S., -있다/없다, and the past stem -았/었/였 and the future stem -겠. The English equivalent of this pattern is "…, but…" or "…and…" or "…so…" or "…so why…", etc.

4. This pattern is used to connect two sentences. It is, therefore, a conjunctive ending.

II. V.S.+-ㄹ(을)거예요: "will probably" or "must"(probable future)

Examples:

그분이 내일 올 거예요. ⌒	He'll probably come tomorrow.
한국말이 어려울 거예요. ⌒	Korean must be difficult.
그분이 여기 있을 거예요. ⌒	He'll probably be here.
그분이 재미있을 거예요. ⌒	It's probably interestion.

Notes:

1. -ㄹ(을) 거예요 is a contraction of -ㄹ(을) 것이에요. The contracted form is used more than the full form.

2. The pattern -ㄹ(을) 거예요 can be used with any verb and indicates probability, indefiniteness, or indirectness, etc.

3. -ㄹ 거예요 after verb stems ending in a vowel; -을 거예요 after verb stems ending in a consonant.

Text II

III. The pattern 만에 : time word + 만에 : "after (of time)"

Examples:

오래간만이에요. ⌒	It's a long time since I saw you last.
닷새 만에 집에 돌아왔어요. ⌒	I came home after five days.
십 년 만에 한국에 왔어요. ⌒	I came to Korea after ten years.

Notes:

1. 만에 added to time expressions indicates a lapse of time. The English equivalent of this pattern is "after (the lapse of such-and-such a stretch of time)".

2. Depending on the context, it can also mean "it took me (him, etc.)…of time". See

the following examples :

닷새 만에 미국에 도착했어요. ⌒ | It took me five days to reach America.

그분은 삼 년 만에 박사가 되었어요. ⌒ | After three years of studying, he became a Ph. D. (It took him three years to become a Ph. D.)

이 주일 만에 그분을 찾았어요. ⌒ | It took me two weeks to find him.

IV. <u>V.S. + -나요?</u>

Examples :

내년에 또 가시나요? ↗ | Are you going again next year?

무엇을 하시나요? ⌒ | What are you doing?

그것이 어디 있나요? ⌒ | Where is it?

Notes :

1. The ending <u>-나요</u> is used with any verb except the verb of identification <u>-이-</u>. It is only used in questions.

2. The ending belongs to the informal polite style and is added to the verb stem or to the verb stem plus <u>-시-</u> and/or <u>-았-</u>, <u>-겠-</u>.

3. It is an informal polite way of asking questions or expressing doubt.

4. By dropping the final particle <u>-요</u> you get the intimate style form used with children and sometimes with close friends.

V. The negative prefix <u>안-</u> + A.V.S.

Examples :

학교에 안 가겠어요. ⌒ | I will not go to school.

공부를 안 했어요. ⌒ | I did not study.

안 먹겠어요. ⌒ | I will not eat.

그분은 한국말을 안 배워요. ⌒ | He does not learn Korean.

Notes :

1. <u>안-</u> is the contracted from of <u>아니</u> "not". The contracted form is used more often than the full form.

2. It is normally used with action verbs, while the <u>-지 않다</u> form is used with

both action verbs and descriptive verbs. Compare Lesson 4, S.P. No. X.

VI. The plain speech style

You have studied the polite informal or yo-style in Lesson 4, SP. No. XIV. Now let's study the plain style. The plain style is used with children, younger brothers and sisters, and sometimes with close friends. It is also used when a superior addresses his inferiors while keeping the posture of formality. (See Lesson 4, S.P. No. XIII.)

(A) Declarative forms :

The ending occurs in two shapes. Look at the diagram below :

A.V.S. + -ㄴ (는) -다 (present)

A.V.S. + -았- -다 (past)

A.V.S. + -겠- -다 (tentative or probable fact, future)

D.V.S. + -다 (present)

D.V.S. + -았- -다 (past)

D.V.S. + -겠- -다 (tentative or probable fact, future)

있 + -다 (present)

있 + -었- -다 (past)

있 + -겠- -다 (tentative or probable fact, future)

-이 + -다 (present)

-이 + -었- -다 (past)

-이 + -겠- -다 (tentative or probable fact, future)

Notes :

1. The -ㄴ(-는)다 shape of this ending occurs in only one case : with action verbs in the present tense -ㄴ다 after verb stems ending in a vowel ; -는다 after verb stems ending in a consonant. In all other cases the ending is just -다.

2. Notice well here that those action and descriptive verbs whose last element is -하다 follow the above rule exactly the same way as all other verbs. Don't be misled by the fact that the dictionary forms of both categories are identical. See

the examples :

Action verb : 공부하다 → 공부한다 "studies"

Descriptive verb : 복잡하다 → 복잡하다 "is complicated"

Examples :

나는 학교에 간다. ↘	I go to school.
나는 점심을 먹는다. ↘	I am taking lunch.
나는 학교에 갔다. ↘	I went to school.
나는 학교에 가겠다. ↘	I will go to school.
이것이 좋다. ↘	This is good.
이것이 좋았다. ↘	This was good.
그것이 좋겠다. ↘	I think that will be wonderful.
그것이 교실에 있다. ↘	That is in the classroom.
그것이 교실에 있었다. ↘	That was in the classroom.
그것이 교실에 있겠다. ↘	I think that thing is in the classroom.
그분이 학생이다. ↘	He is a student.
그분이 학생이었다. ↘	He was a student.
그분이 학생이겠다. ↘	I think he is a student.

(B) Question forms :

The ending of the question form also occurs in two shapes. Look at the diagram
below :

D.V.S. + -냐 or 으냐	(present)
-이 + -냐	(present)
A.V.S. + -느냐	(present)
A.V.S. + -았느냐	(past)
A.V.S. + -겠느냐	(tentative or probable fact, future)
D.V.S. + -았느냐	(past)
D.V.S. + -겠느냐	(tentative or probable fact, future)

있 + -느냐   (present)

있 + -었느냐   (past)

있 + -겠느냐   (tentative or probable fact, future)

-이 + -었느냐   (past)

-이 + -겠느냐   (tentative or probable fact, future)

Note:

The -(으)냐 shape of this ending occurs in two cases: with descriptive verbs in the present tense and with -이- "is" in the present tense(-냐 after verb stems ending in a vowel; -으냐 after verb stems ending in a consonant). In all other cases the ending is -느냐. The -냐(-으냐)/-느냐 form is mostly used in indirect discourse.

Examples:

그것이 좋으냐? ↗	Is that good?
그분이 크냐? ↗	Is she tall?
그분이 학생이냐? ↗	Is he a student?
학교에 가느냐? ↗	Do you go to school?
학교에 갔느냐? ↗	Did you go to school?
학교에 가겠느냐? ↗	Do you intend to go to school?
그것이 좋았느냐? ↗	Was it good?
그것이 좋겠느냐? ↗	Do you think that thing is good?
그것이 어디 있느냐? ⌢	Where is that?
그것이 어디 있었느냐? ⌢	Where was that?
그것이 어디 있겠느냐? ⌢	Where do you think it is?
그분이 학생이었느냐? ↗	Was he a student?
그분이 학생이겠느냐? ↗	Do you think he is a student?

(C) **Propositive forms:**

Examples:

학교에 가자. ↘	Let's go to school.

점심을 ^v먹자. ↘	Let's take lunch.
집에 ^v있자. ↘	Let's stay at home.
한국말을 ^v공부하자. ↘	Let's study Korean.

Note :

To make the propositive form, the ending 　-자　 is attached directly to the verb stem.

(D) Imperative forms :

Examples :

학교에 ^v가라. ↘	Go to school.
이 칠판을 ^v보아라. ↘	Look at this blackboard.
점심을 ^v먹어라. ↘	Eat lunch.
한국말을 ^v공부하여라. ↘	Study Korean.

Note :

To form the imperative form, 　-아(-어, -여)라 is attached to the verb stem. The vowel changes of the ending are as usual : -아라　 after -아- and -오- ; 　-어 라 after any other vowel ; -여라 after 하-, the stem of the verb 하다 "does".

(E) Other imperative expressions :

그것 좀 ^v보여 달라. ↘	Show me that.
거기 좀 ^v가 달라. ↘	Go there (for me).
여기 ^v와 달라. ↘	Come here (for me).
한국말을 ^v가르쳐 달라. ↘	Teach me Korean.
좀 ^v기다려 달라. ↘	Wait a little bit (for me).

Note :

그것 좀 보여 주세요 is a polite imperative expression.(See Lesson 6, S.P. No. II) If you substitute 달라 for 주세요, the result is the plain imperative form.

Remark :

From now on we will practice the plain style forms one by one in the drill material of each lesson.

Text III

VII. The suffix -(으)러 : A.V.S. + -(으)러 : "in order to" (purpose)

Examples :

공부하러 학교에 가겠어요. ⌒	I intend to go to school to study.
여기에 일하러 왔어요. ⌒	I came here to work.
한국말을 배우러 갑시다. ↘	Let's go to learn Korean.
그분이 옷을 입으러 들어와요. ⌒	He is coming in to put on his clothes.

Notes :

1. The suffix -(으)러 is attached to the stem of action verbs and is always followed by either 가다 or 오다 or their compounds.

2. It expresses the purpose of the action. The phrase or clause with -(으)러 always precedes the main clause.

3. -러 after verb stems ending in a vowel ; -으러 after verb stems ending in a consonant.

VIII. The prefix 못-

(A) 못 + Action Verb or Action Verb Stem + -지 못하다

학교에 못 가요. ⌒	I can't go to school.
학교에 가지 못해요. ⌒	
나는 일을 못 해요. ⌒	I can't work.
나는 일을 하지 못해요. ⌒	
영어를 못 배웠어요. ⌒	I could not learn English.
영어를 배우지 못했어요. ⌒	

(B) Descriptive Verb Stem + -지 못하다

이것이 좋지 못해요. ⌒	This is not good.
교실이 크지 못해요. ⌒	The classroom is not big.
그 여자가 예쁘지 못해요. ⌒	That girl is not beautiful.

Notes :

1. When the prefix 못- is used with action verbs, it indicates impossibility.

Therefore, its English equivalent is "can't" or "unable to".

2. Note that in the above examples 못- is used in two kinds of formations without changing the meaning of the sentences.

3. When it is used with a descriptive verb, only the D.V.S. + -지 못하다 form is possible. Moreover the form only means "it is not good, big, beautiful", etc., not "it can't be good, big, beautiful". Remember that D.V.S. + -지 않다 is used much more than D.V.S. + -지 못하다.

IX. The particle -(이)나 : Noun + -(이)나 : "...or something"

(A) Noun + -(이)나

Examples :

한국말이나 배우겠어요. ⌒	I'll learn Korean (or something).
영화나 보러 같이 갈까요? ↗	Shall we see a movie (or something) together?
연필이나 만년필 주세요. ⌒	Give me a pencil or a fountain pen, please.
책이나 신문 주세요. ⌒	Give me a book or a newspaper, please.

Notes :

1. The particle -(이)나 is attached to nominals and indicates selection (choice).

2. -나 after nominals ending in a vowel; -이나 after nominals ending in a consonant.

3. But depending on the context, the particle -(이)나 can also express approximation or "much more than is expected". See the following examples :

선생님이 몇 사람이나 있어요? ⌒	How many teachers are there (approximately)?
몇 개나 사시겠어요? ⌒	About how many will you buy?
벌써 열시 반이나 되었어요. ⌒	It is already 10 : 30. (later than expected)

열 사람이나 왔어요. ⌒   Ten people came. (more than expect-
                                   ed)

(B) <u>Noun + other particle + 나</u>

Examples :

학교에나 갑시다. ↘   Let's go to school (or someplace).

오후에나 갈 것 같아요. ⌒   I think I can go in the afternoon   (or
                                   sometime).

Note :

The particle -나 attached to other particles constitutes a compound particle. It
also indicates selection(choice) of time, place, etc.

DRILLS

─ 〔ADDITIONAL VOCABULARY〕 ─────────────────────

나와요(나오지-)	comes out	들어가요(들어가지-)	goes into
돌아와요(돌아오지-)	goes back	산보해요(산보하지-)	takes a walk
잡수세요(잡수시지-)	eats	가까워요(가깝지-)	is near, is close
빌려요(빌리지-)	lends, loans	도와줘요(도와주지-)	helps

Text I

A. Substitution Drill.

1. 그분이 여기 있을 거예요. ⌒

   He'll probably be here.

왔을,	한국말을 배웠을,
나올,	교실에 들어갈

2. 약 한 달 전에 돌아오셨어요. ⌒

   He came back about one month ago.

두 달,	다섯 달,	일곱 달,
넉 달,	여덟 달,	여섯 달

3. 한 네 시간 후에 오세요. ⌒

   Please come in about four hours.

두 달,	두 추일,	석 달,
넉 달,	일주일	

B. Integration Drill

Teacher : 그것이 좋아요. ⌒ 사지 않으   That's good. Won't you buy it?
시겠어요? ↗

Student : 그것이 좋은데, ⌒ 사지 않으   That's good, (so) won't you buy it?
시겠어요? ↗

1. 그분이 한국말 선생이에요. 왜 여기 왔어요?

   그분이 한국말 선생인데, ⌒ 왜 여기 왔어요? ⌒

2. 날씨가 따뜻해요. 왜 나가지 않으세요?

날씨가 **따뜻한데**, ⌒ 왜 ⌄**나**가지 않으세요? ⌒

3. 날씨가 추워요. 왜 들어가지 않으세요?

   날씨가 **추운데**, ⌒ 왜 ⌄**들**어가지 않으세요? ⌒

4. 한국말이 어려워요. 왜 공부하세요?

   한국말이 ⌄어려운데, ⌒ 왜 ⌄**공**부하세요? ⌒

5. 그것이 싸요. 왜 사지 않으세요?

   그것이 ⌄싼데, ⌒ 왜 ⌄**사**지 않으세요? ⌒

C. Integration Drill

Teacher : **그분이 ⌄공**부해요. ⌒ 왜 ⌄**공**부하지 않아요? ⌒

He is studying. Why don't you study?

Student : **그분이 ⌄공**부하는데, ⌒ 왜 ⌄**공**부하지 않아요? ⌒

He is studying, (so) why don't you study?

1. 저는 학교에 가요. 그분은 가지 않아요.

   저는 ⌄학교에 가는데, ⌒ 그분은 ⌄**가**지 않아요. ⌒

2. 나는 시계가 없어요. 하나 살까요?

   나는 ⌄시계가 없는데, ⌒ 하나 ⌄**살**까요? ↗

3. 그분을 만나야겠어요. 그분이 어디 있어요?

   그분을 ⌄만나야겠는데, ⌒ 그분이 ⌄**어**디 있어요? ⌒

4. 비가 와요. 가시겠어요?

   비가 오는데, ⌒ **가**시겠어요? ↗

5. 바람은 불어요. 춥지 않아요.

   바람은 ⌄부는데, ⌒ **춥**지 않아요. ⌒

D. Pattern Drill

Teacher : **지난 ⌄정월에 ⌄돌**아왔어요. ⌒   I came back last January.

Student : **지난 ⌄정월달에 ⌄돌**아왔어요. ⌒   I came back last January.

1. 사월이 제일 좋아요.   **사월달이 ⌄제일 좋**아요. ⌒

2. 삼월은 날씨가 따뜻해요.   **삼월달은 ⌄날씨가 따뜻**해요. ⌒

3. 유월에 돌아가겠어요.   **유월달에 ⌄돌**아가겠어요. ⌒

4. 팔월은 몹시 더워요.　　　　팔월달은 몹시 더워요. ⌒

5. 십이월은 아주 추워요.　　　십이월달은 아주 추워요. ⌒

6. 시월에 그분을 만났어요.　　시월달에 그분을 만났어요. ⌒

E. Expansion Drill

도착했을 거예요. ⌒

집에 도착했을 거예요. ⌒

지금쯤 집에 도착했을 거예요. ⌒

떠났는데, ⌒ 지금쯤 집에 도착했을 거예요. ⌒

두 시간 전에 떠났는데, ⌒ 지금쯤 집에 도착했을 거예요. ⌒

그분이 두 시간 전에 떠났는데, ⌒ 지금쯤 집에 도착했을 거예요. ⌒

He left two hours ago, (so) he has probably reached home by now.

Text II

F. Substitution Drill

1. 석달 만에 학교에 왔어요. ⌒

   I came to school after three months.

넉 달,	다섯 달,	엿새,
이레,	여드레,	아흐레

2. 무엇을 하시나요? ⌒

   What are you doing?

무엇을 잡수,	몇 시에 떠나,
무엇을 읽으,	어디에서 공부하

G. Pattern Drill

Teacher : 학교에 가지 않겠어요. ⌒　　I will not go to school.

Student : 학교에 안 가겠어요. ⌒　　　I will not go to school.

1. 공부를 하지 않았어요.　　　공부를 안 했어요. ⌒

2. 기차가 떠나지 않았어요.　　기차가 안 떠났어요. ⌒

3. 그 책을 빌리지 않았어요.　　그 책을 안 빌렸어요. ⌒

4. 그분이 들어가지 않아요.　　그분이 안 들어가요. ⌒

5. 그것을 먹지 않아요.　　　그것을 안 먹어요. ⌒

6. 자지 않겠어요.　　　　안 자겠어요. ⌒

H. Response Drill

Teacher : 김 선생님이 벌써 공부했어   Has Mr. Kim studied already?
요? ↗

Student : 아니오, ↗ 아직도 공부하지 않   No, he hasn't studied yet.
았어요. ⌢

1. 그분이 벌써 떠났어요?   아니오, ↗ 아직도 떠나지 않았어요. ⌢
2. 그분이 벌써 나갔어요?   아니오, ↗ 아직도 나가지 않았어요. ⌢
3. 그분이 벌써 들어왔어요?   아니오, ↗ 아직도 들어오지 않았어요. ⌢
4. 그분이 벌써 도착했어요?   아니오, ↗ 아직도 도착하지 않았어요. ⌢
5. 그분이 벌써 그것을 마쳤어요?   아니오, ↗ 아직도 그것을 마치지 않았어
요. ⌢

I. Response Drill

Teacher : 한 선생님이 아직도 공부하지   Hasn't Mr. Han studied yet?
않았어요? ↗

Student : 아니오, ↗ 벌써 공부했어요. ⌢   Yes, he has already studied.

1. 아직도 시작하지 않았어요?   아니오, ↗ 벌써 시작했어요. ⌢
2. 아직도 끝내지 않았어요?   아니오, ↗ 벌써 끝냈어요. ⌢
3. 아직도 드리지 않았어요. ?   아니오, ↗ 벌써 드렸어요. ⌢
4. 아직도 가르치지 않았어요?   아니오, ↗ 벌써 가르쳤어요. ⌢
5. 아직도 일어나지 않았어요?   아니오, ↗ 벌써 일어났어요. ⌢
6. 아직도 떠나지 않았어요?   아니오, ↗ 벌써 떠났어요. ⌢

J. Response Drill

Teacher : 아직도 나빠요? ↗   Is it still bad?

Student : 아니오, ↗ 이젠 나쁘지 않아   No, it is not bad any more.
요. ⌢

1. 아직도 커요?   아니오, ↗ 이젠 크지 않아요. ⌢
2. 아직도 빨개요?   아니오, ↗ 이젠 빨갛지 않아요. ⌢
3. 아직도 하얘요?   아니오, ↗ 이젠 하얗지 않아요. ⌢
4. 아직도 까매요?   아니오, ↗ 이젠 까맣지 않아요. ⌢

5. 아직도 공부하세요?　　　　　　아니오, ↗ 이젠 공부하지 않아요. ⌢

6. 아직도 잡수세요?　　　　　　　아니오, ↗ 이젠 먹지 않아요. ⌢

K. Response Drill

Teacher : 이젠 한국말을 공부하지 않아요? ↗

　　　　　Aren't you studying Korean any more?

Student : 아니오, ↗ 아직도 공부해요. ⌢

　　　　　Yes, I'm still studying.

1. 이젠 이 책을 읽지 않아요?　　　아니오, ↗ 아직도 읽어요. ⌢

2. 이젠 배우지 않아요?　　　　　　아니오, ↗ 아직도 배워요. ⌢

3. 이젠 재미있지 않아요?　　　　　아니오, ↗ 아직도 재미있어요. ⌢

4. 이젠 크지 않아요?　　　　　　　아니오, ↗ 아직도 커요. ⌢

5. 이젠 작지 않아요?　　　　　　　아니오, ↗ 아직도 작아요. ⌢

6. 이젠 피곤하지 않아요?　　　　　아니오, ↗ 아직도 피곤해요. ⌢

L. Level Drill

Teacher : 학교에 가요. ⌢　　　　　I'm going to school.

Student : 학교에 간다. ↘　　　　　I'm going to school.

1. 두시에 도착해요.　　　　　　두시에 도착한다. ↘

2. 여섯시에 일어나요.　　　　　여섯시에 일어난다. ↘

3. 여섯 시간 공부해요.　　　　　여섯 시간 공부한다. ↘

4. 두시 반에 수업이 끝나요.　　두시 반에 수업이 끝난다. ↘

5. 아홉시에 자요.　　　　　　　아홉시에 잔다. ↘

6. 책을 읽어요.　　　　　　　　책을 읽는다. ↘

Text III

M. Substitution Drill

　1. 공부하러 갑시다. ↘

　　Let's go and study.

밥 먹으러,	옷을 입으러,
물건 사러,	그분을 도와주러

2. <u>모레나</u> 글피쯤 어때요? ⌒ (나/이나)

How about the day after tomorrow
or two days after tomorrow?

두 시 — 세 시,   아홉 시 — 열 시,
토요일 — 일요일,   월요일 — 화요일

N. Pattern Drill

Teacher : 나는 오늘 학교에 못 가요. ⌒   I can't go to school.

Student : 나는 오늘 학교에 가지 못해   I can't go to school.
요. ⌒

1. 영어를 못 배웠어요.   영어를 배우지 못했어요. ⌒

2. 시계를 못 샀어요.   시계를 사지 못했어요. ⌒

3. 그 책을 못 읽었어요.   그 책을 읽지 못했어요. ⌒

4. 기차를 못 타겠어요.   기차를 타지 못하겠어요. ⌒

5. 네시에 못 일어나겠어요.   네시에 일어나지 못하겠어요. ⌒

O. Pattern Drill

Teacher : 한국말을 배우겠어요. ⌒   I'll learn Korean.

Student : 한국말이나 배우겠어요. ⌒   I'll learn Korean (or something).

1. 이 책을 읽읍시다.   이 책이나 읽읍시다. ↘

2. 시계를 하나 삽시다.   시계나 하나 삽시다. ↘

3. 영화를 보러 갑시다.   영화나 보러 갑시다. ↘

4. 물건을 사러 갑시다.   물건이나 사러 갑시다. ↘

5. 영어를 공부합시다.   영어나 공부합시다. ↘

P. Pattern Drill

Teacher : 열 사람 왔어요. ⌒   Ten people came.

Student : 열 사람이나 왔어요. ⌒   Ten people came. (more than expected)

1. 다섯 개 먹었어요.   다섯 개나 먹었어요. ⌒

2. 열 사람 갔어요.   열 사람이나 갔어요. ⌒

3. 스무 권 읽었어요.   스무 권이나 읽었어요. ⌒

4. 다섯 시간 가르쳤어요.   다섯 시간이나 가르쳤어요. ⌒

5. 팔 개월간 있었어요.   팔 개월간이나 있었어요. ⌒

Q. Pattern Drill

Teacher : 선생이 몇 사람 있어요?   How many teachers are there?

Student : 선생이 몇 사람이나 있어요?   How many teachers are there? (approximately)

1. 담배를 몇 갑 샀어요?   담배를 몇 갑이나 샀어요?

2. 몇 시간 공부하시겠어요?   몇 시간이나 공부하시겠어요?

3. 몇 병 사시겠어요?   몇 병이나 사시겠어요?

4. 몇 권 읽었어요?   몇 권이나 읽었어요?

5. 종이 몇 장 드릴까요?   종이 몇 장이나 드릴까요?

6. 몇 분 오셨어요?   몇 분이나 오셨어요?

R. Level Drill

Teacher : 지금 무엇을 하세요?   What are you doing?

Student : 지금 무엇을 하느냐?   What are you doing? (the plain style)

1. 저분이 누구예요?   저분이 누구냐?

2. 몇 시에 일어나세요?   몇 시에 일어나느냐?

3. 언제 가시겠어요?   언제 가겠느냐?

4. 몇 사람 왔어요?   몇 사람 왔느냐?

5. 몇 시간 공부하세요?   몇 시간 공부하느냐?

6. 무엇을 배웠어요?   무엇을 배웠느냐?

제십일과 인사와 소개 (Lesson 11 Meeting People)

TEXT I

〔VOCABULARY〕

소개	Introduction	이게	this
누구	who	별고	something wrong, something the matter
정말	really, truly		
만나요(만나지-)	meets	가족	family
몰라요(모르지-)	does not know	덕택	favor, indebtedness, grace

1. 김정우 : **최 선생님 아니세요?** ↗ — Aren't you Mr. Ch'oe?

2. 최인수 : **아니,** ↗ **이게 누구야,** ⌢ **정말 이런 데서 만날 줄은 몰랐군요.** ⌢ — Who is this! I never expected to meet you in a place like this.

3. 김정우 : **그간 별고 없었습니까?** ↗ — Have things been going all right?

4. 최인수 : **나야 밤낮 그렇지요,** ↗ **뭐.** ↘ — Things are always about the same with me.

5. 김정우 : **그래 가족들도 안녕하시구요?** ⌢ — And how is your family?

6. 최인수 : **예,** ⌢ **모두 덕택에 잘 있습니다.** ↘ — Yes, they are all well (thanks to you).

TEXT II

〔VOCABULARY〕

친구	friend	고향	home
서로	each other, one another	충청도	Ch'ungch'ŏng-do
공항	airport	들어요(듣지-)	hears, listens to
처음	the beginning, the start, first		

7. 김정우 : **참,** ↘ **최 선생님 서로 인사하시지요.** ⌢ **이분은 제 친구에요.** ⌢ **지금 공항에서 일하고 계세요.** ⌢ — Oh! Mr. Ch'oe, I'd like to introduce you to my friend. Right now he is working for the airport.

8. 최인수 : **처음 뵙겠어요.** ⌒ **최인수라고** 합니다. ↘

I am glad to meet you. (This is the first time we meet.) My name is Ch'oe In-su.

9. 한지영 : **한지영이에요.** ⌒ **잘 부탁합니** 다. ↘

My name is Han Ji-yŏng. I ask for your goodwill.

10. 최인수 : **고향이 충청도 아니세요?** ↗

Isn't your home (in) Ch'ungchŏng-do?

11. 한지영 : **어떻게 아시지요?** ↗

How did you know? (How do you know?)

12. 최인수 : **김 선생님한테서 말씀 많이 들** 었어요. ⌒

I've heard a lot about you from Mr. Kim.

TEXT III

┌─[VOCABULARY]──────────────────────┐
함께 together   약속 promise, appointment
영화 movie   찾아가요(찾아가지-) visits
다른 another, different
└────────────────────────────────┘

13. 김정우 : **시간이 있으시면,** ⌒ **함께 가실** 까요? ↗

If you have time, how about going out together?

14. 최인수 : **무슨 좋은 일이라도 있으세** 요? ↗

Do you have anything in mind?

15. 김정우 : **그저 영화라도 같이 보고 싶** 어요. ⌒

I would like to see a movie with you.

16. 최인수 : **가고 싶지만** ⌒ **다른 약속이 있** 어요. ⌒

I would like to go. But I have another appointment.

17. 김정우 : **그럼 내일쯤 한번 만날 수 있** 을까요? ↗

Then, can I meet you tomorrow?

18. 최인수 : **예,** ⌒ **제가 내일 저녁때 ·찾아 가** 지요. ⌒

I will visit you tomorrow evening.

19. 김정우 : **그럼 또 뵙겠어요.** ⌐

Well, see you again.

20. 최인수 : **안녕히 가세요.** ⌐

Good-bye.

REMARKS TO THE TEXT

Text I

2. ○아니 is an exclamatory form expressing surprise, annoyance, unbelief, or merely emphasis. It corresponds to English "Oh!," "Bless me!", "Oh my!", "Good heavens!", or "What!", etc. See the examples :

아니, 또 늦었어요?   What! Are you late again?

아니, 또 잡수세요?   Good heavens! Are you eating again?

아니, 누가 이렇게 했어요?   Oh my! Who did this?

○이게 is a contraction of 이것이 ; 그게＝그것이 ; 저게＝저것이. See the following examples :

이게 뭐예요? (이것이 무엇이에요?)   What's this?

그게 좋을 것 같아요.   That seems to be good.

저게 우리 학교예요.   That over there is our school.

○누구야 : Noun + -(이)야 : (1) The question marker -(이)야 is used only after nominals. (2) It is used mostly with children and by children, but also between or for close friends.

저게 누구야?   Who is that man over there?

이게 뭐야?   What's this?

이게 책이야.   This is a book.

이 사람이 학생이야.   This man is a student.

아니, 이게 누구야 means "Oh! Who is this?" It is used when one meets a friend or a well-known person unexpectedly. It usually is not used with strangers or people of higher status.

○정말 is a nominal meaning "truth" or "a true story". Depending on the context, it is also used as an adverbial. 참말 is synonymous with 정말.

See the examples below :

참말이에요. ⌢ (정말이에요. ⌢)   It is true. (nominal)

참말일까요? ↗ (정말일까요? ↗)   Can it be true? (or, I wonder if it is

                                           true.) (nominal)

정말 좋았어요. ⌢   It was really wonderful. (adverbial)

○이런 데서 is a contraction of 이런 데에서. -데 "place" is a dependent noun (bound noun) used with another preceding nominal modifier. Another word for "place" is -곳.

○몰랐군요 : The stem of this verb is 모르- meaning "is ignorant of". It is an irregular verb (we will study this kind of irregular verb in detail later). 알다 "knows" is the opposite of 모르다. By the way, the words 알다 and 모르다 are frequently used with the infix -겠-, but with the meaning of the present tense. See the following examples :

이젠 아시겠어요? ↗   Do you understand now?

예, ⌢ 이젠 알겠어요. ⌢   Yes, now I understand.

아니오, ↗ 아직도 모르겠어요. ⌢   No, I don't understand yet.

3. ○그간 is a time word expressing an undefined time interval. Synonyms are 그동안 and 그새.

○별고 means "something wrong". It is usually used to inquire after someone's well-being. 별고 없이 means "in safety" or "quite well". See the examples :

별고 없으세요? ↗   How are you (getting along)?

모두 별고 없이 잘 있어요. ⌢   Everybody is quite well.

4. ○나야 : Here -야 is an emphasizing particle. It can replace almost all other particles such as -이/-가, -을/-를 ; -은/-는 etc. Depending on the context, this particle is also used for belittling something or as a vocative meaning.

5. ○그래 is a contraction of 그리하여. It is a conjunctive word meaning and it is also used as an exclamatory expression when you challenge someone or as the beginning of an answer to an inferior, younger brother or sister.

See the examples below :

그래, ˇ어땠어요 ? ⌒   And how was it?

그래, ˇ이것을 몰라 ? ↗   Well, you say you don't know this?

그래, ˇ그렇게 하자. ↘   All right. Let's do that way.

그래, ˇ잘 알겠다. ↘   Yes, I understand well.

○가족 means "members of a family" and 가정 means "home".

○안녕하시구요 is slightly less formal than 안녕하시고요.

6. ○덕택에 denotes the speaker's appreciation for interest shown in his personal affairs : "thanks for asking" and/or appreciation for received assistance ; "thanks to you". It always implies favorable or pleasant information.

Text II

7. ○제 is a contraction of 저의 meaning "my".

8. ○처음 is a nominal : 처음이에요 "it's the first time" ; 처음이 아니에요 "it's not the first time". 처음에 "in the beginning" ; 처음부터 "from the beginning" ; 처음으로 "for the first time". Its opposite word is 마지막 or 끝 "end".

○뵙다, meaning "has an audience with," "sees" or "meets", is a contraction of 뵈옵다. It is the honorific verb of 보다 or 만나다 "meets".

○처음 뵙겠어요 meaning "I'm happy to meet you" is used only in introductions as a humble-polite greeting. The infix -겠- used in this construction does not refer to the future.

10. ○고향 is (1) the place where one was born and grew up or (2) the place where one's ancestors have lived for a long time.

○충청도 means "Ch'ungch'ŏng Province". -도 "province" is the largest local administrative division. In South Korea, there are 9 provinces and several special cities. They are 경기도 "Kyŏnggi Province", 강원도 "Kangwŏn Province", 충청북도 "North Ch'ungch'ŏng Province", 충청남도 "South Ch'ungch'ŏng Province", 전라북도 "North Chŏlla Province", 전라남도 "South Chŏlla Province", 경상북도 "North Kyŏngsang Province", 경상남도 "South Kyŏngsang Province", 제주도 "Cheju Province", 서울특별시 "Seoul Special City", 부산직할시 "Pusan Special City", etc.

Text III

13. ○함께 means "together", "with", or "in the company of", etc. It is interchange-able with 같이.

14. ○무슨- is a noun modifier meaning "what (kind of)". With normal initial pitch and the final contour of the intonation of the sentence going up(↗), however, it means "something".

15. ○그저 has several meanings depending on the context: (1) "casually" or "aim-lessly", (2) "just" or "simply", (3) "nothing new", (4) "unconditionally", etc. See the following examples:

그저 이 책을 샀어요. ⌒	I bought this book casually.
그저 들렸어요. ⌒	I have just dropped in at your house.
그분은 그저 울고만 있어요. ⌒	He does nothing but cry. (or, He is just crying.)
그저 그렇지요, ↗뭐. ↘	Well, nothing new.
그저 용서해 주세요. ⌒	Please forgive me once and for all.

17. ○한 번 means "one time". The bound form -번 used with Korean numerals indi-cates "multiplication". See the following examples:

한 번	one time	네 번	four times	아홉 번	nine times
두 번	two times	다섯 번	five times	열 번	ten times
세 번	three times	여섯 번	six times	스무 번	twenty times

STRUCTURAL PATTERNS

Text I

I . Noun Modifiers

As you have seen in Lesson 6, S.P. No 1, Korean uses nouns and verbs to modify nouns and other nominals. You have further learned that verbs when used as modifiers take special suffixes differing in shape according to the nature of the verb in question and its relation to time. Below you will find a diagram showing which suffixes or markers are used with which verbs and for which verb tenses.

1. The modifier marker -는

   -used only with action verbs;

   -refers to the present tense;

   -meaning: "the (man, thing) that is doing (does) (something)";

   -the marker is added either directly to the verb stem or to the verb stem plus the honorific marker -시-;

   -있 becomes 있는 "that exists" or "that someone has";

   -없 becomes 없는 "that is nonexistent" or "that someone does not have".

   Examples:

   공부하는 저 사람이 누구예요? ⌒   Who is that man who is studying?

   공부하시는 사람이 김 선생님이에요. ⌒   The person who is studying is Mr. Kim.

   책상 위에 있는 것이 무엇이에요? ⌒   What is that on the desk?

   없는 것이 없군요. ⌒   They have everything. (There is nothing they don't have.)

2. The modifier marker -ㄴ/-은

   a) -is used with action verbs ("does something");

-refers to the past tense ;

-meaning : "that has done". Example : 이 여자를 본 사람 "the man who has seen her". It can also mean "that someone has done". Example : 이 여자가 본 사람은 "the man she has seen". To make the meaning clear the subject or object particle must be expressed.

-the marker has two shapes : -ㄴ after verb stems ending in a vowel ; -은 after verb stems ending in a consonant.

b) The marker -ㄴ(은) is also used with descriptive verbs ; it refers to the present tense but notice the difference with (a) ; its meaning is "that is". Example : 큰 학교 "a school that is big". Even though the above example can be translated as "a big school", remember that modifiers like 큰 do not mean "big" but "is big".

3. The modifier marker -ㄹ(-을)

-used with action verbs as well as with descriptive verbs ;

-refers to the future ;

-meaning ; "that someone will do" (action verbs) ;

　　　　　　"that will be" (descriptive verbs).

Examples :

공부할 사람이 최 선생이에요. ⌒　　　　The man who is going to study is Mr. Ch'oe.

그것이 좋을지⌒ 나쁠지⌒ 모르겠어요. ⌒　I don't know if it will be good or bad.

Note :

All these expressions with the noun modifier can be made the subject, object, or predicate, etc. of larger sentences. See the examples below :

저기서 공부하는 사람이 누구예요? ⌒　　Who is the man studying over there? (subject)

저는 공부하는 사람을 좋아해요. ⌒　　　I like the man who studies. (object)

김 선생은 한국말을 공부하는 사람이 에요. ⌒　　　　Mr. Kim is the man who is studying Korean. (predicate complement)

II. V.S. + modifier suffix + -줄 알다 : "thinks that…" "knows that…"

Examples : (Please pay attention to the absence of the diacritic ∨ before the phrase 알아요 in the first column and their presence in the second column ; ∨ refers to pause.)

supposition	knowledge
그분이 ˇ공부하는 줄ˇ 알아요? ↗	그분이 ˇ공부하는 줄 ˇ알아요? ↗
Do you think he is studying?	Do you know he is studying?
그분이 ˇ여기 올 줄 알았어요. ⌒	그분이 ˇ여기 올 줄 ˇ알았어요. ⌒
I expected he would come here.	I knew he would come here.
그 여자가 ˇ예쁜 줄 알았어요. ⌒	그 여자가 ˇ예쁜 줄 ˇ알았어요. ⌒
I thought she was beautiful.	I knew she was beautiful.
그분이 ˇ한국에 ˇ있는 줄 알아요. ⌒	그분이 ˇ한국에 ˇ있는 줄 ˇ알아요. ⌒
I think he is in Korea.	I know he is in Korea.

Notes :

1. When there is no pause before the final verb 알아요 and the pitch of the syllable 알- is not simultaneously raised, the pattern expresses supposition or expectation. However, when there is a pause before the final verb 알아요 and the pitch of 알- is raised, the pattern expresses knowledge of a fact or something.

2. When, for the purpose of emphasis, the particle -로 (for supposition) or -을 (for knowledge) is attached to 줄, the above distinction becomes clearer without having to depend on intonation alone. See the examples below :

   그분이 ˇ이태리에 ˇ간 줄로 알아요. ⌒   I think he went to Italy.

   그분이 ˇ이태리에 ˇ간 줄을 ˇ알아요. ⌒   I know he went to Italy.

3. When the final verb 알다 is replaced by such verbs as 모르다, 믿다, etc., there is no such difference in meaning regardless of intonation. See the examples below :

   선생님이 ˇ여기서 ˇ일하는 줄 ˇ몰랐어요. ⌒   I didn't know that you are working here.

그분이 ˇ한국 사람인 줄 ˇ몰랐어요. ⌒   I didn't know he is a Korean.

한국말이 ˇ어려울 줄 믿어요. ⌒   I believe the Korean language will be difficult.

4. Modifier suffix + -줄 알다/모르다 can be used with action verbs as well as with descriptive verbs, 있어요 and -이에요 included.

5. When the pattern -ㄹ(을) 줄(을) 알다/모르다 is used with action verbs, depending on the context, it can also express the idea of "being able to". The English equivalent to this pattern is "(one) knows(does not know) how to do...", e.g., "(one) is able to(is not able to) do...". We will study this pattern again in Lesson 16. See the following examples:

한국말을 ˇ할 줄(을) 아십니까? ↗   Do you know how to speak Korean?

자동차를 ˇ운전할 줄(을) 몰라요. ⌒   I don't know how to drive a car.

III. The polite formal style : -ㅂ니다/-습니다

We have introduced the polite informal style (Lesson 4, S.P. No. XIV) and the plain style (Lesson 10, S.P. No. VI). Now let's study the polite formal style. The polite formal style is used in addressing strangers, casual acquaintances, and superiors and in speaking to social inferiors in formal situations. Polite words are usually used in reference to persons of equal or superior social standing.One of the most complicated phases of the problem for a foreigner is to determine the bases for social inferiority and superiority in the Korean system, and to know when a formal, comparatively stiff style of speech is appropriate and when it is fitting to be informal. The ability to choose the appropriate level for any given situation requires a thorough knowledge of the Korean social structure.(See Lesson 4, S.P. No. XIII.)

(A) In statements:

  a) 학교에 ˇ갑니다. ↘   I go to school.

    한국말을 ˇ공부합니다. ↘   I study Korean.

    이것이 나쁩니다. ↘   This is bad.

    그분이 ˇ선생입니다. ↘   He is a teacher.

  b) 점심을 ˇ먹습니다. ↘   I take lunch.

사람이 ˇ많습니다. ↘   There are many people.

사람이 ˇ많지 않습니다. ↘   There are not many people.

한국말을 ˇ공부하지 않습니다. ↘   I don't study Korean.

c) 교실에 ˇ책상이 ˇ있습니다. ↘   There are desks in the classroom.

교실에 ˇ칠판이 ˇ없습니다. ↘   There is no blackboard in the class-
                                               room.

학교에 ˇ갔습니다. ↘   I went to school.

학교에 ˇ가지 않았습니다. ↘   I didn't go to school.

Notes :

1. -ㅂ니다 after verb stems ending in a vowel ; -습니다 after verb stems ending
   in a consonant.

2. While English verbals are personal, Korean verbals are impersonal and can
   occur by themselves as complete standard sentences. They can indicate the
   occurrence of an action or the existence of a state without grammatical reference
   to a subject.

(B) In questions :

a) 학교에 갑니까? ↗   Do you go to school?

한국말을 ˇ공부하십니까? ↗   Do you study Korean?

이것이 ˇ나쁩니까? ↗   Is this bad?

b) 이것이 ˇ좋습니까? ↗   Is this good?

사람이 ˇ많습니까? ↗   Are there many people?

한국말을 ˇ공부하지 않습니까? ↗   Don't you study Korean?

c) 교실에 ˇ책상이 ˇ있습니까? ↗   Are there desks in the classroom?

학교에 ˇ칠판이 ˇ없습니까? ↗   Isn't there a blackboard in the class-
                                               room?

학교에 ˇ갔습니까? ↗   Did you go to school?

학교에 ˇ가지 않았습니까? ↗   Didn't you go to school?

Note :

-ㅂ니까? after verb stems(or the honorific infix -시-) ending in a vowel ; -습

니까? after verb stems ending in a consonant.

(C) In propositions :

a) 학교에 갑시다. ↘   Let's go to school.

한국말을 공부합시다. ↘   Let's study Korean.

b) 옷을 입읍시다. ↘   Let's get dressed.

여기 놓읍시다. ↘   Let's put (it) here.

Note :

-ㅂ시다 after verb stems ending in a vowel ; -읍시다 after verb stems ending
in a consonant.

(D) In commands :

a) 학교에 가십시오. ↘   Go to school, please.

한국말을 공부하십시오. ↘   Study Korean, please.

b) 옷을 입으십시오. ↘   Get dressed, please.

여기 놓으십시오. ↘   Put (it) here, please.

Note :

-십시오 after verb stems ending in a vowel ; -으십시오 after verb stems ending
in a consonant.

IV. Number (plural and singular)

Examples :

1. 학생들 students   아이들 children (plain)

선생님들 teachers or you   이분들 these persons (honorific)

당신들 you (plain)   그들   they (plain)

2. 짐승들 animals   산들   mountains

3. 어디로들 가십니까? ↘   Where are you going? (more than one
                                                        person)

연필로들 썼어요. ⌒   They (we) wrote with pencils.

한국말로들 말하세요. ⌒   Speak in Korean (all of you).

집에들 갔어요. ⌒   They went home.

집에서들 무엇했어요? ⌒   What did you do at home (all of you)?

학교까지들 갑시다.	Let's go as far as the school.
어머니들께 보였습니다.	They showed it to their mothers.
어서들 가세요.	Please go without delay (all of you).
잘들 공부하세요.	Study well, please (all of you).
빨리들 갑시다.	Let's go quickly.
재미있게들 노십시요.	Have a good time (all of you).
많이들 먹었어요.	We (they) ate satisfactorily.

4. 집집 houses   곳곳 places

    끼리끼리   people, birds, animals, etc. of the same category

Notes :

1. Whenever number is sufficiently clear from the grammatical context and/or the outer circumstances, as a rule, none of the Korean devices of number is used.

2. When for the sake of clarity a plural form is required, Korean makes use of either the particle -들 suffixed to nouns (see Ex. 1, 2) and to particles and adverbials (see Ex. 3) or, in the case of nouns, of duplication (Ex. 4).

3. The use of the plural suffix -들 is relatively frequent with nouns referring to persons, whereas with other nouns the frequency of use is low. The use of duplication of nouns as a device to express number is also rather limited.

4. Use of the plural suffix -들 after the following pronouns is optional :

우리	or	우리들	we (intimate)
저희	or	저희들	we (humble)
너희	or	너희들	you (plain)
여러분	or	여러분들	you (honorific)

Text II

V. Verbal gerund + -있다 : A.V.S. + 고 있다 : "(someone) is doing"

    Examples :

저는 지금 공부하고 있습니다.	I'm studying now.
한국말을 가르치고 있습니다.	I'm teaching Korean.

그분을 기다리고 있습니다. ↘   I'm waiting for him.

Notes :

1. The pattern -고 있다 is used only with action verbs and indicates that an action is actually progressing. In Korean the progressive form is not used as extensively as in English. To express the simple progressive aspect of an action, it is usually sufficient to use the simple present tense form.

2. The pattern -고 있다 must never be used for the immediate future as is done in English, i.e., "I am going" for "I will go".

3. The pattern -고 있다 can also indicate an action or state that began in the past and is still continuing. In this case, a time word + particle like -부터 or -동안 is usually used to indicate when the action began and how long the action or state has been continuing. See the examples below :

    오 년 동안 한국말을 공부하고 있어요. ⌒

    I have been studying Korean for the past five years.

    작년부터 가르치고 있어요. ⌒

    I have been teaching since last year. (Lit. I'm teaching from last year.)

4. The tense, negation, etc., are regularly expressed in the final verb 있다, not in the verb with -고. See the following examples :

    저는 기다리고 있겠어요. ⌒   I will be waiting for you.
    그때 공부하고 있었습니다. ↘   I was studying at that time.
    지금 공부하고 있지 않아요. ⌒   I am not studying now.
    그분이 자고 있지 않았어요. ⌒   He was not sleeping.
    그분은 아직도 주무시고 계실 거예요. ⌒ He must still be sleeping.

5. 있다 may be replaced by its honorific 계시다.

VI. Noun+(이)라고 하다 : "is called"

   Examples :

    이것을 의자라고 합니다. ↘   This is called a chair.
    그것을 무엇이라고 합니까? ↘   What is the name of that thing?
    그것을 책상이라고 합니다. ↘   That is called a desk.

김인수라고 합니다. ↘   My name is Kim In-su.

Notes :

1. The pattern -(이)라고 하다 attached to a nominal tells what the person or thing to which the nominal refers is called.

2. -라고 하다 after nominals ending in a vowel ; -이라고 하다 after nominals ending in a consonant.

Ⅶ. Particles -한테 : "to", -한테서 : "from"

Examples :

1. 누구한테 편지를 씁니까? ↘   To whom are you writing?

   친구한테 편지를 씁니다. ↘   I'm writing to my friend.

   그 책을 김 선생한테 주었어요. ⌒   I gave that book to Mr. Kim.

2. 어머니한테서 편지가 왔어요. ⌒   The letter came from my mother.

   누구한테서 그 책을 받았어요? ⌒   From whom did you receive that
                                         book?

   친구한테서 이 책을 받았어요. ⌒   I received this book from my friend.

Notes :

1. The particles -한테 "to" and -한테서 "from" are used with nouns referring to animate beings. The particle -한테 "to" indicates direction toward a person, etc., and the particle -한테서 "from" indicates direction toward a person, etc., as a source or origin.

2. But the particles -에(다) "to" and -에서 "from" are used with nouns referring to inanimate things. The particle -에(다) "to" indicates an inanimate indirect object and the particle -에서 "from" indicates an inanimate source or origin. See the following sentences :

   a) 어디에(다) 편지를 씁니까? ↘   To whom (lit. where) are you writing?

      집에(다) 편지를 씁니다. ↘   I'm writing home.

      이 책을 어디에(다) 부칩니까? ↘   To whom (lit. where) are you mailing
                                             this book?

      이 책을 이태리에(다) 보냅니다. ↘   I am sending this book to Italy.

b) 어디(에)서 왔습니까?   Where did you come from?

프랑스에서 왔습니다. ↘   I came from France.

사무실에서 옵니다. ↘   I'm coming from the office.

3. -(에)서 : -에 may be dropped after nominals ending in a vowel. -(에)다 : -다 may be omitted.

VIII. Verb stems ending in a final consonant -ㄷ

Examples :

긷(다) draws, pumps	듣(다) hears
붇(다) increases, becomes sodden	싣(다) loads
눋(다) burns, gets scorched	걷(다) walks
일컫(다) designates, calls	묻(다) asks
깨닫(다) perceives, apprehends	

Notes :

Some verbs whose stems end in -ㄷ are irregular ; in certain environments the final stem sound -ㄷ changes into -ㄹ. The examples of the irregular -ㄷ verbs given above form a fairly exhaustive list.

1. When the final -ㄷ of the stem is followed by a vowel, -ㄷ changes into -ㄹ.

See the examples below :

들으면, ⌒	If you listen,
들었습니다. ↘	I heard.
들어야 합니다. ↘	You must listen to (it).
들어라. ↘	Listen. (plain style)
들어 보세요. ⌒	Listen and see.
들어도 ⌒ 좋아요. ⌒	You may listen to (it).

2. But when the final -ㄷ of the stem is followed by a consonant, no such change takes place. See the following examples :

듣자. ↘	Let's listen. (plain style)
듣지 마세요. ⌒	Don't listen.
듣습니다. ↘	I'm listening.

듣느냐? ↗   Do you listen? (plain style)

듣겠습니다. ↘   I'll listen.

3. There are, however, -ㄷ regular verbs which never change their stem, such as 믿다 "believes", 닫다 "shuts", 받다 "receives", etc.

Text III

IX. <u>Noun + -(이)라도</u> : "(this) or something else" ; "even"

Examples :

책이라도 읽읍시다. ↘
(If we can't do that), then let's read a book.

기차라도 탑시다. ↘
(If we can't go that way), then let's ride a train.

한국말이라도 공부하겠어요. ⌒
(If I cant's do that), I will study Korean.

Notes :

1. The particles -(이)라도 are attached to nominals and indicate a lack of finality, forthrightness, or enthusiasm about one's choice.

2. -이라도 after nominals ending in a consonant ; -라도 after nominals ending in a vowel.

3. The particles -(이)라도, depending on the context, can also mean "even". See the following examples :

그것은 아이라도 합니다. ↘
Even a child can do that.

제일 힘센 사람이라도 못해요. ⌒
Even the strongest person can't do that.

X. <u>The pattern -고 싶다/-고 싶어하다</u> : "wants to (or would like to) do so-and-so"

(A) <u>A.V.S. + -고 싶다</u>

Examples :

지금 자고 싶어요. ⌒
I would like to sleep now.

저는 독일에 가고 싶습니다. ↘
I want to go to Germany.

무엇을 하고 싶습니까? ↘   What do you want to do?

한국말을 공부하고 싶습니다. ↘   I would like to study Korean.

이 책을 읽고 싶지 않아요. ⌒   I don't want to read this book.

(B) A.V.S. + -고 싶어하다

Examples :

학생들이 자고 싶어합니다. ↘   The students want to sleep.

김 선생이 영국에 가고 싶어해요. ⌒   Mr. Kim wants to go to England.

당신도 가고 싶어하지만, ⌒   You also want to go, but…

Notes :

1. The pattern -고 싶다 / -고 싶어하다 is used with action verb stem and -있- and indicates the desire of the speaker.

2. The pattern -고 싶다 is usually used with the first person in statements and with the second person in questions only.

3. -고 싶어하다 is used with the third person and with the second person in certain declarative sentences.

4. The tense, negation, etc., are regularly expressed in the final verb 싶다.

XI. The potential -ㄹ(을) 수(가) 있다 : "can do so-and-so" "so-and-so can do"

Examples :

점심을 먹을 수(가) 있습니다. ↘   I can eat lunch.

지금 갈 수(가) 없습니다. ↘   I can't go now.

저도 여기에 있을 수(가) 있습니다. ↘   I can stay here, too.

저도 여기에 있을 수(가) 없습니다. ↘   I can't stay here, either.

Notes :

1. The potential -ㄹ(을) 수(가) 있다 is used with action verbs as well as with the verb 있- and indicates possibility of an action or state. Its negative form is -ㄹ(을) 수(가) 없다. The particle -가 after -수 is optional.

2. -을 수(가) 있다 / 없다 after verb stems ending in a consonant ; -ㄹ 수(가) 있다 / 없다 after verb stems ending in a vowel.

3. The tense is normally expressed in the final verb 있 다. See the following examples:

저는ˇ그때ˇ갈 수(가) 있었어요. ⌒   I was able to go at that time.

그분이ˇ이것을ˇ할 수(가) 있을 거예요. ⌒   He is probably able to do this.

그분이ˇ갈 수(가) 있겠지요. ⌒   I think he can go.

4. We have studied A.V.S. + -ㄹ(을) 줄 알다 / 모르다 "knows/does not know how to do" in this lesson.(See S.P.No. II, Note 5.) While the pattern -ㄹ(을) 수 있다 / 없다 indicates the possibility of an action, the pattern -ㄹ(을) 줄 알다 / 모르다 indicates the understanding of the method or principle.

DRILLS

졸아요(졸지-) dozes, takes a nap   방문해요(방문하지-) visits

농담해요(농담하지-) jokes, jests   운동장 playground

열심히 hard, ardently   편지 letter

아버지 father   비켜요(비키지-) moves aside

어머니 mother   세수해요(세수하지-) washes oneself

등산해요(등산하지-) climbs (up) a   춤춰요(춤추지-) dances
    mountain   수영해요(수영하지-) swims

낚시질해요(낚시질하지-) fishes with   혼자 alone, by oneself
    rod and line   운전해요(운전하지-) drives, operates

Text I

A. Substitution Drill

1. 학교에 갑니다. ↘   I go to school.

2. 한국말을 공부합니다. ↘   I study Korean.

3. 날씨가 좋습니다. ↘   The weather is fine.

4. 그분이 내일 도착합니다. ↘   He will arrive (here) tomorrow.

5. 나는 모레 떠납니다. ↘   I'll leave the day after tomorrow.

6. 그분이 선생입니다. ↘   He is a teacher.

B. Substitution Drill

1. 이것이 나쁩니까? ↗   Is this bad?

2. 한국말을 배웁니까? ↗   Do you learn Korean?

3. 영어를 공부하지 않습니까? ↗   Don't you study English?

4. 교실에 책상이 있습니까? ↗   Are there desks in the classroom?

5. 교실에 칠판이 없습니까? ↗   Isn't there a blackboard in the class-
    room?

6. 학교에 가지 않았습니까? ↗   Didn't you go to school?

C. Substitution Drill

1. 학교에 가십시오. ↘   Go to school, please.
2. 한국말을 공부하십시오. ↘   Study Korean, please.
3. 빨리 일어나십시오. ↘   Get up quickly, please.
4. 두 시에 떠나십시오. ↘   Leave at two o'clock, please.
5. 이 책을 읽으십시오. ↘   Read this book, please.
6, 집에 돌아가십시오. ↘   Go back home, please.

D. Substitution Drill

1. 이런데서 만날 줄 몰랐어요. ⌒   I never expected to meet you in a place like this.

2. 그분이 오실 줄 몰랐어요. ⌒   I didn't know that he would come (here).

3. 그 여자가 예쁠 줄 몰랐어요. ⌒   I didn't know that she would be beautiful.

4. 그렇게 빨리 떠날 줄 몰랐어요. ⌒   I didn't know that he would leave so quickly.

5. 아직도 주무실 줄 몰랐어요. ⌒   I didn't know that he would be still sleeping.

6. 그분이 한국말을 잘 할 줄 몰랐어요. ⌒   I didn't know that he would speak Korean so well.

E. Pattern Drill

Teacher : 어디로 가십니까? ↘   Where are you going?
Student : 어디로들 가십니까? ↘   Where are you going? (more than one person)

1. 한국말로 말하세요.   한국말로들 말하세요. ⌒
2. 집에 갔어요.   집에들 갔어요. ⌒
3. 어서 가세요.   어서들 가세요. ⌒
4. 잘 공부하세요.   잘들 공부하세요. ⌒
5. 빨리 갑시다.   빨리들 갑시다. ↘
6. 재미있게 노십시오.   재미있게들 노십시오. ↘

F. Pattern Drill

Teacher : 학생이 교실에서 공부해요. ⌢   The student is studying in the classroom.

Student : 학생들이 교실에서 공부해요. ⌢   The students are studying in the class-room.

1. 선생님이 가르쳐요.   선생님들이 가르쳐요. ⌢
2. 그분이 기차를 타요.   그분들이 기차를 타요. ⌢
3. 아이가 운동장에서 놀아요.   아이들이 운동장에서 놀아요. ⌢
4. 이분이 한국말을 공부해요.   이분들이 한국말을 공부해요. ⌢
5. 사람이 참 많아요.   사람들이 참 많아요. ⌢

G. Pattern Drill

Teacher : 저분이 한국말을 가르쳐요. ⌢   That person is teaching Korean.

Student : 한국말을 가르치는 저분이 누구예요?   Who is that person teaching Korean?

1. 저분이 영어를 가르쳐요.   영어를 가르치는 저분이 누구예요? ⌢
2. 그분이 기차를 타요.   기차를 타는 그분이 누구예요? ⌢
3. 저 사람이 저기서 기다립니다.   저기서 기다리는 저 사람이 누구예요? ⌢
4. 그분이 책을 읽습니다.   책을 읽는 그분이 누구예요? ⌢
5. 그분이 독일어를 배웁니다.   독일어를 배우는 그분이 누구예요? ⌢
6. 저분이 산보합니다.   산보하는 저분이 누구예요? ⌢

Text II

H. Substitution Drill

1. 이것을 의자라고 합니다. ↘ (라고/이라고)

   This is called "chair".

책,	책상,	분필,
인형,	담배,	지우개

2. 저는 지금 공부하고 있습니다. ↘

   I'm studying now.

책을 읽고,	영어를 배우고,
밥을 먹고,	그분을 도와주고

230   *Drills*

3. <u>아버지</u>한테서 이 책을 받았습니다. ↘

I received this book from my father.

학생,	그 여자,	김 선생님,
어머니,	그 남자,	최 선생님

4. <u>친구</u>한테 이 인형을 드리겠습니다. ↘

I'll give this doll to my friend.

어머니,	학생,	김 선생님,
아버지,	그 여자,	최 선생님

I. Pattern Drill

Teacher : 그분이 졸고 계십니다. ↘   He is taking a nap.

Student : 그분이 졸고 계셨습니다. ↘   He was taking a nap.

1. 그분이 농담하고 계십니다.   그분이 농담하고 계셨습니다. ↘
2. 그분이 주무시고 계십니다.   그분이 주무시고 계셨습니다. ↘
3. 그분이 책을 읽고 계십니다.   그분이 책을 읽고 계셨습니다. ↘
4. 그분이 가르치고 계십니다.   그분이 가르치고 계셨습니다. ↘
5. 그분이 일하고 계십니다.   그분이 일하고 계셨습니다. ↘

J. Pattern Drill (based on this Lesson, S.P. No. I)

Teacher : 저기서 공부하는 사람이 누구입니까? ↘

Who is the man studying over there?

Student : 저기서 공부한 사람이 누구입니까? ↘

Who is the man who studied over there?

1. 저기서 일하는 분이 제 친구입니다.   저기서 일한 분이 제 친구입니다. ↘
2. 저기서 주무시는 분이 아버지입니다.   저기서 주무신 분이 아버지입니다. ↘
3. 한국말을 가르치는 분이 친구입니다.   한국말을 가르친 분이 친구입니다. ↘
4. 저기서 세수하는 분이 노 선생입니다.   저기서 세수한 분이 노 선생입니다. ↘
5. 영어를 배우는 분이 독일 사람입니다.   영어를 배운 분이 독일 사람입니다. ↘

K. Pattern Drill (based on this Lesson, S.P. No. I)

Teacher : 이 교실에서 공부하는 사람이 학생입니다. ↘

The man studying in this classroom is a student.

Student : 이 교실에서 공부할 사람이 학생입니다. ↘

The man who will study in this classroom is a student.

1. 그분은 하는 일이 많습니다. 그분은 할 일이 많습니다. ↘
2. 책을 읽는 분이 김 선생님입니다. 책을 읽을 분이 김 선생님입니다. ↘
3. 저기서 주무시는 분이 아버지입니다. 저기서 주무실 분이 아버지입니다. ↘
4. 저기서 일하는 분이 어머니입니다. 저기서 일할 분이 어머니입니다. ↘
5. 한국말을 가르치는분이 제 친구입니다. 한국말을 가르칠 분이 제 친구입니다. ↘

L. Level Drill

Teacher : 지금 학교에 갑시다. ↘   Let's go to school now.

Student : 지금 학교에 가자. ↘   Let's go to school now.

1. 한국말을 공부합시다.   한국말을 공부하자. ↘
2. 농담이나 합시다.   농담이나 하자. ↘
3. 빨리 일어납시다.   빨리 일어나자. ↘
4. 이 일을 어서 끝냅시다.   이 일을 어서 끝내자. ↘
5. 내일 떠납시다.   내일 떠나자. ↘

Text III

M. Substitution Drill

1. 지금 <u>등산하고</u> 싶습니다. ↘

   I want to climb the mountain.

만나고,	운전하고,	수영하고,
춤추고,	산보하고,	혼자 있고

2. 그분은 <u>한국에 오고</u> 싶어합니다. ↘

   He wants to come to Korea.

자고,	등산하고,	수영하고,
산보하고,	농담하고,	혼자 있고

3. 두시에 <u>그것을 드릴</u> 수 있습니다. ↘

   I can give it (to you) at two o'clock.

도와드릴,	이 방에서 잘,
빨리 끝낼,	그분을 소개할

N. Pattern Drill

Teacher : 이 책을 읽읍시다. ↘   Let's read this book.

Student : 이 책이라도 읽읍시다. ↘   (If we can't do that), then let's read this book.

1. 기차를 탑시다.
기차라도 탑시다. ↘

2. 한국말을 공부합시다.
한국말이라도 공부합시다. ↘

3. 그분을 만나야겠습니다.
그분이라도 만나야겠습니다. ↘

4. 라디오를 들읍시다.
라디오라도 들읍시다. ↘

5. 담배를 피웁시다.
담배라도 피웁시다. ↘

6. 저 만년필을 삽시다.
저 만년필이라도 삽시다. ↘

O. Pattern Drill

Teacher : 그때 갈 수 있었습니다. ↘
I could go at that time.

Student : 그때 갈 수 없었습니다. ↘
I couldn't go at that time.

1. 춤을 출 수 있었습니다.
춤을 출 수 없었습니다. ↘

2. 운전할 수 있습니다.
운전할 수 없습니다. ↘

3. 비킬 수 있었습니다.
비킬 수 없었습니다. ↘

4. 소개할 수 있었습니다.
소개할 수 없었습니다. ↘

5. 등산할 수 있었습니다.
등산할 수 없었습니다. ↘

6. 수영할 수 있습니다.
수영할 수 없습니다. ↘

P. Level Drill

Teacher : 열심히 공부하십시오. ↘
Study hard, please.

Student : 열심히 공부해라. ↘
Study hard.

1. 좀 비키십시오.
좀 비켜라. ↘

2. 수영하십시오.
수영해라. ↘

3. 이 책을 읽으십시오.
이 책을 읽어라. ↘

4. 한 시간 기다리십시오.
한 시간 기다려라. ↘

5. 시작하십시오.
시작해라. ↘

Q. Response Drill

1. 누구한테서 편지를 받았습니까?
친구한테서 편지를 받았습니다. ↘

2. 누구한테 그것을 드렸습니까?
아버지한테 그것을 드렸습니다. ↘

3. 무엇을 공부하고 싶습니까?
한국말을 공부하고 싶습니다. ↘

4. 이것을 무엇이라고 합니까?
이것을 의자라고 합니다 ↘.

5. 어디에들 갔습니까?
학교에들 갔습니다. ↘

제십이과 성당에서 (Lesson 12 In Church)

TEXT I

┌─ [VOCABULARY] ─────────────────────────────────┐

성당 church

주일 Sunday, a holiday

시작되요(시작되지-) begins, starts

미사 Mass

여러 번 many times

머리 head

아파요(아프지-) is painful, aches

└──┘

1. 한옥현 : 아 오늘이 주일이군요.   Oh! Today is Sunday.

         저하고 같이 성당에 갑시다.   Let's go to church together.

2. 최상호 : 몇 시에 미사가 시작되는지요?   What time does Mass begin?

3. 한옥현 : 여러 번 있어요. 열 시 것 갑   There are many sessions. Let's go for

         시다.   the 10 o'clock Mass.

4. 최상호 : 그런데 난 머리가 아프기 때문   (But) I can't go because I have a head-

         에, 갈 수가 없어요.   ache.

5. 한옥현 : 그러지 마시고, 갑시다.   Don't act like that. Let's go.

6. 최상호 : 그럴까?   Shall I go?

TEXT II

┌─ [VOCABULARY] ─────────────────────────────────┐

묵주 the rosary

기도 prayer

가지고 와요(가지고 오지-) brings
                     (something)

마음 mind, spirit, mentality

속 the inner part, the interior

기도해요(기도하지-) prays

앉아요(앉지-) sits, takes a seat

성서 the Bible

└──┘

7. 최상호 : 모두 기도를 드리고 있는데요.   Everyone is saying the prayer, but I

         그런데 난 묵주를 가지고 오지   didn't bring my rosary.

         않았어요.

8. 한옥현 : 그럼 마음속으로 기도하세요. 묵주가 없어도, 괜찮아요. | Then, pray in your heart. Even though you don't have a rosary, it's all right.

9. 최상호 : 어디에 앉을까요? | Where shall we sit?

10. 한옥현 : 저기가 좋겠군요. | Over there will be fine.

11. 최상호 : 그럼 저기 가서 앉읍시다. | All right. Let's go and sit there.

12. 한옥현 : 성서는 가지고 오셨지요? | You brought your Bible, didn't you?

13. 최상호 : 예, 성서는 가지고 왔어요. | Yes, I brought my Bible.

TEXT III

┌─ [VOCABULARY] ─────────────────────────────┐
성가 hymn (holy song)   강론 sermon
성가대 chorus, choir   거짓말 lie
유명해요(유명하지-) is famous   어떻게 how
└──┘

14. 최상호 : 오늘 성가가 참 좋았지요? | The hymn was very good today, wasn't it?

15. 한옥현 : 예, 이 성당의 성가대가 유명해요. 신부님의 강론도 유명하구요. | This church's choir is famous. Father's sermons are famous, too.

16. 최상호 : 그런데 내년에 그분이 미국에 가신다고 해요. | They say he is going to America next year.

17. 한옥현 : 정말이에요? | Is that true?

18. 최상호 : 그럼요, 내가 거짓말 하겠어요? | Of course, would I lie?

19. 한옥현 : 아이구, 어떻게 하나. 그분이 여기 안 계시면. | Oh! What will I do if he is not here.

REMARKS TO THE TEXT

Text I

1. ○성당 : sacred(성) hall(당), or sacred meeting place, is the term generally used for a church building, whereas 교회 "doctrinal(교) assembly(회)" is used to mean the Church as an institution. The term for Catholic Church is 천주교회, 천주 meaning "the Lord of Heaven", i.e., "God". The term for Protestant church is 신교, meaning "the New Religion"; its church building is called 예배당, 예배, meaning "worship".

   ○주일, depending on the context, means either (1) "week", (2) "Sunday" (the day of the Lord). See the following examples :

   다음 주일에 그분을 만나겠어요. ⌒   I'll meet him next week.

   오늘은 주일이에요. ⌒   Today is a holiday(or, Sunday).

2. ○시작되다 "begins" is a non-object verbs used with the particle -가/-이. 시작하다 "begins" is an object verb used with the particle -을/-를. See the following examples :

   두 시에 수업이 시작됩니다. ↘   The lesson begins at two.

   두 시에 수업을 시작합니다. ↘   We start classes at two.

4. ○머리, depending on the context, stands for : "head"(part of the human body) ; "hair"(on the head) ; "brain" or "intellect".

   For the head of animals(birds, fish), the word 대가리 is used. For the hair on parts of the human body other than the head, the word 털 is used. The word 털 is also used for the hair of animals. See the following examples :

   머리가 아픕니다. ↘   I have a headache.

   그분은 머리가 좋습니다. ↘   He has a clear head. (or, he is smart.)

   머리 깎으러 갑시다. ↘   Let's go to get a haircut.

5. ○그러시지 말고 is an abbreviation of 그렇게 하시지 말고. -시- is the honorific infix. See this Lesson, S.P. No. IV, for the pattern -지 말고.

6. ○그럴까? is an abbreviated form of 그렇게 할까? Both forms are used to express a reluctant consent, while the abbreviated form, not the full form, is also used to express doubt about someone's statement.

Text II

7. ○기도(하다), 신공(하다) and 기구(하다): all mean "prays", "prayer". Although they are theoretically interchangeable, in some situations they are not. For example, one never says: 신공해 주세요 "Pray for me, please", but 기도해 주세요 or 기구해 주세요; not 묵주기도, but 묵주신공 "the prayer of the rosary". 기도하다 is used more generally, i.e., both in the protestant and the Catholic Churches. 묵주신공 is a Catholic term.

   ○난 is a contraction of 나는.

   ○드리다 is the honorific verbal of 주다 "gives". It is also used for "offers". For example, 기구를 드리다 "offers a prayer".

   ○가지고 오다 "brings (something somewhere)" means literally "comes holding" or "comes carrying." 가지고 is the gerund of the verbal 가져요 "holds", "has", "owns". Note also 가지고 가다 "takes or brings(something somewhere)".

8. ○속 is a nominal meaning "the inner part", "the interior", "the depth", or "the bottom", etc. 마음속 "the bottom of one's heart": 산속 "the heart of a mountain". The opposite of 속 is 겉 "the face", or "the surface". Note also 안 "the inside" and 밖(바깥) "the outside" or "the exterior".

9. ○앉다 means "takes a seat" or "sits down". Its opposite verbal is 서다 "stands".

Text III

14. ○성가 "hymn" is a Catholic term, derived form Chinese, literally meaning "holy songs," whereas 찬송가 "hymn" is a Protestant term.

15. ○성가대, derived from Chinese, literally means "hymn-choir". It is used for both

choirs in a Protestant church and a Catholic church.

○강론 "sermon" is a term used by Catholics, whereas 설교 "sermon" is more common in the Protestant churches.

○유명하구요 stands for 유명하고요. The substitution of 우 for 오 in non-initial syllable, as in this case, is a characteristic of the Seoul dialect. In Seoul, for example, you can hear 바루 for 바로 "right", "directly", 시굴 for 시골 "countryside", 하구말구 for 하고말고 "of course", etc.

18. ○거짓말 "lie" is the opposite of 참말 or 정말 ; 거짓말쟁이 a "liar" or "a story-teller". See the following examples :

거짓말 하지 마세요. ⌒	Don't tell lies.
절대로 거짓말이 아니에요. ⌒	I mean everything I say.
그 사람은 거짓말쟁이에요. ⌒	That man is a liar.

19. ○아이구 is an exclamatory expression of sickness, disappointment, grief, or surprise. It is frequently used in daily life. 어떻게 하나… 그분이 여기 안 계시면 is an inverted form of 그분이 여기 안 계시면 어떻게 하나. The ending -하나 is intimate style. Here the speaker is talking to himself.

STRUCTURAL PATTERNS

Text I

I. The particle -하고(같이) : "together with"

Examples :

누구하고 (같이) 가세요? ⌒   With whom are you going?

김 선생님하고 (같이) 갑니다. ↘   I'm going with Mr. Kim.

저하고 (같이) 성당에 갑시다. ↘   Let's go to church together.

Notes :

1. The particle -하고(같이) is added to nominals. The particle -하고 means "with", "accompanying"; 같이 means "together". Therefore, the pattern -하고 같이 corresponds to the English "together with". However, the word 같이 can be dropped, just as "together" is sometimes dropped in English.

2. The particle -하고(같이) may be replaced by -와/-과 같이 without change of meaning. In this case, however, we usually do not drop the word 같이. See the following examples :

김 선생님과 같이 기다렸어요. ⌒   I waited with Mr. Kim.

누구와 같이 가시겠습니까? ↘   With whom will you go?

3. -와 같이 after nominals ending in a vowel ; -과 같이 after nominals ending in a consonant.

4. The particle -하고(같이) is used more than -와/-과 같이 in colloquial language.

II. The provisional conjunctive ending V.S. + -아(-어, -여)야 : "provided"

(A) In the affirmative : "provided so-and-so happens or is true"

Examples :

그분이 가야⌒ 저도 가겠어요. ⌒   Provided he goes, I'll go, too.

그것이˅ 좋아야⌒ 사겠어요.⌒   Provided it is good, I'll buy it.

우리들은˅책이 있어야⌒ 공부할 수 있   Provided we have books, we can
어요.⌒   study.

(B) In the negative : "provided so-and-so doesn't happen or isn't true"; "unless so-
and-so happens or is true"

Examples :

김 선생이˅오지 않아야⌒ 공부하겠어요.⌒ I'll study unless Mr. Kim comes.

그것이˅크지 않아야⌒ 사겠어요.⌒   I'll buy it if it is not big.

그분이 여기에˅없어야⌒ 공부할 수 있어 We can study provided he is not here.
요.⌒

Notes :

1. The provisional form −아(−어, −여)야 may be used with action verbs as well
as with descriptive verbs and 있−. The most common English equivalent for
both the conditional and the provisional, in the affirmative is "if…". There is a
slight difference in meaning between the two, but in most cases the two forms are
interchangeable. See the following examples :

그분이˅가면,⌒ 가겠어요.⌒   If he goes, I'll go. (conditional) (This
                                  sentence tells what will happen if he
                                  goes.)

그분이˅가야,⌒ 가겠어요.⌒   I'll go if (provided) he goes. (provi-
                                  sional) (This sentence tells under
                                  what circumstances I go.)

2. In the negative, the English equivalent of the conditional is "if not…", whereas
the negative provisional corresponds to the English "unless…". See the examples below :

김 선생이˅오지 않으면,⌒ 제가˅한국   If Mr. Kim doesn't come, I'll teach
말을˅가르치겠어요.⌒   Korean. (This sentence tells what
                                  will happen if Mr. Kim doesn't
                                  come.)

김 선생이 오지 않아야 제가 한국 I'll teach Korean unless Mr. Kim
말을 가르치겠어요. comes. (This sentence indicates an
intention to teach Korean, provided
Mr. Kim doesn't come.)

3. In the conditional form, the tense infixes (-았-, -겠-) can be used in the
dependent clause if necessary, whereas in the provisional form the tense infixes
can not be used in the dependent clause. The tense is expressed only in the main
clause. While the conditional occurs in sentences referring to the past, present, or
future time, sentences containing a provisional form usually refer to the present
or future only.

4. While the conditional may be used with any form, the provisional can be used only
with the interrogative and declarative, not with the propositive and imperative.

III. Particles used in verb phrases:

Some particles such as -가/-이, -를/-을, -는/-은, or -도, etc. are often used
with any verb phrases.

(A) Particles -가/-이 and -를/-을

한국 음식을 먹을 수가 있어요.   I can eat Korean food.
한국 음식을 먹지를 않아요.   I don't eat Korean food.
한국 음식을 먹을 줄을 몰라요.   I don't know how to eat Korean food.

Note:

Although particles -가/-이 or -를/-을 are inserted in verb phrases as shown
in the examples above, they do not carry added meaning. The forms with a particle
are considered original or full constructions.

(B) The contrast particle -는/-은

한국 음식을 먹을 수는 있어요.   I can eat Korean food (but).
한국 음식을 먹지는 않아요.   I don't eat Korean food (but).
한국 음식을 먹을 줄은 몰라요.   I don't know how to eat Korean food
(but).

Note:

The particle -는/-은 is used instead of -가/-이 whenever you want to bring out a contrast. (See Lesson 4, S.P.No. VII.)

(C) The particle -도

한국 음식을 먹을 수도 있어요. ⌒	I can eat Korean food, too.
한국 음식을 먹지도 않아요. ⌒	I don't eat Korean food, either.
한국 음식을 먹을 줄도 몰라요. ⌒	I don't even know how to eat Korean food.

Note: When the particle -도 is inserted in verb phrases, it has the meaning of "even" or "also" depending on the context.

IV. The pattern -(지) 말고... : "not, but..."

(A) V.S. + -지 말고

Examples:

자지 말고⌒ 공부하십시오. ↘	Don't sleep, (but) study, please.
여기 있지 말고⌒ 가세요. ⌒	Don't stay here, (but) go, please.
먹지 말고⌒ 갑시다. ↘	Let's go without eating. (Lit. Let's not eat but go.)
공부하지 말고⌒ 잡시다. ↘	Let's sleep without studying. (Lit. Let's not study but sleep.)

Notes:

1. When one rejects one action in favor of another, -지 말고 is added to the verb the action of which is not wanted. -지 말고 is used with action verbs and -있.

2. V.S. + -지 말고 is used mostly in imperative or propositive sentences.

(B) Noun + -말고

Examples:

이것말고 그것 주세요. ⌒	Give me that (but) not this.
내일말고 모레 오세요. ⌒	Please come the day after tomorrow, not tomorrow.

이 연필말고 저 시계 삽시다. ↘   Let's buy that watch but not this pen-
                                                  cil.

Notes :

1. When one rejects something in favor of something else, -말고 is added to the
   nominal which expresses that which is not wanted.

2. Noun + -말고 is also regularly used in imperative or propositive sentences.

Text II

V. V.S. + -아(-어, -여)도 좋다(괜찮다)… : "even being or doing so-and-so it's all
   right, or, it doesn't matter" (asking and giving permission)

Examples :

이것을 먹어도, ⌒ 좋습니까?   May I eat this?
  (괜찮습니까?) ↗

집에 가도, ⌒ 좋습니까?   May I go home?
  (괜찮습니까?) ↗

이 문을 열어도, ⌒ 좋습니까?   May I open this door?
  (괜찮습니까?) ↗

추워도, ⌒ 좋습니다. ↘   It's all right even if it's cold.

거기 있어도, ⌒ 좋습니다. ↘   You may stay there.

Notes :

1. The pattern -아(-어, -여)도 좋다(괜찮다) may be used with any verb except
   the verb of identification -이-. It is used in requesting and granting permission. When used as an affirmative, permission to do or be so-and-so is requested
   (in questions) or granted (in statements) ; when used as a negative, permission
   not to do or be so-and-so is requested (in questions) or granted (in statements).

2. 좋다 may be replaced by 괜찮다 without any difference in meaning.

3. -아도 좋다 after -아- and -오- ; -어도 좋다 after any other vowel ; -여도 좋
   다 after 하- or the stem of the verb 하다 "does".

4. An affirmative answer to a request for permission may be a repetition of (A) all

or (B) part of the request with a declarative form or (C) 어서 + affirmative imperative, etc. See the responses to the following question:

집에 가도, ⌒ 좋습니까? ↗	May I go home?
a) 집에 가도, ⌒ 좋습니다. ↘	You may go home.
b) 예, ⌒ 좋습니다. ↘	All right.
c) 어서 가세요. ⌒	Go home, please.

5. In denying permission for someone to do something, the negative imperative form is used.

집에 가도, ⌒ 좋습니까? ↗	May I go home?
a) 가지 마세요. ⌒	Please don't.
b) 가지 말아 주세요. ⌒	Please don't go home. (polite)

6. In denying permission not to do something, the affirmative imperative form is used.

집에 가지 않아도, ⌒ 좋습니까? ↗	Is it alright (even) if I don't go home?
a) 집에 가세요. ⌒	Go home, please.
b) 집에 가 주세요. ⌒	Go home, please. (polite)

VI. The suppositional infix -겠-

In Lesson 5, S.P. No. X, we have studied the intentional infix -겠-, stating or asking for the subject's intention, planning or schedule. The infix -겠- in other situations, however, has the meaning of supposition or conjecture. Now let's study the following examples:

저 책이 좋겠어요. ⌒	I suppose that book over there is good.
오후에 비가 오겠어요. ⌒	It will (probably) rain in the afternoon.
그분이 학생이겠어요. ⌒	I think he is a student.
그분이 벌써 갔겠어요. ⌒	I suppose (-겠-) he must have (-았-) gone already.

Notes:

1. The suppositional infix -겠- is inserted between the stem (or the stem plus

the honorific infix -시- and/or the past tense -았-) and the ending. It expresses the speaker's supposition or conjecture.

2. Pay special attention to the co-occurrence of the two infixes -았-(past tense) and -겠- (suppositional infix) as illustrated above in the last example.

3. While the intentional infix -겠- is used only with action verbs and 있, the suppositional infix -겠- may be used with any verb. The subject is usually the third person.

4. -겠어요 (or -겠습니다) may be replaced with the -겠지요 form without any difference in meaning.(See Lesson 6, S.P. No. III.)

그분이 집에 있겠어요.	He is probably at home. (or I think he is at home.)
그분이 공부하겠지요.	I think he is studying.

VII. <u>A.V.S. + -아(-어, -여)서</u> : "(does) and (does)"

Examples :

1. 집에 가서 공부하겠어요.	I'll go home and study.
2. 여기 와서 말씀하십시오.	Please come here and talk.
3. 나가서 기다리세요.	Please go out and wait.
4. 들어와서 말씀하시지요.	Please come in and talk.
5. 여기 앉아서 기다리세요.	Sit down here and wait, please.
6. 서서 읽으십시오.	Please stand up and read it.
7. 돌아앉아서 담배 피우세요.	Turn around, sit down, and smoke, please.
8. 일어나서 아침 잡수세요.	Please get up and eat breakfast.
9. 그분을 만나서 이야기 하십시오.	Go see him and have a talk, please.
10. 편지를 써서 부쳤습니다.	I wrote the letter and mailed it.

Notes :

1. To tell that the same one person performs "one action <u>and</u> a second one", you can build two complete sentences, connecting them with the conjunctive word 그리고. Another way of telling the same story is adding the "ending" -아(어,

-여)서 to the stem of the <u>first</u> (action) verb while giving the second (action) verb its normal sentence-final ending. Ex. 집에 <u>가서</u> 공부하겠어요. "I'll go home <u>and</u> study".

2. Notice that when using this pattern the subject of both verbs must be the same. If the subjects are different, the gerund form of the verb (V.S. + <u>-고</u>) is used. Ex. 나는 학교에 가고, 그분은 집에 가요. "I am going to school, and he is going home".

3. This pattern is used mostly when the first of the two verbs in question is <u>가다</u> or <u>오다</u> (or their compounds), or some other verb of movement of change of posture, like <u>앉다</u>, <u>서다</u> (or their compounds), or <u>일어나다</u>, etc. (See Ex. 1-8.) However, this is not exclusive. There are cases where the <u>-아(-어, -여)서</u> ending is used with action verbs other than <u>가다</u>, <u>오다</u>, etc. (See Ex. 9-10.)

4. Tenses are expressed in the main verb, not in the verb with <u>-아(-어, -여)서</u>.

5. <u>-아서</u> after <u>-아-</u> and <u>-오-</u>; <u>-어서</u> after any other vowel; <u>-여서</u> after <u>하-</u>, the stem of the verb 하다 "does".

Review :

We have already studied the gerund form of the verb (V.S. + <u>-고</u>) linking two clauses and meaning "and". (See Lesson 8, S.P.No. V.) Let's compare :

1. While in the pattern <u>-아(-어, -여)서</u> the subject must be the same, in the gerund form <u>-고</u> the subject of the two clauses can be either the same or different.

2. The pattern <u>-아(-어, -여)서</u> is used only with action verbs, whereas the pattern <u>-고</u> may be used with any verb. See the following examples :

그것은 싸고, ⌒ 좋아요. ⌒	That is cheap and good. (one subject)
저는 일하고, ⌒ 그분은 주무셔요. ⌒	I am working, and he is sleeping. (two subjects)
그분은 한국말을 공부하고, ⌒ 저는 영어를 공부해요. ⌒	He studies Korean, and I study English. (two subjects)

Text III

Ⅷ. The indirect discourse -고 하다 : "one says that"

If you know well how to handle the plain style studied in Lesson 10, S.P. No. Ⅵ, it is not difficult to understand this pattern -고 하다 which is usually attached to the plain style to express indirect discourse (except in a few cases, e.g., in the case of the verb of identification -이- in the present tense and imperative form). Some quotations repeat the exact words of the original speaker. However, a Korean quotation, particularly in the informal style, usually gives the gist of what is or was said, from the point of view of the person reporting the quotation. The quotation does retain the tense of the original.

(A) The declarative indirect discourse form :

Examples :

그분이 학생이라고 합니다. ↘	He says he is a student.
그분이 학생이었다고 합니다. ↘	He says he was a student.
그분이 학교에 간다고 합니다. ↘	He says he goes to school.
점심을 먹는다고 합니다. ↘	He says he is eating lunch.
학교에 갔다고 합니다. ↘	He says he went to school.
학교에 가겠다고 합니다. ↘	He says he will go to school.
이것이 좋다고 합니다. ↘	He says this is good.
이것이 좋았다고 합니다. ↘	He says this was good.
이것이 좋겠다고 합니다. ↘	He says this will be good.
그것이 교실에 있다고 합니다. ↘	He says it is in the classroom.
그것이 교실에 있었다고 합니다. ↘	He says it was in the classroom.

Note :

The -(이)라고 하다 shape of this ending occurs only in one case : with the copula -이- in the present tense (-라고 하다 after nominals ending in a vowel ; -이라고 하다 after nominals ending in a consonant). In all other cases the ending -고 하다 is attached directly to the plain declarative form of the verb.

(B) The interrogative indirect discourse form:

Examples:

학교에 ˅가느냐고 합니다. ↘	He asks if you (he, she) go to school.
학교에 ˅갔느냐고 합니다. ↘	He asks if you (he, she) went to school.
학교에 ˅가겠느냐고 합니다. ↘	He asks if you (he, she) will go to school.
이것이 ˅좋으냐고 합니다. ↘	He asks if this is good.
이것이 ˅좋았느냐고 합니다. ↘	He asks if this was good.
그것이 ˅어디 ˅있느냐고 합니다. ↘	He asks where it is.
그것이 ˅어디 ˅있었느냐고 합니다. ↘	He asks where it was.
그것이 ˅어디 ˅있겠느냐고 합니다. ↘	He asks where it will be.
그분이 ˅누구냐고 합니다. ↘	He asks who that person is.
그분이 ˅학생이냐고 합니다. ↘	He asks if he is a student.
그분이 ˅학생이었느냐고 합니다. ↘	He asks if he was a student.

Note:

To express the interrogative indirect discourse, the pattern -고 하다 is attached directly to the plain question form of the verb.

(C) The propositive indirect discourse form:

Examples:

학교에 ˅가자고 합니다. ↘	He says, "Let's go to school".
점심을 ˅먹자고 합니다. ↘	He says, "Let's eat lunch".
집에 ˅있자고 합니다. ↘	He says, "Let's stay at home".

Note:

To express the propositive indirect discourse, the pattern -고 하다 is attached directly to the plain propositive form of the verb.

(D) The imperative indirect discourse form:

Examples:

학교에 ˅가라고 합니다. ↘	He says, "Go to school".

점심을 먹으라고 합니다. ↘   He says, "Eat lunch".

한국말을 공부하라고 합니다. ↘   He says, "Study Korean".

교실에서 기다리라고 합니다. ↘   He says, "Wait in the classroom".

Notes :

1. As far as the imperative indirect discourse is concerned, -고 하다 is not attached to the plain imperative forms.

2. To express the imperative indirect discourse, -(으)라고 하다 is attached to the verb stem.

3. -라고 하다 after verb stems ending in a vowel ; -으라고 하다 after verb stems ending in a consonant.

Now let's compare the planin imperative forms (See Lesson 10, S.P.No. VI(D).) with the imperative indirect discourse, particularly noting the vowel changes.

Plain imperative forms :	Imperative indirect discourse forms :
이 칠판을 보아라. ↘	이 칠판을 보라고 합니다. ↘
점심을 먹어라. ↘	점심을 먹으라고 합니다. ↘
옷을 입어라. ↘	옷을 입으라고 합니다. ↘
공부하여라. ↘	공부하라고 합니다. ↘

(E) Another (polite) imperative indirect discourse form :

Examples :

그것 좀 보여 달라고 합니다. ↘   He says, "Show me that, please".

거기에 가 달라고 합니다. ↘   He says, "Go there, please".

여기에 와 달라고 합니다. ↘   He says, "Come here, please".

한국말을 가르쳐 달라고 합니다. ↘   He says, "Teach me Korean, please".

Note :

The pattern -고 하다 is attached directly to the plain imperative form of the verb 달라.

DRILLS

┌─ [ADDITIONAL VOCABULARY] ─────────────────────────┐

입어요(입지-) dresses   벗어요(벗지-) undresses
목사 pastor, church minister   가지고 가요(-가지-) takes
안 the inside   (something somewhere)
밖(바깥) the outside, the exterior   서요(서지-) stands
겉 the face, the surface

└──┘

Text I

A. Substitution Drill

1. **김 선생님**하고 같이 공부하겠어요. ⌒

   I'll study with Mr. Kim.

저 학생,	미스터 리,	목사님,
미스 박,	미스터 최	

2. **김 선생님**과 같이 일하겠어요. ⌒ (과/와)

   I'll work with Mr. Kim.

아버지,	목사님,	미스터 최,
신부님,	저 학생,	미스터 박

3. **머리가 아프기** 때문에 ⌒ 갈 수가 없

   어요. ⌒

   I can't go because I have a head-

   ache.

바쁘기,	시간이 없기,
돈이 없기,	숙제를 해야하기

B. Pattern Drill

Teacher : 그분이 가면 ⌒ 가겠어요. ⌒   If he goes, I'll go. (conditional)

Student : 그분이 가야 ⌒ 가겠어요. ⌒   Provided he goes, I'll go. (provisional)

1. 그분이 그것을 사면 저도 사겠어요.   그분이 그것을 사야 ⌒ 저도 사겠어요. ⌒

2. 그것이 좋으면 사겠어요.   그것이 좋아야 ⌒ 사겠어요. ⌒

3. 책이 있으면 공부할 수 있어요.   책이 있어야 ⌒ 공부할 수 있어요. ⌒

4. 날씨가 좋으면 등산하겠어요.　　　　날씨가 좋아야 ⌒ 등산하겠어요. ⌒

5. 바쁘지 않으면 놀러 가겠어요.　　　바쁘지 않아야 ⌒ 놀러 가겠어요. ⌒

6. 그분이 없으면 재미있게 놀 수 있어요.　그분이 없어야 ⌒ 재미있게 놀수있어요. ⌒

C. Integration Drill

Teacher : 가지 마십시오. ↘ 오십시오. ↘　　Don't go. Come, please.

Student : 가지 말고, ⌒ 오십시오. ↘　　　Don't go,(but) come, please.

1. 자지 마십시오. 공부하십시오.　　　자지 말고, ⌒ 공부하십시오. ↘

2. 공부하지 마십시오. 주무십시오.　　공부하지 말고, ⌒ 주무십시오. ↘

3. 먹지 마십시오. 가십시오.　　　　먹지 말고, ⌒ 가십시오. ↘

4. 놀지 마십시오. 일하십시오.　　　놀지 말고, ⌒ 일하십시오. ↘

5. 읽지 마십시오. 쓰십시오.　　　　읽지 말고, ⌒ 쓰십시오. ↘

6. 벗지 마십시오. 입으십시오.　　　벗지 말고, ⌒ 입으십시오. ↘

D. Response Drill

Teacher : 아직도 공부하지 않았어요? ↗

　　　　　Haven't you studied yet? (Did you not study yet?)

Student : 아니오, ↗ 벌써 공부했어요. ⌒

　　　　　Yes, I've already studied.

1. 그분이 아직도 가지 않았어요?　　아니오, ↗ 벌써 갔어요. ⌒

2. 아직도 숙제를 하지 않았어요?　　아니오, ↗ 벌써 했어요. ⌒

3. 아직도 그 일을 끝내지 않았어요?　아니오, ↗ 벌써 끝냈어요. ⌒

4. 그분이 아직도 일어나지 않았어요?　아니오, ↗ 벌써 일어났어요. ⌒

5. 아직도 세수하지 않았어요?　　　아니오, ↗ 벌써 세수했어요. ⌒

6. 아직도 그분한테 부탁하지 않았어　아니오, ↗ 벌써 부탁했어요. ⌒
　요?

E. Level Drill

Teacher : 학교에 갑시다. ↘　　　　Let's go to school.

Student : 학교에 가자. ↘　　　　　Let's go to school.

1. 점심을 먹읍시다.　　　　　　점심을 먹자. ↘

2. 한국말을 공부합시다.　　　　　　한국말을 공부하자. ↘

3. 그분한테 물어 봅시다.　　　　　　그분한테 물어 보자. ↘

4. 빨리 일어납시다.　　　　　　　　빨리 일어나자. ↘

5. 이 일을 끝냅시다.　　　　　　　　이 일을 끝내자. ↘

6. 여기서 기다립시다.　　　　　　　여기서 기다리자. ↘

F. Expansion Drill

공부하고 싶지 않아요. ⌢

그분하고 같이 공부하고 싶지 않아요. ⌢

엉터리 학생이기 때문에 ⌢ 그분하고 같이 공부하고 싶지 않아요. ⌢

그분이 엉터리 학생이기 때문에 ⌢ 그분하고 같이 공부하고 싶지 않아요. ⌢

I don't like to study with him because he is a clumsy student.

Text II

G. Substitution Drill

1. 이것을 먹어도 ⌢ 좋습니까? ↗	May I eat this?
2. 집에 가도 ⌢ 좋습니까? ↗	May I go home?
3. 그분을 만나도 ⌢ 좋습니까? ↗	May I meet him?
4. 이 책을 집에 가지고 가도 ⌢ 좋습니까? ↗	May I take this book home?
5. 밖에 나가도 ⌢ 좋습니까? ↗	May I go out?
6. 이 문을 열어도 ⌢ 좋습니까? ↗	May I open this door?

H. Substitution Drill

1. 묵주가 없어도 ⌢ 괜찮아요. ⌢	Even though you don't have a rosary, it's all right.
2. 돈이 없어도 ⌢ 괜찮아요. ⌢	Even though you don't have any money, it's all right.
3. 공부하지 않아도 ⌢ 괜찮아요. ⌢	Even though you don't study, it doesn't matter.

4. <u>그분을 만나지 않아도</u> 괜찮아요. It's all right even if you don't meet him.

5. <u>지금 숙제 하지 않아도</u> 괜찮아요. You don't have to do your homework now.

6. <u>지금 가르치지 않아도</u> 괜찮아요. You don't have to teach now.

I. Substitution Drill

1. <u>저 책이 좋겠어요.</u> I suppose that book over there is good.

2. <u>그분은 예쁘겠어요.</u> She must be beautiful. (or, I think she is beautiful.)

3. <u>그분이 벌써 도착했겠어요.</u> I suppose he must have arrived already.

4. <u>그분이 벌써 갔겠어요.</u> I suppose he must have gone already.

5. <u>오후에 비가 오겠어요.</u> It will (probably) rain in the afternoon.

6. <u>그것이 여기 있겠어요.</u> I think it's here. (or, it must be here.)

J. Integration Drill

Teacher : 그분을 만나십시오. 이야기 하십시오.

See him, please. Talk (with him), please.

Student : 그분을 만나서 이야기 하십시오.

See him and talk (with him), please.

1. 편지를 썼습니다. 부쳤습니다.　　편지를 써서 부쳤습니다.

2. 집을 팔았습니다. 자동차를 샀습니다.　　집을 팔아서 자동차를 샀습니다.

3. 나가세요. 기다리세요.　　나가서 기다리세요.

4. 들어오시지요. 말씀하시지요.　　들어와서 말씀하시지요.

5. 나오세요. 담배 피우세요.　　나와서 담배 피우세요.

6. 일어나세요. 아침 잡수세요.　　일어나서 아침 잡수세요.

K. Response Drill

Teacher : 집에 가도 좋습니까?　　May I go home?

Student : 아니오, 집에 가지 말아 주세요.　　No, please don't go home.

1. 이것을 먹어도 좋습니까?　　아니오, 이것을 먹지 말아 주세요.

2. 그분을 만나도 좋습니까?　　　　아니오, ↗ 그분을 만나지 말아 주세요. ⌒

3. 내일 와도 좋습니까?　　　　　　아니오, ↗ 내일 오지 말아 주세요. ⌒

4. 여기 앉아도 좋습니까?　　　　　아니오, ↗ 거기 앉지 말아 주세요. ⌒

5. 이 문을 열어도 좋습니까?　　　　아니오, ↗ 그 문을 열지 말아 주세요. ⌒

6. 이 문을 닫아도 좋습니까?　　　　아니오, ↗ 그 문을 닫지 말아 주세요. ⌒

L. Response Drill

Teacher : 집에 가지 않아도 ⌒ 좋습니까? ↗　　Is it all right (even) if I don't go home?

Student : 아니오, ↗ 집에 가 주세요. ⌒　　No, go home, please.

1. 그분을 만나지 않아도 좋습니까?　　아니오, ↗ 그분을 만나 주세요. ⌒

2. 내일 오지 않아도 좋습니까?　　아니오, ↗ 내일 와 주세요. ⌒

3. 이것을 가지고 가지 않아도 좋습니　　아니오, ↗ 그것을 가지고 가 주세요. ⌒
   까?

4. 그분을 기다리지 않아도 좋습니까?　　아니오, ↗ 그분을 기다려 주세요. ⌒

5. 숙제를 하지 않아도 좋습니까?　　아니오, ↗ 숙제를 해 주세요. ⌒

6. 이 문을 닫지 않아도 좋습니까?　　아니오, ↗ 그 문을 닫아 주세요. ⌒

M. Expansion Drill

만나 주세요. ⌒

그분을 만나 주세요. ⌒

선생님이 그분을 만나 주세요. ⌒

학교에 가서 ⌒ 선생님이 그분을 만나 주세요. ⌒

내일은 학교에 가서 ⌒ 선생님이 그분을 만나 주세요. ⌒

지금은 가지 않아도 괜찮지만, ⌒ 내일은 학교에 가서 ⌒ 선생님이 그분을 만나 주세요. ⌒

Even if you don't go now, it's all right, but go to school tomorrow and see him, please.

Text III

N. Substitution Drill (Descriptive verbs)

1. 한국말이 참 어렵다고 합니다. ↘   They say Korean is difficult.

2. 물건 값이 비싸다고 합니다. ↘   They say prices of things are high.

3. 날씨가 참 시원하다고 합니다. ↘   They say the weather is very cool.

4. 날씨가 참 따뜻하다고 합니다. ↘   They say the weather is very warm.

5. 한국말은 참 복잡하다고 합니다. ↘   They say Korean is very complicated.

O. Substitution Drill (action verbs : present)

1. 그분은 책을 읽는다고 합니다. ↘   He says he is reading a book.

2. 지금 학교에 간다고 합니다. ↘   He says he is going to school.

3. 한국말을 공부한다고 합니다. ↘   He says he is studying Korean.

4. 그분은 일찍 일어난다고 합니다. ↘   He says he gets up early.

5. 날마다 일한다고 합니다. ↘   He says he works every day.

P. Substitution Drill (D.V. and A.V.: past)

1. 학교에 갔다고 합니다. ↘   He says he went to school.

2. 그것이 참 좋았다고 합니다. ↘   He says it was very good.

3. 그분이 그분을 만났다고 합니다. ↘   He says he met him.

4. 그분이 학생이었다고 합니다. ↘   He says he was a student.

5. 이것이 교실에 있었다고 합니다. ↘   He says this was in the classroom.

Q. Substitution Drill

1. 학교에 가느냐고 합니다. ↘   He asks if you go to school.

2. 학교에 갔느냐고 합니다. ↘   He asks if you went to school.

3. 학교에 가겠느냐고 합니다. ↘   He asks if you will go to school.

4. 이것이 좋으냐고 합니다. ↘   He asks if this is good.

5. 이것이 좋았느냐고 합니다. ↘   He asks if this was good.

6. 그분이 누구냐고 합니다. ↘   He asks who that person is.

7. 그분이 학생이냐고 합니다. ↘   He asks if that person is a student.

R. Substitution Drill

1. 학교에 가자고 합니다. ↘   He says, "Let's go to school".

2. 점심을 먹자고 합니다. ↘   He says, "Let's eat lunch".

3. 집에 있자고 합니다.   He says, "Let's stay at home".

4. 한국말을 공부하자고 합니다.   He says, "Let's study Korean".

5. 빨리 시작하자고 합니다.   He says, "Let's start quickly".

S. Level Drill

Teacher : 학교에 가십시오.   Go to school, please.

Student : 학교에 가라.   Go to school.

1. 이 칠판을 보십시오.   이 칠판을 보아라.

2. 점심을 잡수십시오.   점심을 먹어라.

3. 한국말을 공부하십시오.   한국말을 공부해라.

4. 그분을 만나십시오.   그분을 만나라.

5. 이 책을 읽으십시오.   이 책을 읽어라.

6. 어서 가르치십시오.   어서 가르쳐라.

T. Level Drill

Teacher : 그것 좀 보여 주십시오.   Show me that, please.

Student : 그것 좀 보여 달라고 합니다. He says, "Show me that".

1. 거기 좀 가 주십시오.   거기 좀 가 달라고 합니다.

2. 여기 와 주십시오.   여기 와 달라고 합니다.

3. 한국말을 가르쳐 주십시오.   한국말을 가르쳐 달라고 합니다.

4. 좀 기다려 주십시오.   좀 기다려 달라고 합니다.

5. 문 좀 열어 주십시오.   문 좀 열어 달라고 합니다.

제십삼과 거리에서 (Lesson 13 On the Street)

TEXT I

[VOCABULARY]

거리 street
나와요(나오지-) comes out
세종문화회관 The Sejong Cultural
          Center
네거리 intersection
북쪽 north(direction)
올라가요(올라가지-) goes up
가까와요(가깝지-) is close, is near

1. 김철수 : 어디에 가시려고 이렇게 나오셨어요?

   (Having come out like this) where do you intend to go?

2. 매 리 : 예, 지금 세종문화회관에 좀 가려고 해요.

   I intend to go to the Sejong Cultural Center now.

3. 김철수 : 무슨 좋은 일이라도 있으신가요?

   Do you have anything good coming up?

4. 매 리 : 예, 친구를 좀 만날 일이 있어요. 그런데 세종문화회관이 어디쯤 있지요?

   I have to meet a friend on business. By the way, where is the Sejong Cultural Center?

5. 김철수 : 광화문 네거리 아시지요? 네거리를 건너서 북쪽으로 조금만 올라가세요.

   You know the Kwanghwamun intersection, don't you? Cross the intersection and just go north a short distance.

6. 매 리 : 여기서 멀어요?

   Is it far from here?

7. 김철수 : 아니오, 멀지 않아요. 가까와요.

   No, it's not far. It's close.

TEXT II

[VOCABULARY]

차 tea
-잔 a cup of (classifier)
슬슬 slowly, softly
쓸데없이 vainly, in vain, to no pur-
          pose

8. 김철수 : **차**나 한잔 **하**고서 **가**시지요.

   그렇게 **바**쁘지 않으시면,

   Have a cup of tea and then go.
   If you aren't busy, (why not)···

9. 매 리 : **아**니오, **지금 가** 봐야겠어요.

   늦게 가면 그 **친**구를 **만**나지

   못해요.

   No, I think I'll have to go now. If I'm
   late, I won't be able to meet my friend.

10. 김철수 : **그**럼, **왜 그**렇게 **슬**슬 **걸**어가

    시지요? **어**서 **택**시라도 **타**고

    가세요.

    Well then, why are you walking so
    slowly? Quickly take any taxi and
    go.

11. 매 리 : **아**니오, **버**스를 **타**고 **가**지

    요, 뭐. **쓸**데없이 **돈** 쓸

    필요 **없**잖아요?

    No, I am going to take the bus. There is
    no reason to waste money, is there?

12. 김철수 : **그**럼, **잘** 다녀오세요.

    Well, good-bye.

13. 매 리 : **예**, **갔**다 오겠어요.

    Good-bye.

TEXT III

┌─ [VOCABULARY] ─────────────────────────────────┐

물어요(묻지-) asks	바로 rightly, honestly
중앙우체국 the Central Post Office	돌아가요(돌아가지-) turns, makes a
낯선사람 a stranger	detour
길 road, way, street	신세계 Sinsegye
쭉 all the way, in a line	백화점 department store
내려가요(내려가지-) goes down	앞 in front of, before
오른쪽 right side, toward or to the	꼭 exactly, just, precisely
right	대단히 very much

└──┘

14. 매 리 : **실**례합니다. **미**안하지만,

    말씀 좀 **물**읍시다.

    중앙우체국이 **어**디 **있**어요?

    Excuse me. May I bother you for a
    moment? Where is the Central Post
    Office?

15. 낯선 사람 : 중앙우체국요?↗ 이 길로 쭉 내려가세요.⌒ 내려가다가↗ 오른쪽으로 돌아가세요.⌒ 바로 신세계 백화점 앞이에요.⌒

The Central Post Office?　Go all the way down this street and after a little while turn to the right.　It's directly in front of the Shinsegye department store.

16. 매　리 : 여기서 몇 분쯤 걸릴까요?⌒

How many minutes does it take from here?

17. 낯선 사람 : 글쎄요.⌐ 한 십 분쯤 걸릴까요?↗ 저도 꼭 한번 가 본 일이 있어요.⌒

Mm! About ten minutes. I've been there only once myself.

18. 매　리 : 대단히 감사합니다.⌐

Thank you very much.

19. 낯선 사람 : 천만의 말씀이에요.⌐

That's quite all right.

REMARKS TO THE TEXT

Text I

5. ○네거리 means literally "four(네) streets(거리)" and is used for any intersection of two streets. A three-forked road is called 삼거리. The vowel 어 in 거리 is long. 거리 with short 어 would mean "matter, business, or material". 북쪽 : 북 means "the north" and -쪽(bound form) means "direction", so 북쪽 means "the north". In the West the four directions are usually listed in the order of north-south-east-west, whereas in the Far East they are listed east-west-south-north. So Koreans say 동서남북.

해가 동쪽에서 뜹니다. ↘	The sun rises in the east.
해가 서쪽으로 집니다. ↘	The sun sets in the west.
남쪽은 따뜻합니다. ↘	The south is warm.
북쪽은 춥습니다. ↘	The north is cold.

○올라가다 means basically "goes up", "ascends". Pay attention to the different situations expressed in the following examples. :

어서 올라가십시오. ↘	Step in (to the house), please. (The 마루 "wooden floors" of Korean houses are above street level.)
산에 올라갑시다. ↘	Let's climb the mountain.
그분은 서울에 올라갔어요. ⌒	He travelled to Seoul. (Seoul is always "up".)
물건 값이 올라갔어요. ⌒	Prices have gone up.
그분은 대위로 올라갔어요. ⌒	He has been promoted to the rank of captain.

○올라오다 means "come up".

올라오십시오. ↘   Come in, please (into the house) ; or,
                                        Come up this staircase (or hill or any
                                        high place).

그분이 서울에 올라왔어요. ⌒   He came to Seoul. (Seoul is always
                                        "up".)

The opposite meaning "goes down" and "comes down" is conveyed by the following
verb combination. 내려가다 "goes down", 내려오다 "comes down". See the examples below :

그분이 부산에 내려갔어요. ⌒   He went (down) to Pusan (from Seoul).
산에서 내려갑시다. ↘   Let's go down the mountain.
물가가 내려가고 있어요. ⌒   Prices are falling.

6. ○여기서 is a contraction of 여기에서 "from here".

7. ○가깝다 means "is near". 가까운 : noun modifier form "near", "close". 가까이 or
가깝게 : adverbial form "closely". See the examples below :

여기서 학교까지 가깝습니다. ↘   It's close (not far) from here to the
                                        school.

학교는 우리 집에서 가까운 곳에 있어   My school is situated within easy reach
요. ⌒   of my house.

그분과 가까이하지 마세요. ⌒   Don't make friends with him. (Don't con-
                                        tract a friendship with him.)

Text II

8. ○차나 한잔 하고서 가시지요. 그렇게 바쁘지 않으시면 : this is an inverted
sentence. The dependent clause ending with …않으시면 is put after the main
clause, whereas dependent clauses usually come before the main clause. The inversion of the order sometimes makes the language more lively.

○차나 : 차 means "tea" but is also used as a general term for drinks sold in the
다방 "tearoom". For the particle -(이)나, see Lesson 10, S.P. No. IX. 한잔 means

"a cup of tea". -잔 is a classifier meaning "a cup (of)". It is used with the Korean numerals.

○하고서 : 하다 means "does" but in this sentence it stands for "drinks". For the ending -고서, see this lesson, S.P. No. Ⅴ.

Words for eating and drinking :

잡수시다   You (etc.) eat. (honorific)

들다   You (etc.) eat, drink. (honorific)

먹다   I eat.

마시다   You drink (not "eat").

먹다   The dog (etc.) eats.

이 음식 좀 잡수세요. ⌒	Help yourself to this food, please.
무엇을 잡수시겠읍니까? ↘	What would you like to eat?
자, ↘ 듭시다. ↘	Let's begin eating.
더 드시지요. ⌒	Will you take another helping?
많이 먹었습니다. ↘	I have had my fill.
너무 많이 마시지 마세요. ⌒	Don't drink too much.

10. ○걸어가다 is a compound verb of 걷다 "walks" and 가다 "goes". Therefore, 걸어가다 means literally "walks and goes". Note also 걸어오다 "comes on foot". For "direction" expressed by the verbs 가다 and 오다, see Lesson 5, Remarks to the Text, No. 2.

○택시라도 : 택시 "taxi" is derived from English. For the particle -(이)라도, see Lesson 11, S.P. No. Ⅸ.

○타다 means "gets on (a vehicle)", "takes (a vehicle)" or "rides"; the opposite of this is 내리다 "gets off (a vehicle)". 태우다 is an object verb meaning "gives (someone) a ride", or "takes (someone) on board". See the examples below :

어서 타십시오. ↘	Please get on.
어서 내리십시오. ↘	Please get off.
저는 자동차를 타고 싶어요. ⌒	I'd like a ride in the car.
좀 태워 주세요. ⌒	Please take me on board.

11. ○쓰다, depending on the context, can mean (1) "writes", (2) "uses", (3) "puts on" (hat, glasses, etc.) (4) "is bitter", etc.

여기에 이름을 쓰십시오. ↘   Write your name here, please.

영어를 쓰지 마세요. ⌒   Don't use (speak) English.

교실에서는 모자를 쓰지 마세요. ⌒   Don't put on your hat in the classroom.

좋은 약은 씁니다. ↘   Good medicine tastes bitter.

   ○필요 없잖아요 is a contraction of 필요 없지 않아요. 필요 is a nominal meaning "necessity, requirement"; 필요하다 is a descriptive verb meaning "is necessary".

13. ○갔다 오겠어요 is less polite than 다녀 오겠어요 which is the expression of farewell used when leaving "home". It is the reply to 다녀 오세요.

Text III

14. ○말씀 좀 물읍시다 means literally "May I ask you a question". 묻다 "asks" belongs to that group of irregular verbs whose stem ends with -ㄷ : See Lesson 11, S. P. No. Ⅷ.

15. ○오른쪽 means "right side", "toward the right". Its opposite is 왼쪽 "left side", "toward the left". Other words of the same meaning are : 바른쪽 or 우측 "right side" 좌측 "left side". -측 is of Chinese origin, equivalent to -쪽.

   ○바로, depending on the context, can mean (1) "rightly", "honestly", "correctly", "directly", "erectly", (2) "only", "just", etc.

책상 위에 바로 놓으세요. ⌒   Put that right on the desk.

바로 말씀하세요. ⌒   Tell me honestly.

바로 집으로 돌아가세요. ⌒   Go straight home.

바로 그때에 그분이 왔어요. ⌒   Just at that time he came.

바로 내 옆에 그분이 앉아 있었어요. ⌒   He was sitting right beside me.

앞	"before", "front"	안	"inside"(something spacious)
뒤	"behind", "back"	속	"inside"(something small or full)
위	"above", "(on) top of"	밖	"outside"

가운데	"center", "between"	왼편	"left side (of)"
아래	"below", "underneath"	바른편	"right side (of)"
밑	"(at the) bottom of"	맞은편	"across from"
옆	"beside", "side"	사이	"between"
다음	"next (to)"		

All these words are nominals and occur with the following particles: -가/-이, -를/-을, -에, -에서, -으로, etc.

STRUCTURAL PATTERNS

Text I

I. The suffix -(으)려고 : A.V.S. +-(으)려고 : "in order to" (purpose)

Examples :

한국말을 공부하려고⌒ 한국에 왔어요.⌒   I came to Korea to study Korean.

점심을 먹으려고⌒ 여기 왔어요.⌒   I came here to eat lunch.

공부하려고⌒ 일찍 일어났어요.⌒   I got up early to study.

Notes :

1. The suffix -(으)려고 is attached to the stem of action verbs and expresses the purpose of the action. The phrase or clause with -(으)려고 always precedes the main clause.

2. The suffix -(으)러 also expresses purpose but it is used only when followed by either 가다 or 오다 or their compounds (See Lesson 10, S.P.No. Ⅶ), whereas the suffix (으)려고 can be followed by any action verb.

3. -려고 after verb stems ending in a vowel ; -으려고 after verb stems ending in a consonant.

4. The tense is regularly expressed in the main clause, not in the verb with -(으)려고.

II. The pattern -(으)려고 하다 : "be going to do"(intention)

Examples :

1. Present affirmative forms :

한국말을 공부하려고 합니다. ↘   I am going to study Korean.

영어를 가르치려고 합니다. ↘   I am going to teach English.

여기에 있으려고 합니다. ↘   I am going to stay here.

2. Present negative forms :

그분을 ˘만나지 않으려고 합니다. ↘   I am not going to meet him.

그 책을 ˘사지 않으려고 합니다. ↘   I am not going to buy that book.

학교에 ˘가지 않으려고 합니다. ↘   I am not going to go to school.

3. Past affirmative forms:

영어를 ˘가르치려고 했어요. ⌢   I was going to teach English.

그분을 ˘만나려고 했어요. ⌢   I was going to meet him.

그 책을 ˘사려고 했어요. ⌢   I was going to buy that book.

4. Past negative forms:

그분을 ˘만나지 않으려고 했어요. ⌢   I was not going to meet him.

그때 ˘자지 않으려고 했어요. ⌢   I was not going to sleep at that time.

점심을 ˘먹지 않으려고 했어요. ⌢   I was not going to eat lunch.

5. Question forms:

그분을 ˘만나려고 합니까? ↗   Are you going to meet him?

그분을 ˘만나지 않으려고 합니까? ↗   Aren't you going to meet him?

그분을 ˘만나려고 했습니까? ↗   Were you going to meet him?

그분을 ˘만나지 않으려고 했습니까? ↗   Weren't you going to meet him?

Notes:

1. The pattern -(으)려고 하다 is attached to the stem of action verbs or -있 and indicates the subject's intention, planning or schedule. It corresponds to English "is going to".

2. The meaning of the pattern -(으)려고 하다 is roughly similar to that of the intentional infix -겠-. (See Lesson 5, S.P. No. X.) However, the pattern -(으)려고 하다 is slightly weaker than the intentional infix -겠-.

3. While the intentional infix -겠- is used with the first and second person, the pattern -(으)려고 하다 can be used with all persons.

4. -려고 하다 after verb stems ending in a vowel; -(으)려고 하다 after verb stems ending in a consonant.

5. The past tense is regularly expressed in the final verb 하-, not in the verb with -(으)려고.

III. The informal polite speech ending -는가요? (-ㄴ(은)가요?)

Examples:

(A) 그것이 좋은가요? ↗   Is that good?

그 여자가 예쁜가요? ↗   Is she beautiful?

그분이 학생인가요? ↗   Is he a student?

(B) 무엇을 하시는가요? ⌢   What are you doing?

그분이 갔는가요? ↗   Did he go?

그분이 예뻤는가요? ↗   Was she so beautiful?

그분이 돈이 있는가요? ↗   Does he have money?

그분이 돈이 있었는가요? ↗   Did he have money?

그분이 선생이었는가요? ↗   Was he a teacher?

Notes:

1. The -ㄴ(은)가요 shape of this ending occurs in two cases: with descriptive verbs in the present tense and with -이- in the present tense. In all other cases the ending is -는가요.

2. The ending -ㄴ(은, 는)가요, used with any verb, is similar in meaning to the ending -나요. (See Lesson 10, S.P. No. IV.)

3. It is an informal polite way of asking questions or expressing doubt.

4. By dropping the final particle -요, you get the intimate style form. With children and sometimes with close friends you use the intimate style form.

IV. The pattern -ㄹ(을) 일이 있다 : A.V.S.+-ㄹ(을) 일이 있다 : "has something to do"

Examples:

지금 할 일이 있습니다. ↘   I have something to do now.

그분을 만날 일이 있어요. ⌢   I have to meet him.

기차를 탈 일이 있어요. ⌢   I have to catch the train.

Notes:

1. The pattern -ㄹ(을) 일이 있다 is attached to action verbs and expresses "has something to do in the future"; the negative of this is -ㄹ(을) 일이 없다.

2. The tense is regularly expressed in the final verb 있다 or 없다. See the fol-

lowing examples:

할 일이 있었습니다. ↘   I had something to do.

할 일이 없었습니다. ↘   I had nothing to do.

3. -ㄹ 일이 있다 after verb stems ending in a vowel; -을 일이 있다 after verb stems ending in a consonant.

Text II

V. A.V.S. + -고서: "(does) after (doing)"

Examples:

아침을 먹고서⌒ 왔어요. ⌒   I came after (having taken) breakfast.

공부하고서⌒ 갑시다. ↘   Let's study first and then go.

차 한잔 들고서⌒ 가겠어요. ⌒   I'll go after taking a cup of tea.

숙제를 하고서⌒ 주무세요. ⌒   Please go to sleep after doing the homework.

Notes:

1. To tell that the same one person performs a second action <u>after</u> having previous-ly completed another one, you add the ending -고서 to the verb stem of the first (action) verb, while giving the second verb its normal sentence-final ending.

2. Notice that when using this pattern the subject of both verbs must be the same.

3. Any action verb can go with this ending except the verbs 가다, 오다 (or their compounds), and some other verbs of movement or change of posture, like 앉다, 서다 (or their compounds), 일어나다, etc. These verbs always go with the -아(-어, -여)서 ending.

4. In the -아(-어, -여)서 "(does) and (does)" pattern studied in Lesson 12, S.P. No. VII, there is a certain continuation from the first action to the second. Look again at the examples given in Lesson 12; then look at the following examples:

그분을 만나서⌒ 이야기 하십시오. ↘   See him and talk (to him). (the same person)

편지를 ˇ써서⌒ 부쳤습니다. ↘   I wrote a letter and mailed it.

집을 ˇ팔아서⌒ 차를 ˇ샀습니다. ↘   I sold the house (and used that money) to buy a car.

In the -고서 "(does) after (doing)" pattern, this continuation is not necessarily present. A clear-cut discontinuation sometimes appears in sentences with the -고서 "(does) after (doing)" pattern. Compare the following minimal pair sentences :

a) 그분을 ˇ만나서⌒ 이야기 합시다. ↘   Let's meet him and talk (to him). (the same person)

    그분을 ˇ만나고서⌒ 이야기 합시다. ↘   Let's talk (the two of us) after you meet that man.

b) 편지를 ˇ써서⌒ 드리겠습니다. ↘   I'll write this letter and give it to you.

    편지를 ˇ쓰고서⌒ 드리겠습니다. ↘   I'll give it (e.g., the money you have asked for) to you after I have finished writing this letter.

5. The pattern -고서 "(does) after (doing)" answers the non-expressed question "when?", while the pattern -아(-어, -여)서 "(does) and (does)" answers the question "what?"

6. You can drop -서 in colloquial speech, but it sounds more stressed (emphatic) or formal when -서 is used. Therefore, in the beginning stage it is better to practice this pattern with -서. After you have mastered the pattern you are free to drop it.

7. The tense is regularly expressed in the final clause, not in the first clause with -고서.

VI. The pattern -ㄹ(을) 필요가 있다(없다) : "it is (not) necessary to do"

Examples :

가실 필요가 ˇ있습니까? ↗   Is it necessary to go?

한국말을 ˇ공부할 필요가 ˇ있어요. ⌒   It is necessary to study Korean.

그분을 도와줄 필요가 없어요. ⌒   It is not necessary to help him.

여기에 있을 필요가 없어요. ⌒   It is not necessary to stay here.

Notes :

1. The pattern -ㄹ(을) 필요가 있다 is attached to action verbs or 있- and expresses necessity ; the negative of this is -ㄹ(을) 필요가 없다 "it is not necessary". After 필요, the particle -가 is optional.

2. The tense is regularly expressed in the final verb 있다 or 없다. See the following examples :

   그분을 만날 필요가 있었어요. ⌒   It was necessary to meet him.

   그분을 도와줄 필요가 없었어요. ⌒   It was not necessary to help him.

   지금 갈 필요가 없겠어요. ⌒   I think it's not necessary to go now.

3. -ㄹ 필요가 있다(없다) after verb stems ending in a vowel ; -을 필요가 있다 (없다) after verb stems ending in a consonant.

Text III

VII. The pattern -ㄹ(을)까요?

   Examples :

   여기서 몇 분쯤 걸릴까요? ⌒   How many minutes do you think it takes from here?

   몇 사람쯤 왔을까요? ⌒   How many people do you think came?

   그분이 무엇을 했을까요? ⌒   What do you think he did?

   Notes :

1. The sentence-final -ㄹ(을)까요? with the final intonation contour going up indicates that someone is inquiring about the second person's opinion. The subject of the sentence is usually the third person.

2. -ㄹ까요? after verb stems ending in a vowel ; -을까요? after verb stems ending in a consonant.

3. By dropping the final particle -요, you get the intimate style form. See Lesson 5, S.P. No. IV, and compare with this pattern.

Ⅷ. The pattern -는 일이 있다(없다) :

(A) A.V.S. + -는 일이 있다 : "sometimes does", "does indeed (on occasion)"

그분을 만나는 일이 있어요. ⌒   I sometimes meet him. (There are times when I meet him.)

그분은 담배를 피우는 일이 있어요. ⌒   He sometimes smokes. (There are times when he smokes.)

저는 술을 마시는 일이 있어요. ⌒   I sometimes drink. (There are times when I drink.)

(B) A.V.S. + -는 일이 없다 : "never does", "doesn't ever do"

그분은 산보하는 일이 없어요. ⌒   He doesn't ever take a walk. (There is never a time when he takes a walk.)

그분은 술을 마시는 일이 없어요. ⌒   He never drinks. (There is never a time when he drinks.)

택시로 가지 않는 일이 없어요. ⌒   I always go by taxi. (There is never a time when I don't go by taxi.)

Notes :

1. The pattern -는 일이 있다(없다) means literally "the act, fact, or experience of doing exists(or does not exist)". It is used only with action verbs. (The modifier marker -는 used with action verbs refers to the present tense.)

2. It corresponds to the English "there are times(or there is never a time) when (someone) does(or doesn't do) so-and-so".

3. The tense is regularly expressed in the final verb 있다 or 없다.

그분하고 공부하는 일이 있었어요. ⌒   I sometimes studied with him.

그분하고 공부하는 일이 없었어요. ⌒   I never studied with him.

Ⅸ. The pattern -ㄴ(은) 일이 있다(없다) : "(someone) has ever (never) done so-and-so"

Examples :

서울에 간 일이 있습니까? ↗   Have you ever been to Seoul?

서울에 간 일이 없습니다. ↘   I've never been to Seoul.

그분을 만난 일이 있어요. ⌒   I've met him.

그 책을 읽어 본 일이 없어요. ⌒   I've never read that book.

Notes:

1. The pattern -ㄴ(은) 일이 있다(없다) means literally "the act, fact, or experience of <u>having done</u> something exists (or doesn't exist)". This pattern expresses one's past experience.

2. This pattern corresponds to the English "(someone) has (never) done so-and-so". In question form, it is equivalent to English "have (you) ever done so-and-so?".

3. The pattern -ㄴ(은) 일이 있다 is interchangeable with <u>-아(-어, -여) 본 일이</u> <u>있다</u> or <u>-아(-어, -여) 보았다</u> without any difference in meaning. See the examples below:

그분을 만난 일이 있어요? ↗

그분을 만나 본 일이 있어요? ↗   Have you ever met him?

그분을 만나 보았어요? ↗

4. <u>-ㄴ 일이 있다</u> after verb stems ending in a vowel; <u>-은 일이 있다</u> after verb stems ending in a consonant.

DRILLS

┌─ 〔ADDITIONAL VOCABULARY〕 ─────────────────────┐

동	the east	올라와요(-오지-)	comes up
서	the west	내려가요(-가지-)	goes down
남	the south	내려와요(-오지-)	comes down
북	the north	중요해요(-하지-)	is important
노래불러요(-부르지-)	sings a song	급해요(급하지-)	is urgent
마셔요(마시지-)	drinks	걸어와요(-오지-)	comes on foot
들어요(들지-)	eats or drinks	내려요(내리지-)	gets off
태워요(태우지-)	gives(someone) a ride or takes(someone) on board	마차	coach, carriage
		뒤	back, rear
왼쪽	left side	놓아요(놓지-)	puts, places, lays
위	over, above, top	밑	bottom, the base
아래	the lower part, under, base	가운데	middle
옆	side	배	boat, ship

└──┘

Text I

A. Substitution Drill

1. 무슨 급한 일이라도 있으신가요? ↗
   Is there any urgent business?

┌─────────────────────────────────────┐
| 좋은,   중요한,   재미있는, |
| 바쁜,   복잡한,   기분 나쁜 |
└─────────────────────────────────────┘

B. Substitution Drill

1. 한국말을 공부하려고 합니다. ↘   I am going to study Korean.

2. 영어를 가르치려고 합니다. ↘   I am going to teach English.

3. 여기에 있으려고 합니다. ↘   I am going to stay here.

4. 그분을 만나려고 합니다. ↘   I am going to meet him.

5. 내일 아침에 일찍 일어나려고 합니다. ↘   I am going to get up early tomorrow morning.

C. Substitution Drill

1. **지금** 할 일이 **있습니다**. ↘   I have something to do now.

2. **볼** 일이 **있습니다**. ↘   I have some business to attend to.

3. **학교에 갈** 일이 **있습니다**. ↘   I have to go to school.

4. **기차를 탈** 일이 **있습니다**. ↘   I have to catch the train.

5. **그분한테 부탁할** 일이 **있습니다**. ↘   I have to ask him for something.

6. **그분을 찾**아갈 일이 **있습니다**. ↘   I have to visit him.

D. Pattern Drill

Teacher : **그분을 만나려고** 합니다. ↘   I am going to meet him.

Student : **그분을 만나지** 않으려고 합   I am not going to meet him.
니다. ↘

1. 그 책을 사려고 합니다.   그 책을 **사**지 않으려고 합니다. ↘

2. 학교에 가려고 합니다.   **학교에 가**지 않으려고 합니다. ↘

3. 점심을 먹으려고 합니다.   **점**심을 **먹**지 않으려고 합니다. ↘

4. 서울에 올라오려고 합니다.   서울에 **올라오**지 않으려고 합니다. ↘

5. 부산에 내려가려고 합니다.   부산에 **내려가**지 않으려고 합니다. ↘

6. 노래를 부르려고 합니다.   노래를 **부르**지 않으려고 합니다. ↘

E. Pattern Drill

Teacher : **그것이 좋습니까**? ↗   Is that alright?

Student : **그것이 좋**은가요? ↗   Is that alright?

1. 그 여자가 예쁩니까?   그 여자가 **예쁜**가요? ↗

2. 그분이 학생입니까?   그분이 **학생인**가요? ↗

3. 무엇을 하십니까?   무엇을 **하시는**가요? ⌒

4. 그분이 어디에 갔습니까?   그분이 **어디에 갔는**가요? ⌒

5. 그분이 돈이 있습니까?   그분이 **돈이 있는**가요? ↗

6. 무엇을 가르치십니까?   무엇을 **가르치시는**가요? ⌒

F. Integration Drill

Teacher : **한국말을 공**부하려고 했습니다. ↘ **한국에 왔**습니다. ↘

I was going to study Korean. I came to Korea.

Student : 한국말을 공부하려고 한국에 왔습니다.

I came to Korea to study Korean.

1. 그분을 만나려고 했습니다. 교실에 갔습니다.

　그분을 만나려고 교실에 갔습니다.

2. 점심을 먹으려고 했습니다. 여기에 왔습니다.

　점심을 먹으려고 여기에 왔습니다.

3. 프랑스에 가려고 합니다. 불어를 공부합니다.

　프랑스에 가려고 불어를 공부합니다.

4. 공부하려고 했습니다. 일찍 일어났습니다.

　공부하려고 일찍 일어났습니다.

5. 친구한테 주려고 했습니다. 이 책을 샀습니다.

　친구한테 주려고 이 책을 샀습니다.

6. 극장에 가려고 합니다. 옷을 입고 있습니다.

　극장에 가려고 옷을 입고 있습니다.

G. Pattern Drill

Teacher : 학교에 가십시오.　　　　　Go to school, please.

Student : 학교에 가라고 합니다.　　　He says, "Go to school".

1. 공부하십시오.　　　　　　공부하라고 합니다.

2. 영어를 가르치십시오.　　　영어를 가르치라고 합니다.

3. 여기서 기다리십시오.　　　여기서 기다리라고 합니다.

4. 서울에 올라가십시오.　　　서울에 올라가라고 합니다.

5. 빨리 이 일을 끝내십시오.　빨리 이 일을 끝내라고 합니다.

6. 이 책을 읽으십시오.　　　　이 책을 읽으라고 합니다.

H. Expansion Drill

오려고 합니다.

다시 오려고 합니다.

내일 다시 오려고 합니다.

그분이 계시지 않기 때문에 내일 다시 오려고 합니다.

학교에 왔지만⌒ 그분이 계시지 않기 때문에⌒ 내일 다시 오려고 합니다. ↘

김 선생님을 만나려고⌒ 학교에 왔지만⌒ 그분이 계시지 않기 때문에⌒ 내일 다시 오려고 합니다. ↘

I came to school to meet Mr. Kim, but since he is not here, I'll come again tomorrow.

Text II

I. Substitution Drill

1. 공부할 필요가 있어요. ⌒

It is necessary to study.

만날,	가르칠,	기다릴,
배울,	도와줄,	일어날

2. 늦게 가면, ⌒ 그 친구를 만나지 못해요. ⌒ (을/를)

If I go late, I won't be able to meet my friend.

내일 — 그분,
금요일 — 한 선생님,
너무 일찍 — 그 친구

3. 어서 택시라도 타고 가세요. ⌒

Quick! Take any taxi and go.

배,	기차,	버스,
전차,	마차,	비행기

J. Integration Drill

Teacher : 공부합시다. ↘ 갑시다. ↘   Let's study. Let's go.

Student : 공부하고서⌒ 갑시다. ↘   Let's study first and then go.

1. 아침을 먹었어요. 왔어요.   아침을 먹고서⌒ 왔어요. ⌒
2. 숙제를 하세요. 주무세요.   숙제를 하고서⌒ 주무세요. ⌒
3. 이 일을 끝내세요. 집에 가세요.   이 일을 끝내고서⌒ 집에 가세요. ⌒
4. 이 책을 읽으세요. 그분을 만나세요.   이 책을 읽고서⌒ 그분을 만나세요. ⌒
5. 세수하세요. 아침을 잡수세요.   세수하고서⌒ 아침을 잡수세요. ⌒

K. Pattern Drill

Teacher : 한국말을 가르쳐 주십시오. ↘

Teach me Korean, please.

Student : 한국말을 가르쳐 달라고 합니다. ↘

He says, "Please teach me Korean".

1. 좀 도와 주십시오.   좀 도와 달라고 합니다. ↘
2. 이 책을 읽어 주십시오.   이 책을 읽어 달라고 합니다. ↘
3. 그분을 소개해 주십시오.   그분을 소개해 달라고 합니다. ↘
4. 이 구두를 닦아 주십시오.   이 구두를 닦아 달라고 합니다. ↘
5. 노래를 불러 주십시오.   노래를 불러 달라고 합니다. ↘

L. Response Drill

Teacher : 한국말을 공부할 필요가 있어요? ↗

         Is it necessary to study Korean?

Student : 아니요, ↗ 한국말을 공부할 필요가 없어요. ⌒

         No, it is not necessary to study Korean.

1. 그분을 만날 필요가 있어요?   아니오, ↗ 그분을 만날 필요가 없어요. ⌒
2. 지금 가르칠 필요가 있어요?   아니오, ↗ 지금 가르칠 필요가 없어요. ⌒
3. 그분을 도와줄 필요가 있어요?   아니오, ↗ 그분을 도와줄 필요가 없어요. ⌒
4. 그분한테 부탁할 필요가 있어요?   아니오, ↗ 그분한테 부탁할 필요가 없어
                                       요. ⌒
5. 일찍 일어날 필요가 있어요?   아니오, ↗ 일찍 일어날 필요가 없어요. ⌒

M. Pattern Drill

Teacher : 그분이 여기서 일했어요. ⌒

         He worked here.

Student : 여기서 일한 그분이 누구예요? ⌒

         Who was that person who worked here?

1. 그분이 한국말을 가르쳤어요.   ·   한국말을 가르친 그분이 누구예요? ⌒
2. 그분이 편지를 썼어요.   편지를 쓴 그분이 누구예요? ⌒
3. 그분이 김 선생님을 소개했어요.   김 선생님을 소개한 그분이 누구예요? ⌒
4. 그분이 이 구두를 닦았어요.   이 구두를 닦은 그분이 누구예요? ⌒
5. 그분이 어제 돌아왔어요.   어제 돌아온 그분이 누구예요? ⌒

N. Expansion Drill

갈 필요가 없어요. ⌒

저는 ˇ갈 필요가 ˇ없어요. ⌒

그분이 ˇ왔기 때문에⌒ 저는 ˇ갈 필요가 ˇ없어요. ⌒

만나러 ˇ가려고 했지만⌒ 그분이 ˇ왔기 때문에⌒ 저는 ˇ갈 필요가 ˇ없어요. ⌒

그분을 ˇ만나러 ˇ가려고 했지만⌒ 그분이 ˇ왔기 때문에⌒ 저는 ˇ갈 필요가 ˇ없어요. ⌒

숙제를 마치고서⌒ 그분을 ˇ만나러 ˇ가려고 했지만⌒ 그분이 ˇ왔기 때문에⌒ 저는 ˇ갈 필요가 ˇ없어요. ⌒

After finishing my homework I intended to go and meet him, but because he came (himself), there is no need to go.

Text III

O. Substitution Drill

1. 그것을 ˇ책상 ˇ오른쪽에 ˇ놓으세요. ⌒
   Put that on the right side of the desk.

위,	뒤,	아래,	왼쪽,
옆,	앞,	가운데	

2. 내려가다가⌒ 왼쪽으로 ˇ돌아가세요. ⌒
   On the way down, turn left, please.

동,	서,	남,	북,	학교,	우체국

P. Substitution Drill

1. 그분을 ˇ만나는 일이 ˇ있어요. ⌒

I sometimes meet him. (There are times when I meet him.)

2. 그분은 ˇ담배를 피우는 일이 ˇ있어요. ⌒

He sometimes smokes. (There are times when he smokes.)

3. 저는 ˇ술을 마시는 일이 ˇ있어요. ⌒

I sometimes drink. (There are times when I drink.)

4. 비행기로 ˇ가는 일이 ˇ있어요. ⌒

I sometimes go by airplane. (There are times when I go by plane.)

5. 그분은 ˇ산보하는 일이 ˇ있어요. ⌒

He sometimes takes a walk. (There are times when he takes a walk.)

6. 집에 ˇ늦게 가는 일이 ˇ있어요. ⌒

I sometimes go home late. (There are times when I go home late.)

Q. Pattern Drill

Teacher : 그분을 만나는 일이 있어요. ⌒   I sometimes meet him.

Student : 그분을 만난 일이 있어요. ⌒   I've met him.

1. 영어를 가르치는 일이 있어요.   영어를 가르친 일이 있어요. ⌒

2. 그분은 담배를 피우는 일이 있어요.   그분은 담배를 피운 일이 있어요. ⌒

3. 그분하고 공부하는 일이 있어요.   그분하고 공부한 일이 있어요. ⌒

4. 그분하고 산보하는 일이 있어요.   그분하고 산보한 일이 있어요. ⌒

5. 집에 늦게 가는 일이 있어요.   집에 늦게 간 일이 있어요. ⌒

R. Response Drill

Teacher : 그분이 산보하는 일이 있어요? ↗   Does he sometimes take a walk? (Are there times when he takes a walk?)

Student : 아니오, ↗ 그분이 산보하는 일이 없어요. ⌒   No, he never takes a walk.(No, there is never a time when he takes a walk.)

1. 그분은 술을 마시는 일이 있어요?   아니오, ↗ 그분은 술을 마시는 일이 없어요. ⌒

2. 그분이 담배를 피우는 일이 있어요?   아니오, ↗ 그분이 담배를 피우는 일이 없어요. ⌒

3. 집에 늦게 가는 일이 있어요?   아니오, ↗ 집에 늦게 가는 일이 없어요. ⌒

4. 그분한테 부탁하는 일이 있어요?   아니오, ↗ 그분한테 부탁하는 일이 없어요. ⌒

5. 그 여자를 만나는 일이 있어요?   아니오, ↗ 그 여자를 만나는 일이 없어요. ⌒

S. Response Drill

Teacher : 한국말을 공부한 일이 있습니까? ↗

Have you ever studied Korean?

Student : 아니오, ↗ 한국말을 공부한 일이 없습니다. ↘

No, I've never studied Korean.

1. 그분을 만난 일이 있습니까?   아니오, ↗ 그분을 만난 일이 없습니다. ↘

2. 그 영화를 본 일이 있습니까?   아니오, ↗ 그 영화를 본 일이 없습니다. ↘

3. 거기서 시계를 산 일이 있습니까? 아니오, ↗ 거기서 시계를 산 일이 없습니다. ↘

4. 그 여자하고 산보한 일이 있습니까? 아니오, ↗ 그 여자하고 산보한 일이 없습니다. ↘

5. 그분하고 술을 마신 일이 있습니까? 아니오, ↗ 그분하고 술을 마신 일이 없습니다. ↘

T. Response Drill

1. 여기서 몇 분쯤 걸릴까요? 여기서 십 분쯤 걸릴 것 같습니다. ↘

2. 몇 사람쯤 왔을까요? 열 사람쯤 왔을 것 같습니다. ↘

3. 그분이 그 여자를 만났을까요? 예, ⌒ 그분이 그 여자를 만났을 것 같습니다. ↘

4. 그분이 몇 시쯤 도착할까요? 그분이 세 시쯤 도착할 것 같습니다. ↘

5. 그분이 지금 집에 계실까요? 예, ⌒ 그분이 지금 집에 계실 것 같습니다. ↘

제십사과 우체국에서 (Lesson 14 In the Post Office)

TEXT I

[VOCABULARY]

과장 the chief of a section	부쳐 줘요(부쳐 주지-) mails for me
전보 telegram	우표 stamp
쳐요(치지-) telegraphs	-짜리 value, worth
곧 soon, at once	

1. 김수경 : 우체국에 좀 다녀오겠습니다. ↘
   지금 갔다와도⌒ 괜찮을까요?↗

   I am going to the post office. Is it all right if I go now?

2. 과 장 : 예,⌒ 어서 다녀오세요.⌒ 그러
   나 할 일이 많으니까,⌒ 빨리
   돌아오세요.⌒

   Please go. But since there is a lot to do, hurry back.

3. 김수경 : 전보 한 장 치고서⌒ 곧 돌아
   오지요.⌒

   I'll send a telegram and come right back.

4. 과 장 : 그러면⌒ 가는 길에 이 편지 좀
   부쳐 주세요.⌒ 그리고 우표도
   석 장 사 주시고요.⌒

   (Then) on the way please mail this letter and also buy three stamps for me.

5. 김수경 : 얼마짜리 우표 사 드릴까요?⌒

   What (price) stamps shall I buy for you?

6. 과 장 : 팔십 원짜리 우표로 사 주세요.⌒

   Eighty wŏn stamps, please.

TEXT II

[VOCABULARY]

담당계원 person in charge	저리 there
항공편 airmail	아무 anyone, any
선편 sea mail, surface mail	자리 seat
용지 (blank) form	

7. 김수경 : **이** 편지 **미국에 부치려고 해**
   요. ⌢ **얼마짜리 우표를 붙여야**
   하지요? ↗

I want to send this letter to America. What does it cost? (What price stamp must I affix?)

8. 우표담당계원 : **항공편** 말이에요, ⌢ **선**
   편 말이에요? ⌢

Do you mean airmail or sea mail?

9. 김수경 : **항공편으로요.** ⌢

Airmail!

10. 우표담당계원 : **사백** 사십 원짜리 우표
    를 붙이면 ⌢ **돼요.** ⌢

A 440 wǒn stamp will do.

11. 김수경 : **고맙습니다.** ⌐ **그런데 전보**
    용지 한 장 주시겠어요? ↗

Thank you. Would you give me a blank form for telegram, please?

12. 우표담당계원 : **저리로 가세요.** ⌢

Go over there.

    아, ⌢ **자리에 아무도 없군요.** ⌢

Oh! There is no one there.

    잠깐 기다려 주세요. ⌢

Wait a moment, please.

TEXT
III

┌─ 〔VOCABULARY〕 ─

국내 the interior, domestic	사람 man, human being
지급전보 fast telegram	소용없어요(소용없지-) is of no use,
열자 ten letters	needless
이내 within, under	그만둬요(그만두지-) stops, ceases,
도착해요(도착하지-) reaches,	gives up
arrives at	

13. 김수경 : **국내 지급전보는 얼마지요?** ↗

What does it cost to send a domestic fast telegram, please?

14. 전보담당계원 : **열** 자 이내에 **오백 원이**
    에요. ⌢

Under ten letters (it costs) 500 wǒn.

15. 김수경 : **오전 열시** 차로 **사람이 부산**
    으로 떠났는데요. ⌢ **사람이 도**
    착하기 전에 ⌢ **전보가 먼저 갈**
    까요? ↗

This morning at ten someone left for Pusan. Will the telegram get there before he arrives?

16. 전보담당계원 : 지금 세 시니까, ⌒ 글 Since it's already three o'clock, it will
    쎄⌐ 좀 어렵겠는데요. ⌒ be difficult.

17. 김수경 : 그럼 지금 쳐도⌒ 소용없겠군 Then if I send it, it would be of no value.
    요. ⌒

18. 전보담당계원 : 예, ⌒ 그만두시는 것이 Yes, I agree. You shouldn't send it.
    좋겠군요. ⌒

REMARKS TO THE TEXT

Text I

3. ○전보 is a nominal meaning "telegram"; 전보치다 or 전보하다 "telegraphs", "wires","cables", etc.

　○곧 is an adverbial meaning "at once", "soon", "instantly", "without delay", etc. See the examples below:

　　곧 비가 올 것 같아요. ⌒　　　　　　It looks like it will rain.

　　곧 그분한테 전보치세요. ⌒　　　　　Send him a telegram without delay.

4. ○부치다 : "mails", "sends", is different in meaning and spelling from 붙이다 "pastes" or "sticks" but it is the same in pronunciation.

　　이 편지 미국으로 부쳐 주세요. ⌒　　Please send this letter to America.

　　이 편지에 우표를 붙여 주세요. ⌒　　Please put a stamp on this letter.

　○가는 길에 "on the way to" means literally "on the going road".

　○-는 길에 always goes together with verbs denoting movement, like 가다, 오다 and their compounds.

Text II

8. ○항공편 is a contraction of 항공 우편 meaning "airmail". 항공 "aerial naviga-tion", "aviation". Other compounds : 항공 기지 "air base"; 항공로 "air route"; 항공 회사 "aviation company"; 항공 모함 "an (aircraft) carrier". Another word for 항공편 is 비행기편 "airplane letters".

　○선편 means literally "shipping (steamer) service"; 선편으로 "by ship". But here 선편 actually means "regular or surface mail". Another word for 선편 is 배편 "ship mail". 인편으로 보내다 "sends by a person".

　○담당계원, 담당해요 "is in charge". 담임선생 (pronounce 다님선생) "teacher in charge".

10. ○돼요 is a contraction of 되어요 meaning "becomes". Depending on the context, this non-object verb has several meanings, some of which are illustrated in the following examples:

앞으로 무엇이 되고 싶습니까?	What do you want to be in the future?
저는 선생이 되고 싶어요.	I want to become a teacher.
잘 되었습니다.	It has turned out well.
빨갛게 되었습니다.	It turned red.
갈 시간이 되었습니다.	It is time to go.
나무로 되어 있습니다.	It is made of wood.

11. ○용지 "form"; 메모용지 "memo paper"; 편지지 "stationery".

Text III

13. ○국내 "the interior" is a nominal derived from Chinese: 국(國) means "country", "nation" and 내(內) "inside", "within". Therefore, 국내 means literally "within the country". The opposite of 국내 is 국외 "outside the country", "overseas". 외국(外國) means "foreign country" and 외국어(外國語) is "the language of a foreign country". 외국인(外國人) means "foreigner".

   ○지급전보 "fast telegram". 보통전보 "normal telegram".

14. ○열 자 "ten letters", -자 is a classifier meaning "letter", "character", "ideograph". It is used with the native Korean numerals. 이내 "within" or "not more than" occurs directly following a number (or a number+classifier) and is most commonly used when indicating a period of time or an amount of money. The opposite of 이내 is 이외 "outside of", "except for". It occurs following nominals in general. See the examples below:

한 시간 이내에 돌아오겠어요.	I'll be back within an hour.
오백 원 이내면 사세요.	If it's not more than 500 wŏn, buy it.
한국말 이외는 모릅니다.	I don't understand (any language) except Korean.

17. ○소용없다 means "is needless", "is unnecessary". See the examples below :

그렇게 많이는 소용없어요. ⌒   I don't need so many.

책은 저한테 소용없어요. ⌒   Books are of little use for me.

18. ○그만두다 means "quits", "stops", "gives up", or "retires". The opposite of this is 계속하다 "continues". See the following examples :

저는 이 학교를 그만두겠어요. ⌒   I intend to leave (give up) this school.

이야기를 계속하세요. ⌒   Go on with your story.

STRUCTURAL PATTERNS

Text I

Ⅰ. The causal conjunctive ending (-으)니까 : "because" or "so"

Examples :

비가 오니까, ⌒ 학교에 가지 않겠습니 다. ↘

I'm not going to school because it's raining.

그분이 일찍 일어나니까, ⌒ 문제 없어 요. ⌒

There is no problem because he gets up early.

한국말이 어려우니까, ⌒ 공부하지 맙시 다. ↘

Let's not study Korean because it is difficult.

저는 바쁘니까, ⌒ 갈 수 없습니다. ↘

I can't go because I am busy.

저는 책이 있으니까, ⌒ 사지 않으려고 합니다. ↘

I don't intend to buy books because I have (some).

그분이 한국 사람이니까, ⌒ 한국말을 가르칩니다. ↘

He is teaching Korean because he is a Korean.

Notes :

1. The causal conjunctive ending -(으)니까 may be used with any verb and expresses reason or cause. It corresponds to English "because", "since", "therefore", or "so".

2. This pattern -(으)니까 is similar in meaning to the causal conjunctive ending -기 때문에 studied in Lesson 8, S.P. No. VIII. However, it is less colloquial than -기 때문에.

3. In this pattern, -(으)니 까 usually ends with a comma intonation (a rise on the last syllable of the phrase), and, if necessary the tense infixes (-았-, -겠-) can be used in this dependent clause. The past tense infix (-았-) is used in

this pattern when the causal event has been concluded before the resulting event. See the examples below :

그분도 거기 갔으니까, ⌒ 걱정하지 마세요. ⌒　　　　　He went there too, so please don't worry.

제가 꼭 가겠으니까, ⌒ 기다리세요. ⌒　　I'll go by all means, so please wait.

4. This pattern is used most frequently when you give a reason as the answer to a question. Consequently the final clause (the main clause) is either left unstressed or replaced with a verbal such as 그렇다 (it is so) or completely omitted. When the final clause is completely omitted, the polite particle -요 is added to make the expression polite.

왜 안 가시겠읍니까? ↘　　　　Why won't you go?

비가 오니까, ⌒ 안 가겠어요. ⌒　　Because it's raining, I won't go.

비가 오니까, ⌒ 그렇지요, ↗뭐. ↘　　Because it's raining, I won't go. (Lit, it is so.)

비가 오니까요. ⌒　　　　　Because it's raining.

5. -니까 after verb stems ending in a vowel ; -으니까 after verb stems ending in a consonant.

II. The particle -(으)로 : Noun+-(으)로 : "as", "function" or "manner"

As we have already seen, the particle -(으)로 (1) denotes the means by which one moves about or does something (See Lesson 5, S.P. No. III) or (2) denotes direction (See Lesson 9, S.P. No. VIII). In addition to the above-mentioned meanings, depending on the context, it can also mean function or manner.

Examples :

그분은 선생으로 일하고 있어요. ⌒　　He is working as a teacher.

이것을 사무실로 쓰고 있어요. ⌒　　We are using this as an office.

일반적으로 좋지 않아요. ⌒　　Generally speaking, it's not good.

Notes :

1. The particle -(으)로 is used after nominals in certain cases and denotes function or manner.

2. -로 after nominals ending in a vowel or in the consonant -ㄹ ; -으로 after nominals ending in a consonant except the consonant -ㄹ.

III. Gender :

Korean knows no grammatical gender. For example 그분 and 그이 are used for both "he's" and "she's". In cases where discrimination must be expressed, special words indicating the sex of the person being referred to are used : 그 남자 "that man", 그 여자 "that woman" : or, in general, (a) for persons 남- "male", 여- "female", (b) for animals 수- "male", 암- "female". Below you will finds group of words that "by nature" or by additional words like 남-, etc., refer to either sex.

Masculine	Feminine
할아버지 grandfather	할머니 grandmother
아버지 father	어머니 mother
남편 husband	아내 wife, 부인 wife(honorific)
아들 son	딸 daughter
아저씨 (숙부) uncle	아주머니 (숙모) aunt
형제 brothers	자매 sisters
형님 elder brother (man's)	언니 elder sister (woman's)
오빠 elder brother (woman's)	누나 elder sister (man's)
남동생 younger brother	여동생 younger sister
시아버지 father-in-law (husband's father)	시어머니 mother-in-law (husband's mother)
장인 father-in-law (wife's father)	장모 mother-in-law (wife's mother)
사위 son-in-law (daughter's busband)	며느리 daughter-in-law (son's wife)
조카 nephew	조카딸 niece
총각 bachelor	처녀 virgin
사내 male person	계집 female person (low word)
황소 ox	암소 cow

수캐	male dog	암캐	female dog
수탉	rooster	암탉	hen

Text II

IV. The pattern <u>V.S. + -(으)면 되다</u> : "(one) only has to do…"

"all (one) must do is…"

Examples :

천원만 있으면⌢ 됩니다.↘	All I need is one thousand wŏn.
마음만 좋으면⌢ 됩니다.↘	All you have to be is good.
내일까지 오시면⌢ 됩니다.↘	If you can come tomorrow, that'll be fine.

Notes :

1. The pattern <u>-(으)면 되다</u> means literally "if one does something, it's all right (or that's all, or it's possible)". The English equivalent of this pattern is "(one) only has to do" or "all (one) must do is". It indicates the only sensible action in a given situation.

2. It may be used with any verb.

3. <u>-면 되다</u> after verb stems ending in a vowel ; <u>-으면 되다</u> after verb stems ending in a consonant.

V. 아무도 + negative verb : "nobody does" or "nobody is"

Examples :

교실에 아무도 없어요.⌢	There is nobody in the classroom.
아무도 공부하지 않아요.⌢	Nobody is studying.
아무도 자지 못 했어요.⌢	Nobody could sleep.
아무도 바쁘지 않아요.⌢	Nobody is busy.

Notes :

1. The word <u>아무도</u> is always followed by a negative predicate.

2. <u>아무것도 + negative</u> corresponds to the English "nothing". See the examples below :

교실에 ˇ아무것도ˇ 없어요. ⌒   There is nothing in the classroom.

아무것도ˇ 먹지 않았어요. ⌒   I didn't eat anything. (I ate nothing.)

아무것도ˇ 하지 마세요. ⌒   Don't do anything.

VI. <u>Verb stems ending in a final consonant -ㄹ</u>

Examples :

갈(다) tills, plows	놀(다) plays	날(다) flies
말(다) rolls	불(다) blows	알(다) knows
줄(다) decreases, lessens	비틀(다) twists, twirls	팔(다) sells
헐(다) destroys, pulls down	울(다) cries	살(다) lives

Notes :

Some verbs whose stems end in -ㄹ are irregular in that the final stem sound -ㄹ is dropped in certain environments.

1. When the final -ㄹ of the stem is followed by the consonants -ㄴ, -ㅂ (m -sound), -ㅅ or the vowel -오, the final stem sound -ㄹ is dropped. See the examples :

그분을ˇ 아는가? ↗   Do you know him? (intimate style)

그분을ˇ 저는ˇ 아니까요. ⌒   Because I know him.

저는ˇ 그분을ˇ 압니다. ↘   I know him.

그분을ˇ 아십니까? ↗   Do you know him?

그분을ˇ 아오. ⌒   I know him.

2. But when the final -ㄹ of the stem is followed by other consonants or vowels no such change takes place. See the following examples :

그것을ˇ 알아야 합니다. ↘   You must know that.

그것을ˇ 알지 않으면⌒ 안 됩니다. ↘   You must know that.

잘 알겠습니다. ↘   I understand well.

알고말고요. ⌒   Of course I know that.

Text III

VII. The pattern <u>-기 전에</u> : <u>A.V.S. + -기 전에</u> : "before doing so-and-so", "before so-and-so happens or happened"

Examples:

주무시기 전에, ⌢ 이것을 잡수세요. ⌢   Before you go to bed, eat this.

한국에 오기 전에, ⌢ 한국말을 배웠어   Befor I came to Korea, I learned
요. ⌢   Korean.

비가 오기 전에, ⌢ 가세요. ⌢   Go home before it starts raining.

Notes:

1. The pattern <u>-기 전에</u> is usually used with action verbs and is followed by another sentence (the main clause). For <u>-기</u> see Lesson 8, S.P. No. X.

2. The tense, negation, etc., are regularly expressed in the final sentence (the main clause). See the following examples:

그분이 오기 전에, ⌢ 공부했어요. ⌢   Before he came, I studied.

그분이 오기 전에, ⌢ 공부하겠어요. ⌢   Before he comes, I intend to study.

그분이 오기 전에, ⌢ 공부하지 않겠어요. ⌢ Before he comes, I will not study.

3. In this pattern, <u>-기 전에</u> usually ends with a comma intonation.

4. This pattern <u>-기 전에</u> may be followed by any of the particles <u>-도</u>, <u>-는</u>, etc., depending upon its relation to what follows in the sentence. See the examples below:

한국에 오기 전에도 한국말을 공부했   I studied Korean even (also) before
어요. ⌢   coming to Korea.

그분이 오기 전에는 가지 마세요. ⌢   Please don't go before he comes.
                                         (contrast)

VIII. The concessive conjunctive ending <u>V.S. + -아(-어, -여)도</u> : "even if", "even though"

Examples:

비가 와도 ⌢ 가고 싶습니다. ↘   Although it's raining, I want to go.

292 *Structural Patterns*

들어도∩ 모르겠습니다. ↘   Even if I listen, I won't understand.

멀어도∩ 가겠어요. ∩   Even though it's far, I intend to go.

바빠도∩ 공부해야 합니다. ↘   Even though we are busy, we have
                             to study.

돈이 ˘있어도∩ 사지 않겠어요. ∩   Even though I have money, I'll not
                             buy it.

Notes :

1. The pattern <u>-아(-어, -여)도</u> may be used with any verb except the copula
   <u>-이-</u> and forms a concessive clause which is followed by a main clause.

2. It corresponds to the English "even being or doing so-and-so", "even if it is
   so-and-so", or "even if (someone) does so-and-so", etc.

3. <u>-아도</u> after -아- and -오- ; <u>-어도</u> after any other vowel ; <u>-여도</u> after 하-, the
   stem of the verb 하다 "does".

IX. The pattern <u>V.S. + -는 것</u>

Examples :

학교에 ˃가는 것이 ˘어떻습니까? ↘   How about going to school?

그분은 ˘공부하는 것을 ˘좋아해요. ∩   He likes to study.

여기 계시는 것이 ˘좋겠어요. ∩   I think it's better for you to stay here.

Notes :

1. The pattern <u>-는 것</u> is directly attached to the stem of action verbs or <u>있-</u>
   and expresses the idea, act, or manner of doing something, whereas the nominalizing suffix <u>-기</u> added to verb stems indicates the activity or the state of being
   as a concrete thing.

2. It corresponds to English "-ing" or to the infinitive marker "to", etc. Verbal
   nouns made with <u>-는 것</u> are used as a subject or an object.

DRILLS

Text I

A. Substitution Drill

1. 지금 갔다 와도 괜찮을까요?

   Is it alright if I go now?

내일 떠나,	그분을 만나,
늦게 일어나,	지금 시작해

2. 나가는 길에 이 편지 좀 부쳐 주세요.

   On your way out please mail this letter.

내려가,	올라가,	들어가,
내려오,	올라오,	들어오

3. 얼마짜리 책을 사 드릴까요?(을/를)

   What (price) book shall I buy for you?

가방,	연필,	시계,
공책,	종이,	만년필

4. 그분은 선생으로 일하고 있어요.

   (으로/로)

   He is working as a teacher.

신부,	목사,	선교사,
비서,	점원,	과학자

B. Pattern Drill

Teacher : 비가 ˇ오기 때문에, ⌒ 학교에 ˇ가지 않겠습니다. ↘

I'm not going to school because it's raining.

Student : 비가 ˇ오니까, ⌒ 학교에 ˇ가지 않겠습니다. ↘

I'm not going to school because it's raining.

1. 그분이 일찍 일어나기 때문에, 문제 없어요.

그분이 ˇ일찍 ˇ일어나니까, ⌒ 문제 없어요. ⌒

2. 그분이 저를 기다리고 있기 때문에, 지금 가야 합니다.

그분이 ˇ저를 ˇ기다리고 있으니까, ⌒ 지금 ˇ가야 합니다. ↘

3. 한국말이 어렵기 때문에, 공부하지 않겠어요.

한국말이 ˇ어려우니까, ⌒ 공부하지 않겠어요. ⌒

4. 저는 바쁘기 때문에, 갈 수 없습니다.

저는 ˇ바쁘니까, ⌒ 갈 수 없습니다. ↘

5. 이것이 싸기 때문에, 이것을 사겠어요.

이것이 ˇ싸니까, ⌒ 이것을 ˇ사겠어요. ⌒

C. Pattern Drill

Teacher : 이 교실에서 ˇ공부하는 사람이 ˇ학생입니다. ↘

The man studying in this classroom is a student.

Student : 이 교실에서 ˇ공부할 사람이 ˇ학생입니다. ↘

The man who will study in this classroom is a student.

1. 여기서 일하는 사람이 김 선생입니다.   여기서 ˇ일할 사람이 ˇ김 선생입니다. ↘

2. 그분을 찾아가는 사람이 저의 아버   그분을 ˇ찾아갈 사람이 ˇ저의 아버지입니
   지입니다.   다. ↘

3. 한국말을 공부하는 사람이 제 동생   한국말을 ˇ공부할 사람이 ˇ제 동생입니다. ↘
   입니다.

4. 그분은 하는 일이 많습니다.   그분은 ˇ할 일이 ˇ많습니다. ↘

5. 그 책을 읽는 분이 우리 아저씨예요.   그 책을 ˇ읽을 분이 ˇ우리 아저씨예요. ⌒

6. 만년필을 사는 분이 노 선생님이에요.   만년필을 ˇ살 분이 ˇ노 선생님이에요. ⌒

D. Response Drill

1. 지금 갔다 와도 괜찮을까요?　　　예,⌒ 지금 갔다 와도⌒ 괜찮아요.⌒
2. 지금 할 일이 많습니까?　　　　　예,⌒ 지금 할 일이 많습니다.↘
3. 공부하시고서 어디에 가시겠습니까?　공부하고서⌒ 집에 가겠습니다.↘
4. 얼마짜리 우표를 사 드릴까요?　　팔십원짜리 우표를 사 주세요.⌒
5. 이 일을 할 사람이 어디에 갔습니까?　이 일을 할 사람이 부산에 갔습니다.↘

Text II

E. Substitution Drill

1. 항공편 말이에요,⌒ 선편 말이에요?⌒
   Do you mean airmail or regular mail?

동생 — 형,	담배 — 성냥,
누나 — 오빠,	남자 — 여자

2. 전보 용지 한 장 주시겠어요? ↗
   Could I have a telegram (blank),
   please?

책 한 권,	연필 한 자루,
잉크 한 병,	자동차 한 대,
담배 한 갑,	생선 한 마리

3. 천 원만 있으면⌒ 됩니다.↘
   All I need is one thousand wǒn.

내일까지 오,	학생은 공부하,
그분은 가르치,	아홉 시까지 가

F. Response Drill

Teacher : 모두 교실에 있습니까? ↗　　Is everybody in the classroom?
Student : 아니오, ↗ 교실에 아무도 없습　No, there is nobody in the classroom.
니다. ↘

1. 모두 공부합니까?　　　　아니오, ↗ 아무도 공부하지 않습니다.↘
2. 모두 주무십니까?　　　　아니오, ↗ 아무도 주무시지 않습니다.↘
3. 모두 바쁩니까?　　　　　아니오, ↗ 아무도 바쁘지 않습니다.↘
4. 모두 그분을 기다립니까?　아니오, ↗ 아무도 그분을 기다리지 않습
　　　　　　　　　　　　　니다. ↘
5. 모두 책을 샀습니까?　　　아니오, ↗ 아무도 책을 사지 않았습니다.↘

6. 모두 늦게 일어납니까? 아니오, ↗ 아무도 늦게 일어나지 않습니다. ↘

G. Response Drill

Teacher : 무엇을 샀습니까? ↘   What did you buy?

Student : 아무것도 사지 않았습니다. ↘   I didn't buy anything.

1. 무엇을 사시겠습니까?   아무것도 사지 않겠습니다. ↘

2. 무엇을 공부하시겠습니까?   아무것도 공부하지 않겠습니다. ↘

3. 무엇을 보았습니까?   아무것도 보지 않았습니다. ↘

4. 무엇을 잡수시겠습니까?   아무것도 먹지 않겠습니다. ↘

5. 무엇을 부탁하시겠습니까?   아무것도 부탁하지 않겠습니다. ↘

H. Response Drill

Teacher : 아직도 공부하지 않았어요? ↗   Haven't you studied yet?

Student : 아니오, ↗ 벌써 공부했어요. ⌢   Yes, I have studied already.

1. 아직도 그분을 만나지 않았어요?   아니오, ↗ 벌써 그분을 만났어요. ⌢

2. 아직도 주무시지 않았어요?   아니오, ↗ 벌써 잤어요. ⌢

3. 아직도 그분을 찾아가지 않았어요?   아니오, ↗ 벌써 그분을 찾아갔어요. ⌢

4. 아직도 그분이 도착하지 않았어요?   아니오, ↗ 벌써 그분이 도착했어요. ⌢

5. 아직도 그 일을 마치지 않았어요?   아니오, ↗ 벌써 그 일을 마쳤어요. ⌢

I. Expansion Drill

1. 만나십시오. ↘

   그분을 만나십시오. ↘

   내일 가서 ⌢ 그분을 만나십시오. ↘

   지금 가지 말고 ⌢ 내일 가서 ⌢ 그분을 만나십시오. ↘

   지금 비가 오니까, ⌢ 지금 가지 말고 ⌢ 내일 가서 ⌢ 그분을 만나십시오. ↘

   It's raining now, so don't go, (but) go and meet him tomorrow.

2. 부쳐 주세요. ⌢

   가는 길에 부쳐 주세요. ⌢

   학교에 가는 길에 부쳐 주세요. ⌢

   내일 학교에 가는 길에 부쳐 주세요. ⌢

지금�‿ 갈 수 없으니까⌒ 내일˿ 학교에 가는 길에 부쳐 주세요. ⌒

지금˿ 부치는 것이˿ 좋겠지만⌒ 지금˿ 갈 수 없으니까⌒ 내일˿학교에 가는 길에˿부쳐 주세요. ⌒

It would be good to mail it now, but you can't go, so on your way to school tomorrow please mail it for me.

Text III

O. Substitution Drill

1. 집에 가는 것이˿ 좋겠어요. ⌒   It's better to go home, I suppose.

2. 그분한테˿ 부탁하는 것이˿ 좋겠어요. ⌒   It's better to ask him for a favor, I suppose.

3. 산에˿ 올라가는 것이˿ 좋겠어요. ⌒   It's better to climb the mountain, I suppose.

4. 한국말을˿ 가르치는 것이˿ 좋겠어요. ⌒   It's better to teach Korean, I suppose.

5. 내일˿ 떠나는 것이˿ 좋겠어요. ⌒   It's better to leave tomorrow, I suppose.

P. Substitution Drill

1. 지금˿ 네시니까⌒ 좀˿ 어렵겠는데요.⌒   It will be difficult because it's (already) four o'clock.

2. 벌써˿ 일을˿ 시작했으니까, ⌒ 좀˿ 어렵겠는데요. ⌒   It will be difficult because he has already started his work.

3. 아직도˿ 그분이˿ 오지˿ 않았으니까, ⌒ 좀˿ 어렵겠는데요. ⌒   I will be difficult because he didn't come yet.

4. 너무˿ 사람이˿ 많으니까, ⌒ 좀˿ 어렵겠는데요. ⌒   It will be difficult because there are too many people.

5. 지금˿ 시간이˿ 없으니까, ⌒ 좀˿ 어렵겠는데요. ⌒   It will be difficult because we have no time.

L. Substitution Drill

1. 지금˿ 쳐도⌒ 소용없겠군요. ⌒   Even if I send it (the cable) now, it would be to no avail.

2. 지금 가도⌢ 소용없겠군요.⌢   Even if I go now, it'll be useless.

3. 내일 그분을 만나도⌢소용없겠군요.⌢   Even though I will meet him tomorrow, it'll be useless.

4. 한국말을 공부해도⌢ 소용없겠군요.⌢   Even if I study Korean, it'll be useless.

5. 계속해도⌢ 소용없겠군요.⌢   Even if I continue (it), it'll be useless.

M. Pattern Drill

Teacher : 저는 가지만⌢ 그분은 가지 않아요.⌢   I am going, but he is not.

Student : 저는 가도⌢ 그분은 가지 않아요.⌢   Even if I go, he is not going.

1. 비가 오지만 가고 싶습니다.   비가 와도⌢ 가고 싶습니다.↘

2. 멀지만 가려고 합니다.   멀어도⌢ 가려고 합니다.↘

3. 바쁘지만 공부해야 합니다.   바빠도⌢ 공부해야 합니다.↘

4. 그분은 가지 않지만 나는 가야 합니다.   그분은 가지 않아도⌢ 나는 가야 합니다.↘

5. 돈은 있지만 사지 않겠어요.   돈은 있어도⌢ 사지 않겠어요.⌢

N. Pattern Drill

Teacher : 그분이 가면⌢ 저는 가야 합니다.↘   If he goes, I have to go.

Student : 그분이 가기 전에⌢ 저는 가야 합니다.↘   Before he goes, I have to go.

1. 그분이 주무시면 이것을 잡수세요.   그분이 주무시기 전에⌢ 이것을 잡수세요.⌢

2. 한국에 가면 한국말을 배우겠어요.   한국에 가기 전에⌢ 한국말을 배우겠어요.⌢

3. 기차가 도착하면 나가야 합니다.   기차가 도착하기 전에⌢ 나가야 합니다.↘

4. 비가 오면 빨리 가야 합니다.   비가 오기 전에⌢ 빨리 가야 합니다.↘

5. 내가 그분을 만나면 산에 올라가세요.   내가 그분을 만나기 전에⌢ 산에 올라가세요.⌢

O. Response Drill

1. 한국에 오시기 전에 어디에 계셨어 요?

한국에 오기 전에⌒ 미국에 있었어요.⌒

2. 몇 시 차로 그분이 부산으로 떠났어 요?

다섯 시 차로 그분이 부산으로 떠났어요.⌒

3. 무엇을 공부하는 것이 좋겠습니까?

한국말을 공부하는 것이 좋겠습니다.↘

4. 가는 길에 이 편지 좀 부쳐 주시겠 읍니까?

예,⌒ 가는 길에 부쳐 드리지요.⌒

5. 교실에 아무도 없습니까?

예,⌒ 교실에 아무도 없습니다.↘

6. 얼마 있으면 됩니까?

천 원만 있으면⌒ 됩니다.↘

P. Expansion Drill

좋겠어요.⌒

만나는 것이 좋겠어요.⌒

그분을 만나는 것이 좋겠어요.⌒

떠나기 전에⌒ 그분을 만나는 것이 좋겠어요.⌒

그분이 떠나기 전에⌒ 그분을 만나는 것이 좋겠어요.⌒

내일 그분이 떠나기 전에⌒ 그분을 만나는 것이 좋겠어요.⌒

만나기가 어려우니까⌒ 내일 그분이 떠나기 전에⌒ 그분을 만나는 것이 좋겠어요.⌒

지금 가도⌒ 그분을 만나기가 어려우니까⌒ 내일 그분이 떠나기 전에⌒ 그분을 만나 는 것이 좋겠어요.⌒

Even if you go now, it will be difficult for you to meet him, so I think it's better for you to meet him tomorrow before he leaves.

제십오과 이발관에서 (Lesson 15 At the Barber's)

TEXT I

— [VOCABULARY] —

이발관	barber shop	단골	regular customer
높아요(높지-)	is high	손님	guest, customer
낮아요(낮지-)	is low	자라요(자라지-)	grows
깎아요(깎지-)	trims, sharpens, cuts	겨우	barely, hardly, narrowly
이발사	barber	그래도	but, still, and yet
뒷	the back	오래	long, for a long while
면도	shaving	정신	spirit, soul

1. 이발사 : 높게 깎아 드릴까요, 낮게 깎아 드릴까요?

Do you want it cut short or left long (this time)?

2. 김경모 : 그저 보기 좋도록 깎아 주세요. 그런데 뒷 면도는 하지 말아 주세요.

Just cut it so that it looks good, but please don't shave the neck.

3. 이발사 : 예, 알고 있어요. 단골손님인데요, 뭐.

Yes, I know. You are a regular customer.

4. 김경모 : 그동안에 머리가 많이 자랐지요?

My hair has grown long, hasn't it?

5. 이발사 : 아니오, 이발하신 지 겨우 이 주일 되었는데요, 뭐.

No, it's only about two weeks since you got a haircut.

6. 김경모 : 그래도 오래 된 것 같아요. 요즘 너무 바쁘기 때문에 정신이 없어요.

But it seems like a long time. I am so busy these days that I can't even think.

TEXT II

7. 이발사 : 자, ↘ 다 되었어요. ⌒ 머리 감으시지요. ⌒

It's finished. You will have a shampoo, won't you?

8. 김경모 : 그럽시다. ↘ 야 ⌒ 시원하다. ↘ 머리 감을 때만큼 ⌒ 기분 좋을 때는 없어. ⌒

All right. Oh, how refreshing! There is nothing quite as nice as a shampoo.

9. 이발사 : 자, ↘ 이 수건으로 얼굴 닦으시지요. ⌒

Wipe your face with this towel.

10. 김경모 : 예, ⌒ 수고하셨어요. ⌒

Thank you.

11. 이발사 : 기름 발라 드릴까요? ↗

Shall I use hair oil?

12. 김경모 : 목욕한 후에 ⌒ 바르고 싶은데요. ⌒ 가만히 있자, ⌝ 지금 바를까? ↗

I would like to do that after I've taken my bath. Just a second! Perhaps I might as well have you do it for me now.

13. 이발사 : 머리카락이 참 부드럽군요. ⌒ 머리카락이 부드러우면 ⌒ 마음이 좋대요. ⌒

Your hair is very soft. People with soft hair are said to be good.

14. 김경모 : 오원짜리 비행기 태우지 마세요. ⌒

No soft soap for me! (Don't take me on a five wŏn plane ride.)

┌─〔VOCABULARY〕────────────────────────────┐

젊어요(젊지-) is young	한창 in the prime of
늙어요(늙지-) is old, grows old	나이 age, years
자꾸 repeatedly, continually	들어요(들지-) becomes (ages)
놀려요(놀리지-) makes fun of	

└──┘

15. 이발사 : 이발하시니까, ⌒ 참 젊어 보입니다. ↘   After a haircut you look very young.

16. 김경모 : 늙은 사람 자꾸 놀려 대지 마세요. ⌒   Stop fooling an old man. (Do not fool an old man all the time.)

17. 이발사 : 이제 한창이신데 ⌒ 무슨 그런 말씀을 하세요? ⌒   You are in your prime now. Why are you talking like that?

18. 김경모 : 마음이야 젊었지만 ⌒ 어디 그래요? ↗   I am young in heart but not in age.

19. 이발사 : 아니, ↗ 이제부터 일하실 나인데요. ⌒   You have only reached the age when a man (really) begins to work.

20. 김경모 : 나이가 들면 ⌒ 다 소용 없어요. ⌒   When a person gets old, nothing matters.

REMARKS TO THE TEXT

Text I

1. ○<u>이발관</u>(or <u>이발소</u>) means "a barber shop"; <u>이발하다</u> is an action verb meaning "has a haircut"; <u>이발사</u> means "a barber".

   ○<u>높다</u> is a descriptive verb meaning "is high" as to place, position, or voice, etc. The opposite is <u>낮다</u> "is low"; <u>높은</u> and <u>낮은</u> are noun modifiers; <u>높게</u> and <u>낮게</u> are adverbials.

   ○<u>깎다</u>, depending on the context, can mean "cuts (hair)", "shaves (beard)" or "beats down (price)", etc.

머리를 깎아 주세요. ⌒	I want to have a haircut.
수염 좀 깎으세요. ⌒	Please shave yourself.
너무 비싸요. ⌒ **좀 깎읍시다.** ↘	It's too expensive. Can you lower the price a little?

   Another word for <u>깎다</u> is <u>치다</u> "cuts, trims". To tell the barber you want the hair cut close, you can say: <u>쳐 주세요.</u> If you like to specify your instruction to either the top(윗머리), the sides(옆머리) or the back(뒷머리) of the head, you say: 윗머리를 쳐 주세요, etc. If you don't want a close cut you could say: 그냥 두세요. "Leave it (more or less) as it is".

3. ○<u>단골 손님</u> means "a regular customer", "a patron", or "a client"; <u>단골집</u> "one's favorite shop"; <u>단골 의사</u> "one's family doctor"; <u>단골 여관</u> "one's favorite hotel".

4. ○<u>자라다</u> is an action verb meaning "grows" or "is brought up".

아이는 빨리 자랍니다. ↘	Children grow up fast.
봄은 자라는 계절입니다. ↘	Spring is the growing season.

5. ○<u>겨우</u> depending on the context, can mean "barely", "hardly", "narrowly", "with difficulty", "only", or "just", etc. <u>힘들게</u> can be used with about the same meaning

as 겨우.

겨우 ˇ살아갑니다. ↘   I barely make a living.

겨우 ˇ두 사람만 ˇ남았어요. ⌒   Only two of us are left.

6. ○정신이 없어요 : 정신 means "mind", "spirit", "soul", etc. Therefore, the literal
meaning of the sentence is : "I have no spirit". The expression is used :

  a) when one is absent-minded ;

  b) when one forgot something completely ;

  c) when it is noisy or clamorous.

Text II

7. ○자 is an exclamatory expression to arouse one to action or to call one's attention to something.

  ○머리 감다 means "washes one's hair". 실을 감다 means "winds a thread".

8. ○야 is an exclamatory expression of admiration or excitement.

  ○기분 means "feeling", "humor", "mood", or "frame of mind", etc.

기분이 ˇ좋습니다. ↘   I feel well (fine). Or : I am pleased.

기분이 ˇ나쁩니다. ↘   I don't feel well. Or : I am out of sorts.

기분이 ˇ안 나요. ⌒   I am in no mood (to do it).

11. ○기름 means "pomade", "oil", "fat", "lard", "tallow", etc. 바르다 means
"pastes", "sticks", "applies", "powders", etc. See the examples below :

그분은 벽에다 ˇ종이를 ˇ바르고 있어요. ⌒   He is covering the wall with paper.

그 여자는 ˇ얼굴에 ˇ분을 ˇ바릅니다. ↘   That girl puts powder on her face.

그 여자는 ˇ입술에 ˇ연지를 ˇ바릅니다. ↘   She paints her lips.

12. ○가만히 있자 : Its literal meaning is "Let's stay quiet". It is used when one is
hesitating or when one gets a sudden idea.

13. ○부드럽다 is a descriptive verb meaning "is soft", "is tender" or "is gentle". Its
opposite word is 단단하다 (or 딱딱하다) "is hard", or "is solid", said of wood or
stone, etc.

그분의 음성은 ˇ부드러워요. ⌒   His voice is soft.

이 나무는 단단해요. ⌢   This wood is very hard.

○좋대요 is a contraction of 좋다고 해요 "is said to be good".

14. ○오 원짜리 비행기 태우지 마세요. ⌢ 비행기 means "an airplane" and 태우다 "takes on". The expression refers to those toy airplanes found in the amusement park areas of Seoul's 창경원 and 덕수궁, which used to cost 5 wŏn per ride, and means: "Don't try to fool me."

Text III

15. ○젊다 is a descriptive verb meaning "is young". The opposite word is 늙다 "is old"; 젊은 and 늙은 are noun modifiers. 늙다 always goes with the past tense.

그분은 젊어요. ⌢   He is young.

그분은 늙었어요. ⌢   He is old (lit. he has become old).

16. ○놀리다, depending on the context, can mean (1) "makes fun of", "pokes fun at, (2) "lets something rest (or play)".

사람을 놀리지 마세요. ⌢   Quit your kidding.

할 일이 없기 때문에⌢ 직공을 놀리고   Because there is no work to do, he is

있어요. ⌢   laying off workers.

17. ○한창 means (1) "prime", "flower", "bloom", (2) "the height", "the summit", "the zenith".

그 여자는 지금 한창이에요. ⌢   She is now in the prime of youth.

한창 때는 지났어요. ⌢   I'm past my prime. Or: I am on the
                                       wane.

18. ○마음이야 : -(이)야 is an emphasizing particle of contrast. It is stronger than -는/-은 and is used in belittling and, occasionally, in flattering.

좋은 선생이 많으니까, ⌢ 나야 소용있습니까? ↗

Since there are many good teachers, what need is there for me?

19. ○나이 means "age", "years", "time of life". A few other words for "age" are the following: -살 "age", "years" is a dependent noun used with preceding noun modi-

fiers, like 몇 살 "how old?; 연세 and 춘추 are the honorific words for age.

그분은 나이가 몇이에요? ⌒	How old is he?
그분은 몇 살이에요? ⌒	How old is he?
연세가 몇이십니까? ↘	How old are you?
춘추가 몇이십니까? ↘	How old are you?

20. ○나이들다 means "grows old", "becomes old". 나이들다＝나이를 먹다.

○소용없다 means "is of no use", "is useless".

책은 저한테 소용없어요. ⌒	Books are of no use to me.
소용없는 걱정을 하지 마세요. ⌒	No need to worry.

STRUCTURAL PATTERNS

Text I

Ⅰ. The pattern V.S. + -도록

The pattern -도록 has many different English equivalents depending on the context. Study the following examples carefully:

(A) V.S. + -도록 : "until"

   Examples:

그분은 두시가 되도록 오지 않았어요.	He did not come until two o'clock.
어젯밤에 늦도록 놀았어요.	We played until late last night.

(B) V.S. + -도록 : "so that", "so as to", "in such a way that", or "in order to"

   Examples:

기차 시간에 늦지 않도록 일찍 일어났습니다.	I got up early in order to be on time for the train.
잊어버리지 않도록 배운 것을 복습하세요.	Review what you have learned, so that you will not forget it.

   Note:

The pattern -도록 is used with all verbs except the verb -이다. It indicates the extension of time to a certain limit or point as well as the condition or state of matter to a certain limit or point. Thus, it has the two distinct meanings of "until" and "so that" (result).

(C) A.V.S + -도록 하다

   Examples:

그분을 학교에 가도록 합시다.	Let's try to send him to school.
이것을 먹지 않도록 하세요.	Please try not to eat this.

Note :

When the action verb stem + -도록 is followed by 하다, it expresses the idea of causing or influencing for a definite purpose, like the causative pattern "Verb Stem + -게 하다". (You will study this pattern later.)

(D) A.V.S. + -도록 말하다 : "tell someone to (do)"

그분한테 한국말을 공부하도록 말했   I told him to study Korean.
어요.

빨리 주무시도록 말씀해 주세요.   Please tell him to sleep quickly.

II. The negative imperative form A.V.S. + -지 말다 : "Don't do"

Examples :

지금 가지 마십시오.   Please don't go now.

이 의자에 앉지 말라.   Don't sit on this chair. (plain style)

오늘 밤에 주무시지 마세요.   Please don't sleep tonight.

영어는 배우지 말아 주세요.   Please don't learn English.

Notes :

1. The pattern -지 말다 is always used with action verbs and the verb 있-(the imperative form usually does not go with descriptive verbs). It expresses prohibition or dissuasion.

2. Variant forms "마세요", "마십시오", "말아요", "말라", or "말아 주세요" are also used for the negative imperative expression. 말다 means literally "gives up", "quits", "stops", or "discontinues".

III. A.V.S. + -ㄴ (은) 지(가) + time expression + 되다 : "it has been such-and-such a time since"

Examples :

서울에 온 지(가) 이틀 되었어요.   It has been two days since I came to
                                      Seoul.

그분은 미국에 간 지(가) 석달 되었   It has been three months since he went
어요.   to America.

Notes:

1. This pattern (A.V.S. + -ㄴ〈은〉지) expresses an interval of time extending from the moment when a certain action occurred up to the present.

2. -지 is a dependent noun, always modified by the modifier marker -ㄴ(은). The particle -가 after -지 is optional.

3. -ㄴ지 after verb stems ending in a vowel. -은지 after verb stems ending in a consonant.

Text II

IV. The particle -만큼 : Noun + -만큼 : "as (so)...as"

Examples:

한국말은 영어만큼 어렵습니다.   Korean is as difficult as English.

그 여자는 김 선생님만큼 커요.   That girl is as tall as Mr. Kim.

그분만큼 좋은 분은 없어요.   Nobody is as good as he is.

시간만큼 중요한 것은 없어요.   Nothing is so important as time.

Note:

The particle -만큼 is attached to nominals and expresses extent or degree. (The pattern A.V.S. + -ㄹ(을) 만큼 meaning "as much as one can" will be studied later.)

V. The conjunctive form -ㄴ(은) 후에 : A.V.S. + -ㄴ(은) 후에 : "after"

Examples:

공부한 후에 집으로 돌아왔습니다.   I came home after I studied.

저녁을 먹은 후에 무엇을 할까요?   What shall we do after (having) supper?

Notes:

1. The pattern -ㄴ(은) 후에 is always used with action verbs. The English equivalent to this pattern is "after" (as you remember 후에 "later on" is used with nominals). The tense is expressed in the main (final) clause.

2. When <u>one</u> subject performs two actions in sequence, the pattern -고서 is used

rather than this pattern -ㄴ (은) 후에 (See Lesson 13, S.P. No. V).

3. -ㄴ 후에 after verb stems ending in a vowel ; -은 후에 after verb stems ending in a consonant.

Text III

VI. <u>D.V.S. + -아(-어, -여) 보이다</u> : "it looks or seems"

Examples :

이 책이 좋아 보입니다. ↘	This book seems to be good.
그분이 젊어 보입니다. ↘	He looks young.
그분이 늙어 보입니다. ↘	He looks old.

Notes :

1. -아(-어, -여) 보이다 is a main verb plus auxiliary verb pattern. (See Lesson 4, S.P. No. II, 2-3-5 and No. VIII.) The main verb of this pattern is always descriptive. The pattern expresses resemblance, likeness or what seems or appears to be.

2. Independently used <u>보이다</u> is a non-object verb, used with the particle <u>-가/ -이</u>(-는/-은), and its meaning is "is visible". Do not be misled by the English translation.

이발소가 보입니다. ↘	I can see the barber shop. (The barber shop is visible.)
제가 보입니까 ? ↗	Can you see me? (Am I visible?)

3. -아 보이다 after <u>-아-</u> and <u>-오-</u> ; -어 보이다 after any other vowel ; -여 보이다 after <u>하-</u> the stem of the verb 하다 "does".

VII. The non-final ending -아(-어, -여) 대다

Examples :

놀려 대지 마세요. ⌒	Stop fooling an old man (all the time).
떠들어 대지 마세요. ⌒	Don't make such a noise continuously.
그분이 웃어 댔습니다. ↘	He kept laughing.
그 여자가 울어 댔습니다. ↘	She cried continuously.

개가 짖어 댔습니다. ↘   The dog was barking very much.

그분한테 책을 사 달라고⌒ 졸라 댔습   I pestered him to buy that book.

니다. ↘

그가 지껄여 댔습니다. ↘   He went on talking.

Notes :

1. The non-final ending -아(-어, -여) 대다 is attached directly to the verb
stems of action verbs and indicates continuation or excessiveness of an action.
In most cases, this pattern is used with the words 자꾸 "continuously",
"repeatedly" or 너무 "very much".

2. Tense or negation is expressed in the final verb -대다, not in the verb with
-아(-어, 여).

Ⅷ. Particles -에게 "to", -에게서 "from"

Examples :

a) 그 책을 저에게 주십시오. ↘   Please give that book to me.

친구에게 편지를 씁니다. ↘   I'm writing to my friend.

b) 친구에게서 편지가 왔어요. ⌒   The letter came from my friend.

이 말을 어머님에게서 들었어요. ⌒   I heard this from my mother.

Notes :

1. The particles -에게 "to" and -에게서 "from" are used with nouns referring to
persons, animals, or birds (animate beings). They are similar in meaning to
the paticles -한테 "to" and -한테서 "from" studied in Lesson 11, S.P. No. Ⅶ.

2. The particle -에게 "to" indicates direction toward a person, and the particle
-에게서 "from" indicates a person as a source or origin. The particles -에게
and -에게서 are not used as freqently as -한테 and -한테서.

3. The particle -께 is the honorific form of -한테 and -에게.

Ⅸ. Verb stems ending in a final consonant -ㅅ

Examples :

굿(다) draws (a line),   잇(다) unites,   젓(다) rows,

determines   connects   stirs

낫(다) recovers,   붓(다) pours,   짓(다) makes
     gets well   puts (water in   builds
                                  a bowl)

Notes :

Some verbs whose stems end in -ㅅ are irregular in that the final stem sound -ㅅ is dropped in certain environments.

1. When the final -ㅅ of the stem is followed by a vowel, the final stem sound -ㅅ is dropped. See the examples below :

지으세요. ⌒   Make (it), please.

지어 보세요. ⌒   Try making (it).

2. But when the final -ㅅ of the stem is followed by a consonant, no such change takes place. See the following examples :

짓자. ↘   Let's make (it). (plain style)

짓습니다. ↘   I'm making (it).

짓느냐? ↗   Do you make it?

짓겠습니다. ↘   I'll make (it).

3. There are, however, regular -ㅅ verbs which never change their stems such as :

벗(다) takes off   솟(다) gushes out, springs

웃(다) laughs   빗(다) combs

씻(다) washes   (빼)앗(다) takes (a thing) away from

DRILLS

Text I

A. Substitution Drill

1. **뒷** 면도는 **하**지 말아 주세요.

    Please don't shave the neck.

지금 나가,	산에 올라가,
지금 떠나,	늦게까지 일하

2. **이발한** 지가 **한** 달 되었어요.

    It's been a month since I got a hair-
    cut.

그분이 떠난 ─ 세 시간,
그분이 나간 ─ 한 시간,
그 일을 시작한 ─ 육 개월

B. Pattern Drill

Teacher : 그분한테 한국말을 공부하라고   Tell him to study Korean, please.
         하세요.

Student : 그분한테 한국말을 공부하도   Tell him to study Korean, please.
         록 말씀하세요.

1. 그분을 여기에 오라고 하세요.   그분을 여기에 오도록 말씀하세요.

2. 빨리 주무시라고 하세요.   빨리 주무시도록 말씀하세요.

3. 내일 그분을 만나라고 하세요.　　　내일 그분을 만나도록 말씀하세요.

4. 그분을 찾아가라고 하세요.　　　　그분을 찾아가도록 말씀하세요.

5. 내일 도착하라고 하세요.　　　　　내일 도착하도록 말씀하세요.

6. 노래를 부르라고 하세요.　　　　　노래를 부르도록 말씀하세요.

C. Pattern Drill

Teacher : 어젯밤에 열두 시까지 공부했　　I studied until midnight last night.
　　　　　어요.

Student : 어젯밤에 열두 시가 되도록　　I studied until midnight last night.
　　　　　공부했어요.

1. 네 시까지 기다렸어요.　　　　　네 시가 되도록 기다렸어요.

2. 밤까지 놀았어요.　　　　　　　밤이 되도록 놀았어요.

3. 늦게까지 일했어요.　　　　　　늦도록 일했어요.

4. 세 시까지 책을 읽었어요.　　　　세 시가 되도록 책을 읽었어요.

5. 죽을 때까지 사랑했어요.　　　　죽도록 사랑했어요.

6. 해가 뜰 때까지 잤어요.　　　　　해가 뜨도록 잤어요.

D. Pattern Drill

Teacher : 일찍 일어나면 늦지 않습　　We won't be late if we get up early.
　　　　　니다.

Student : 늦지 않도록 일찍 일어납시　　Let's get up early so that we will not be
　　　　　다.　　　　　　　　　　　　late.

1. 쉬면, 피곤하지 않습니다.　　　　피곤하지 않도록 쉽시다.

2. 빨리 가면, 그분을 만날 수 있습니다.　그분을 만날 수 있도록 빨리 갑시다.

3. 일찍 자면, 일찍 일어날 수 있습니다.　일찍 일어날 수 있도록 일찍 잡시다.

4. 빨리 가면, 늦지 않습니다.　　　　늦지 않도록 빨리 갑시다.

5. 먹을 것을 주면, 울지 않습니다.　울지 않도록 먹을 것을 줍시다.

6. 복습하면, 잊어버리지 않습니다.　잊어버리지 않도록 복습합시다.

Text II

E. Substitution Drill

1. 머리 감을 때만큼, 좋은 때는(은)
   없어요. ⌒

   There is nothing as nice as a shampoo.

그분 — 좋은 분,	시간 — 중요한 것,
그 여자 — 예쁜 분,	이책 — 어려운 것

2. 머리카락이 부드러우면, ⌒ 마음이
   좋대요. ⌒

   If a person has soft hair, he is said to
   be good.

비가 오 — 좋지 않,
이 옷을 입으 — 예쁘,
사람이 많으 — 나쁘

F. Integration Drill

Teacher : 공부했어요. ⌒ 산보했어요. ⌒   I studied. I took a walk.

Student : 공부한 후에 ⌒ 산보했어요. ⌒   After I studied, I took a walk.

1. 그분을 만나겠어요. 공부하겠어요.   그분을 만난 후에 ⌒ 공부하겠어요. ⌒
2. 공부했어요. 집으로 돌아왔어요.   공부한 후에 ⌒ 집으로 돌아왔어요. ⌒
3. 선생님이 갔어요. 그분이 왔어요.   선생님이 간 후에 ⌒ 그분이 왔어요. ⌒
4. 비가 왔어요. 나무가 잘 자랐어요.   비가 온 후에 ⌒ 나무가 잘 자랐어요. ⌒
5. 그분이 저녁을 잡수셔요. 저는 가겠   그분이 저녁을 잡수신 후에 ⌒ 저는 가겠
   어요.   어요. ⌒

G. Pattern Drill

Teacher : 한국말은 영어보다 어렵습니   Korean is more difficult than English.
         다. ↘

Student : 한국말은 영어만큼 어렵습니   Korean is as difficult as English.
         다. ↘

1. 그 여자는 김 선생보다 커요.   그 여자는 김 선생만큼 커요. ⌒
2. 이 책은 그 책보다 좋아요.   이 책은 그 책만큼 좋아요. ⌒
3. 이것은 그것보다 예쁘지 않아요.   이것은 그것만큼 예쁘지 않아요. ⌒
4. 한국은 영국보다 추워요.   한국은 영국만큼 추워요. ⌒

5. 오늘은 어제보다 피곤해요.　　오늘은 ˇ어제만큼 ˇ피곤해요. ⌢

H. Response Drill

1. 어떻게 깎아 드릴까요?　　보기 좋도록⌢ 깎아 주세요. ⌢

2. 한국에 오신 지 얼마나 되셨습니　한국에 온 지⌢ 일곱 달 되었습니다. ⌄
　까?

3. 김 선생이 누구만큼 큽니까?　　김 선생이 ˇ박 선생만큼 ˇ큽니다. ⌄

4. 어제 밤에 늦도록 무엇을 했어요?　어제 밤에 ˇ늦도록⌢ 공부했어요. ⌢

5. 아이들이 울지 않도록 무엇을 줄까　아이들이 ˇ울지 않도록⌢ 먹을 것을 ˇ주세
　요?　　　　　　　　　　　　요. ⌢

I. Expansion Drill

1. 복습하세요. ⌢

　배운 것을 ˇ복습하세요. ⌢

　잊어버리지 않도록⌢ 배운 것을 ˇ복습하세요. ⌢

　잊어버리기 쉬우니까, ⌢ 잊어버리지 않도록⌢ 배운 것을 ˇ복습하세요. ⌢

　복습하지 않으면, ⌢ 잊어버리기 쉬우니까, ⌢ 잊어버리지 않도록⌢ 배운 것을 ˇ복습
　하세요. ⌢

　If you don't review, you'll easily forget, so please review what you have learned,
　　so that you may not forget it.

2. 말하지 못해요. ⌢

　김 선생님만큼 ˇ말하지 못해요. ⌢

　일년이 되었지만, ⌢ 김 선생님만큼 ˇ말하지 못해요. ⌢

　한국말을 ˇ공부한 지가 ˇ일년이 되었지만⌢ 김선생님만큼 ˇ말하지 못해요. ⌢

　한국에 와서⌢ 한국말을 ˇ공부한 지가 ˇ일년이 되었지만, ⌢ 김 선생님만큼 ˇ말하지
　못해요. ⌢

　It has been a year since I came to Korea and began studying Korean, but I don't
　　speak as well as Mr. Kim.

Text III

J. Substitution Drills

1. 참ˇ 좋은데⌒ 무슨ˇ 그런 말씀을ˇ 하세요?⌒

   Why are you talking like that? It's very good.

참ˇ 예쁜데,	참ˇ 따뜻한데,
아직도ˇ 젊은데,	아주ˇ 가까운데,
한창ˇ 일하실 나이인데	

2. 그분이ˇ 젊어 보입니다.↘

   He looks young.

저분이ˇ 작아,	그 여자는ˇ 예뻐,
그분은ˇ 부지런해,	저 학생은ˇ 피곤해

3. 자꾸ˇ 놀려 대지 마세요.⌒

   Stop fooling an old man continuously.

웃어,	울어,	먹어,	떠들어

4. 김ˇ 선생님께ˇ 물어보세요.⌒

   Ask Mr. Kim, please.

신부님,	목사님,	아버님,	어머님

K. Pattern Drill

Teacher : 저는ˇ 학생들한테ˇ 한국말을ˇ 가르칩니다.↘   I'm teaching Korean to (some) students.

Student : 저는ˇ 학생들에게ˇ 한국말을ˇ 가르칩니다.↘   I'm teaching Korean to (some) students.

1. 그분한테 낚시질 가라고 했어요.   그분에게ˇ 낚시질 가라고 했어요.⌒

2. 김 선생님한테 수영하라고 했어요.   김 선생님에게ˇ 수영하라고 했어요.⌒

3. 저 학생한테 춤 추자고 하세요.   저 학생에게ˇ 춤 추자고 하세요.⌒

4. 저 아이한테 몇 살이냐고 물어보세요.   저 아이에게ˇ 몇ˇ 살이냐고⌒ 물어보세요.⌒

5. 어머님한테 시간이 있느냐고 물어보세요.   어머님에게ˇ 시간이 있느냐고⌒ 물어보세요.⌒

L. Pattern Drill

Teacher : 친구한테서ˇ 편지가ˇ 왔어요.⌒   The letter came from my friend.

Student : 친구에게서ˇ 편지가ˇ 왔어요.⌒   The letter came from my friend.

1. 어머님한테서 이 말을 들었어요.   어머님에게서ˇ 이 말을ˇ 들었어요.⌒

2. 아버님한테서 받지 않았어요.　　　　아버님에게서 `받지 않았어요. ⌒

3. 부산에 있는 친구한테서 전보가 왔　　부산에 있는 `친구에게서 `전보가 `왔어요. ⌒
　　어요.

4. 저 여자한테서 이 책을 받았어요.　　저 여자에게서 `이 책을 `받았어요. ⌒

M. Response Drill

1. 저 학생은 참 피곤해 보이지요?　　　예, ⌒ 저 학생은 `참 `피곤해 보입니다. ⍂

2. 한국에 오신 지 몇 년 되었습니까?　　한국에 온 지 ⌒ 육 년 되었습니다. ⍂

3. 무엇으로 얼굴을 닦아 드릴까요?　　　수건으로 `얼굴을 `닦아 주세요. ⌒

4. 늙은 사람을 놀려대는 사람이 누구　　늙은 사람을 `놀려대는 사람이 `이발사예
　　예요?　　　　　　　　　　　　　　　요. ⌒

5. 사람은 나이가 들면 소용이 없지요?　예, ⌒ 사람은 `나이가 들면 소용없어요. ⌒

N. Expansion Drill

놀려대지 마세요. ⌒

자꾸 `놀려대지 마세요. ⌒

늙은 사람 `자꾸 `놀려대지 마세요. ⌒

다 `이렇게 되니까, ⌒ 늙은 사람 `자꾸 `놀려대지 마세요. ⌒

늙으면 ⌒ 다 `이렇게 되니까, ⌒ 늙은 사람 `자꾸 `놀려대지 마세요. ⌒

Everyone becomes this way when they grow old, so stop kidding an old person.

GLOSSARY

Notes :

All verbs are given in their lexical forms. The Arabic figures refer to the lessons. The capital letters RT stands for Remarks to the Text, SP stands for structural Patterns, D stands for Drills. The alphabetical sequence used here is according to the newly revised one announced by the governmant on Jan. 14, 1988.

【ㄱ】

가깝다 10D
가꾸다 2
가다 4SP
가로수 2
가르치다 4
가물다 8D
가요 3
가운데 13RT
가을 8
가족 11
가지다 12
각본 2
갈다 14SP
갈대 2
갈비 2
갈퀴 2
감기 2

감다 15
감동 2
감사하다 3
감자 2
갑시다 5
강 5RT
강론 12
강원도 11RT
같다 6
같이 10
개 15SP
개 6SP
개다 8
개월 10RT
갸륵하다 2
거꾸로 2
거리 13
거짓말 12
걱정 8

건강 2
건망증 2
걷다 8
걸다 9RT
걸리다 9
걸어오다 13D
걸음 8SP
검디검다 2
겁나다 2
겉 12SP
겨우 15
겨울 8
격려 2
겸비 2
겹겹이 2
-경 9
경기도 11RT
경상도 11RT
계란 2

계속 7
계속하다 14D
계절 8
계집 14SP
고구마 2
고기 2
고삐 2
고추 2
곧 14
곧이듣다 2
골자 2
곰 2
곱배기 2
곱셈 2
곳 4SP
공부 2
공부하다 3
공사 2
공중 2

난로 2
난류 2
난 2
날다 8SP
날마다 9
날씨 3
남 13D
남동생 14SP
남자 4D
남편 14SP
낫 2
낫다 15SP
낭비 2
낮 9
낮다 15
낮잠 2
낮 2
낱 2
낱낱이 2
낱말 2
낳다 2
내 4
내년 9RT
내려가다 13
내려오다 13D
내리다 13D
내일 10
너무 6

너희 11SP
넓다 8SP
넝쿨 2
넣다 2
네거리 5
넷(네-) 4SP
넷째 6RT
년 6SP
노랗다 6RT
노래부르다 13D
노인 2
논둑 2
놀다 4D
놀리다 15
농담하다 11D
높다 6RT
놓다 11SP
누구 4RT
누나 14SP
누렇다 2
눈 8
눕다 11SP
느리다 2
-는 3
늘 5
늙다 15
늦다 9D
늦바람 2
-님 3

【ㄷ】

다 15
다니다 7RT
다르다 9RT
다섯 4SP
다섯째 6RT
다음 13RT
다음해 9RT
다행하다 6RT
단골 15
단골여관 15D
단골의사 15D
단골집 15RT
단단하다 15RT
달 10
달밤 2
담 2
담당계원 14
담당하다 14RT
담배 6
담임선생 14RT
닷새 9SP
당신 11SP
닿다 9RT
대 6SP
대가리 12SP
대개 9
대단히 13

대위 13RT
대포 2
더 7
더디다 2
덕택 11
덥다 8
-도 3
도망가다 10RT
도착하다 9
독 2
독나비 2
독일 7D
독일말 8D
돈 6
돋보기 2
돌도끼 2
돌아가다 5
돌아오다 10
돕다 10D
동 13D
동녘바람 2
동복 2
동안 10
돼지 2
되다 8
두껍다 8SP
두더지 2
두시 9
둘(두-) 4SP

둘째 6RT

뒤 5

뒷 15

뒷머리 15RT

드리다 3

듣다 11

들다 2

들다 6

들어오다 10

등기우편 14D

등불 2

등뼈 2

등산하다 11D

따뜻하다 8

딱딱하다 15D

딸 14SP

땅 2

때 2

떠나다 9

떠들다 15D

떡 2

또 3

-데 4SP

뚱보 2

뜨다 13RT

뜻 2

띠 2

【ㄹ】

-(으)로 5

리을 2

【ㅁ】

마귀 2

마루 2

마리 6SP

마시다 13RT

마음 6

마음보 2

마지막 11RT

마치 13D

마치다 9D

마흔 4

만 5SP

-만 7

만나다 11

만년필 6

만이에요 3

많다 4

맏며느리 2

맏이 2

말 3

말갛다 6RT

-말고 12SP

말다 14SP

말더듬이 2

말썽 2

말씀 8

말이에요 5

망조 2

맞은편 13RT

매년 9D

매우 8

매월 9D

매일 9

매주 9RT

머리 12

머리카락 15

먹다 10SP

먼저 5

멀다 10RT

멀리 10

며느리 14SP

면도 15

명도원 4

몇 9

몇 분 4

모두 4

모레 10

모르다 11

모범 2

모자 13RT

모자 2

목사 12D

목요일 9D

몰지각 2

몸짓 2

몹시 8

못- 8SP

몽둥이 2

묘지 2

무겁다 8SP

무 2

무덥다 8D

무슨 4

무엇 4

묵주 12

문방구점 7

문법 2

문자 2

묻다 11SP

물가 13RT

물가 2

물개 2

물건 6

물고기 2

물독 2

미국 7D

미사 12

미신 2

밀고 2

밉다 2

밑 13RT

【ㅂ】

바람 8
바로 13
바르다 15
바른쪽 13RT
바쁘다 3
박람회 2
박사 10SP
밖 7
반 9
받다 6
발달 2
발췌 2
밤 9
밥 7D
방 4D
방금 10
방문 10
방바닥 2
방울 2
밭 2
배 9
배우다 4D
백 4SP
백만 5SP
백화점 13
버스 5D
번개 8D

번 6SP
번번이 2
벌써 10
법 2
법률 2
벗다 12D
베다 2
벽 9RT
별고 11
병 7
볕 8
보다 7D
-보다 8
보름 9SP
보리 2
보슬비 2
보얗다 6RT
보이다 6
보통전보 14RT
복잡하다 5
본과 2
봄 8
봄비 2
뵙다 3
부드럽다 15
부부 2
부산 5D
부산직할시 11RT
부엌기구 2

부인 3D
부치다 13SP
부탁하다 14D
-부터 9
부풀다 2
북 13D
북쪽 13
-분 4SP
분(分) 9
분(粉) 15RT
분필 4D
붇다 11SP
불놀이 2
불능 2
불다 8
불법 2
불쾌 2
붓다 15SP
붙이다 14RT
비 8
비뇨 2
비다 10RT
비밀 2
비싸다 6
비키다 11D
비틀다 14SP
비행기 9
빌리다 10D
빗 2

빗다 15SP
빙과 2
빚 2
빚돈 2
빛 2
빠르다 2
빨갛다 6D
빨래 2
빨리 5
(빼)앗다 15SP
뺨 2
뼈 2
뽀뽀 2
뽀얗다 6RT
뽕나무 2
뿌리 2

【ㅅ】

사거리 2
사고 2
사 5SP
사내 14SP
사다 4D
사람 4RT
사랑 2
사르르 2
사만 5SP
사모 2
사무실 11SP

사백 5SP	상과 2	성과 2	수술 2
사십 5SP	상자 2	성냥 7D	수업 9
사월 10RT	상장 2	성당 12	수영하다 11D
사의 2	상점 7D	성서 12	수캐 14SP
사이 13RT	상징 2	세계 6	수탉 14SP
사전 6D	상처 2	세모꼴 2	숙녀 2
사제 2	상표 2	세상 2	숙제 13SP
사죄 2	새벽 9RT	세수하다 11D	순경 9RT
사천 5SP	새집 2	세종문화회관 13	술 13SP
사치 2	새해 2	셋(세-) 4SP	숯가마 2
사탕 2	생도 2	셋째 6RT	쉬다 2
사흘 5RT	서 13D	소개 10D	쉰 4SP
산 13RT	서거 2	소금기 2	쉽다 8D
산림 2	서늘하다 8D	소나기 8D	스무날 9SP
산보 2	서다 12D	소련 7D	스물(스무-) 4SP
산보하다 10D	서대문 5	소련말 8D	스승 2
산불 2	서로 10D	소용없다 14	스톱 5
살결 2	서른 4SP	속 12	스페인말 8D
살 6SP	서리 2	손님 15	슬슬 13
살다 8SP	서울특별시 11RT	손등 2	-시- 4SP
삶 8SP	석달 10	손재주 2	시 6SP
삼 5SP	선교사 14D	손짓 2	시간 5
삼등 2	선생 3	솔 2	시내 2
삼만 5SP	선선하다 8	솟다 15SP	시렁 2
삼백 5SP	선편 14	쇄도 2	시민 2
삼십 5SP	설교 12SP	쇠고기 2	시아버지 14SP
삼월 10RT	성가 12	수건 15	시어머니 14SP
삼천 5SP	성가대 12	수고 5	시원하다 8D
삼키다 2	성격 2	수선 2	시월 10

시작되다 12
시작하다 8
시장 7
시조 2
식 2
식당 5D
식모 2
신다 2
신라 2
신문 10SP
신부 3D
신세계 13
신자 2
싣다 11SP
실 2
실증 2
십 5SP
십리 2
십만 5SP
십이월 10RT
십일월 10RT
싸다 6
쌀겨 2
쌀 2
쌀쌀하다 8D
썰매 2
쏘다 2
쓰다 8SP
쓸데없다 13

씨름 2
-씩 7
씻다 15SP

【ㅇ】

아 2
아내 14SP
아니요 4
아들 14SP
아래 13RT
아무 4SP
아버지 11D
아이 2
아저씨 14SP
아주 3
아주머지 14SP
아침 9
아프다 12
아홉 4SP
아흐레 9SP
아흔 4SP
악몽 2
악사 2
안 12D
안녕 3
안부 3
앉다 12
알다 14SP
암소 14SP

암캐 14SP
암탉 14SP
압록강 2
앞 13
앞뒤 2
앞발 2
애기 2
애인 2
애호 2
야근 2
야심 2
야초 2
약 9
약속 11
얕잡다 2
어깨 2
어느 4SP
어디 3
어때요 4
어떠세요 3
어떻게 4SP
어렵다 8D
어머니 11D
어서 5
어제 10RT
어쩌면 8
억 5SP
언니 14SP
언제 4RT

얼굴 15
업무 2
없다 5
엉터리 4
-에 4
에미 2
-(에)서 4
에우다 2
에이다 2
여가 2
여기 5
여덟 4SP
여동생 14SP
여드레 9SP
여든 4SP
여러 번 12
여러분 11SP
여름 8
여름밤 2
여섯 4SP
여자 4D
여쭈다 2
연세 15D
연필 4D
연지 15RT
열 4SP
열 다섯 4
열쇠 2
열심히 11D

열홀 9SP	오전 9	우그리다 2	육백 5SP
염가 2	오천 5SP	우량 2	육십 5SP
염전 2	오후 9	우리 11SP	육천 5SP
엿새 9SP	오히려 2	우승 2	윷놀이 2
영어 5D	온천 2	우울 2	으뜸 2
영화 11	온화하다 8D	우유 2	으례 2
옆 13RT	올 9RT	우체국 13D	으쓱하다 2
옆머리 15	올라가다 13	우표 14	-은 4
예배 12RT	옷 4SP	운동 2	은혜 2
예배당 12RT	옷감 2	운동장 11D	-을 4
예쁘다 5D	와언 2	운전하다 11RT	음계 2
예순 4SP	와해 2	울다 14SP	의견 2
예의 2	왜간장 2	웃다 15SP	의미 2
예정 2	왜곡 2	웃도리 2	의사 2
오 5SP	왜식 2	웃마을 2	의의 2
오늘 5	외교 2	워낙 2	의자 4D
오다 4SP	외국 14RT	월요일 9	의지 2
오뚜기 2	외국인 14RT	웬 10	-이 4
오래간만 3	왼쪽 13RT	위 13RT	이것 4
오래 9	요령 2	위치 2	이게 11
오른쪽 13	요망 2	위험 2	이끌다 2
오리 2	요새 3	윗머리 15	이 5SP
오만 5SP	요인 2	유람 2	이내 14RT
오백 5SP	요즈음 3	유명하다 12	이따금 2
오빠 14SP	욕심 8	유서 2	이레 9SP
오십 5SP	용기 2	유월 10	이름 2
오염 2	용법 2	유치원 2	이마 2
오월 10RT	용서하다 11RT	육 5SP	이만 5SP
오인 2	용지 14	육만 5SP	이발관 15

이발사 15 입술 15RT 장 7 젖 2
이발하다 15D 잇다 15SP 장독대 2 제구 6SP
이백 5SP 있다 3 장마철 8D 제사 4
이불 2 잊어버리다 15D 장모 14SP 제삼 3
이성 2 잎만 2 장인 14SP 제십 6SP
이십 5SP 재미 3 제오 5
-이에요 4 【ㅈ】 저것 4RT 제육 6SP
이외 14RT 저기 5 제주도 11RT
이웃 2 자 6 저녁 9RT 제칠 6SP
이웃집 2 자가 2 저리 14 제팔 6SP
이월 10RT 자꾸 15 저분 5 저희 11SP
이젠 10 자다 4SP 저울 2 조사 2
이천 5SP 자동차 5D 전라도 11RT 조카 14SP
이태리말 8D 자라다 15 전보 14 조카딸 14SP
이틀 9SP 자루 7 전(前) 9 졸다 11D
인기 2 자리 14 전진 2 좀 6
인사 3 자본 2 전차 2 좀도둑 2
일곱 4SP 자전거 5D 전하다 3 종이 6D, 7
일 5SP 자정 9RT 절교 2 좋다 3
일본말 8D 작년 9 절규 2 좌우 2
일어나다 9 작은 것 6 젊다 15 죄인 2
일요일 9 -잔 13 점원 6 주다 3
일월 10RT 잔돈 6 젓다 15SP 주무시다 4SP
일찍 5 잔소리하다 15D 정가 2 주일 12
일컫다 11SP 잘 3 정각 9 죽다 9
일하다 4SP 잠 2 정동 4 준비 2
일혼 4SP 잠깐 6 정말 11 줄 11RT
읽다 4SP 잡수다 10D 정신 15 줄다 14SP
입다 4SP 잡지 7SP 정오 9RT -중 8
장갑 2

중국 7D
중국말 8D
중앙우체국 13
중요하다 13D
즉시 2
증기 2
지게 2
지급전보 14
지껄이다 15SP
지난해 9RT
지내다 3
지다 13RT
지다 8SP
지도 2
-지만 8
지우개 4D
지하철 5
직공 15RT
질주 2
집 4D
집념 2
집다 8SP
짓다 15SP
짖다 15SP
-짜리 6
짝짝이 2
쩔쩔매다 2
쪼개다 2
쭈그리다 2

쭉 13
-쯤 9
찌다 2

【ㅊ】

차(茶) 13
찰나 2
참 3
참말 12SP
참외 2
참조 2
창고 2
찾아가다 11
채 6SP
채소 2
책가방 6D
책 4
책상 4D
처녀 14SP
처음 11
처지 2
처치 2
천 5SP
천만 5SP
천주교 12RT
천천히 5
철 8
첫물 2
첫째 6RT

체육 2
초 2
초사흘 9SP
초이틀 9SP
초하 2
초하루 9SP
촛불 2
총각 14SP
추다 8SP
추리 2
추수 2
축배 2
춘천 15D
출가 2
춤 8SP
춥다 8
충청도 11
췌담 2
취미 2
-측 13RT
측면 2
층 6SP
치다 8D
친구 11
칠 5SP
칠만 5SP
칠백 5SP
칠십 5SP
칠월 10RT

칠천 5SP
칠판 7D
침대 2

【ㅋ】

크다 6
큰코 2

【ㅌ】

타국 2
타다 5
태우다 13D
태풍 8D
택시 5
턱 2
토끼 2
토요일 9
톱 2
틈 10

【ㅍ】

파괴 2
파도 2
파랗다 6RT
판단 2
팔 5SP
팔다 14RT
팔만 5SP
팔방 2

팔백 5SP

팔십 5SP

팔월 10RT

팔천 5SP

팥밥 2

퍼렇다 2

편지 11SP

편지지 14RT

폐물 2

포도 2

폭포 2

폭풍우 8D

풀 2

풀비 2

프랑스 7D

프랑스말 8D

피곤하다 5

피리 2

【ㅎ】

하나(한-) 4SP

하늘 2

하다 4SP

하루 9

하얗다 6SP

하의 2

학교 4

학생 4

학적 2

한- 10RT

한 갑 6

한국 3

한국말 3

-한테 3

한파 2

함께 11

함부로 2

합니다 2

항공우편 14

항공편 14

항상 9

허리 2

허리띠 2

허파 2

헌병 2

험담 2

협력 2

호기심 2

호흡 2

혼자 11D

화요일 9D

효험 2

후 10

후사 2

훼손 2

휴양 2

휘파람 2

흐리다 8

힘 2

힘세다 11SP

GUIDE TO STRUCTURAL PATTERNS

Note :

    The Arabic number appearing first at the end of each item refers to Lesson number ; the Roman number refers to Structural Patterns therein ; the last Arabic number refers to page number.

-ㄹ 줄 알다 (one) knows how to do. 11, XI, 227

-ㄹ 필요가 있다(없다) it is (not) necessary to do. 13, VI, 269

-라고 하다 is called. 11, VI, 222

-라도 (this) or something else, even. 11, IX, 225

-러 in order to. 10, VII, 199

-려고 in order to. 13, Ⅰ, 265

-려고 하다 be going to do. 13, Ⅱ, 265

-로 by means of. 5, Ⅲ, 89

    to. 9, VIII, 175

    as, function, manner. 14, Ⅱ, 288

-를 object particle. 4, IV, 67

-ㅁ/-음 verbal noun marker. 8, X, 155

-마다 every. 9, Ⅰ, 170

-만 only. 7, VII, 131

-만에 after (of time). 10, Ⅲ, 193

-만큼 as (so)... as. 15, IV, 310

-말고 not, but. 12, IV, 242

-면 if 8, VII, 151

-면 되다 (one) only has to do..., all(one) must do is.... 14, IV, 290

못- negative prefix. 10, VIII, 199

-ㅂ니다 polite formal style. 11, Ⅲ, 218

-ㅂ시다 the propositive form polite informal style. 5, Ⅱ, 88

-밖에 없다 There is no one (nothing, no other) but.... 7, Ⅲ, 128

-보다 particle of comparison. 8, Ⅲ, 148

-부터 from. 9, IV, 172

-ㅅ verb stems ending in a final consonant. 15, IX, 312

-습니다 polite formal style. 11, Ⅲ, 218

-시- the honorifix infix. 4, V, 67

-씩 (so much) at a tie, (so much) per (person). 7, Ⅱ, 128

About the Revisor-Author : Yunsook Hong

1970-date : Professor of Linguistics, Dept. of English Language & Literature,
    Hanyang University, Seoul, Korea
1984-1986 : Lecturer in Korean, Korean Section, Oriental Studies Dept.,
    University of Pennsylvania, Philadelphia, PA,. U.S.A.

Education : Ewha Women's University, English Dept., Seoul, Korea
    University of Pennsylvania (B.A. in English Literature)
    University of Pennsylvania (M.A. & Ph. D. in Linguistics)

Activities : The Sociolinguistic Society of Korea, Vice-President
    The English Language & Literature Association of Korea. Editorial Board Member
    The Korean Language Research Society of the Korea Broadcasting System,
    Advisory Board Member

Publications : *A Sociolinguistic Study of Seoul Korean*(Ph.D. dissertation)
    *A Comparative Study of Language Change and Culture in North and South
    Korea*(남북한의 언어문화 비교 연구)

Myŏngdo's Korean 제 1 권

1991년 7월 20일 2판 1쇄 인쇄
1992년 11월 20일 2판 4쇄 발행

저 자 Anthony V. Vandesande
    홍   연   숙
발행인 노   양   환
발행소 도서출판 우 신 사
    서울 서초구 양재동 2-1
    FAX 571-1618
    Tel. 571-1615~7
    출판등록 1979년 5월 7일
    제3-96호

값 15,000원

U-SHIN SA PUBLISHING CO.,
2-1 YANGJAE-DONG, SŎCH'O-GU
SEOUL 137-130, KOREA

ISBN 89—7131—052—9